The Lively Experiment

The Shaping of Christianity in America

y[r] petitioners have it much in their hearts . . .
to hold forth a lively experiment, that a
flourishing civill State may stand, yea, and
best be maintain'd . . . with a full liberty in
religious concernm[ts]

John Clarke

The Lively Experiment

The Shaping of Christianity in America

Sidney E. Mead

Harper & Row, Publishers

New York, Hagerstown, San Francisco, London

First Harper & Row paperback edition published in 1976.

LIBRARY OF CONGRESS CATALOG CARD NUMBER: 63-10750

ISBN: 0-06-065545-6

76 77 78 79 80 81 10 9 8 7 6 5 4 3 2 1

To my three deans:

Ernest Cadman Colwell
Bernard M. Loomer
Jerald C. Brauer

"Yet if I were asked what single thing American education needed most, I should reply that it needed such men. . . ."   —R. M. Hutchins

Contents

Preface

When Philip Schaff returned to Germany in 1854 after ten years
in the United States and, on invitation, attempted to explain his
adopted country to erstwhile German colleagues, he must have
sounded distressingly American to many of the churchmen who
heard him.[1]

Schaff, one of their most brilliant young scholars, had been
their answer to a Macedonian call from their Reformed brethren
of Mercersburg Seminary in Pennsylvania. Concerned as they
were about what was reputed to be going on among Protestants
in America, they had sent him forth with the injunction "to
smite with incurable wounds" the "many-headed monster of
pantheism and atheism . . . as it has there become flesh and broken
forth into actual life, in concrete form, spreading desolation and
terror." Their tendency to believe the worst about America was
probably confirmed when Schaff was tried for heresy for expressing ideas in his Mercersburg Inaugural that had become a part of
conventional learning among the German scholars.

Then, after ten years, while his report on the results of his
errand into the wilderness might not justify charges of having
embraced the particular many-headed monster they had had in
mind, what he said was in its way even more shocking. In effect
he informed them that they had better take a good look at what
was going on in the United States because it was only a question
of time before religious developments there would make most of
their European churchmanship obsolete. That had become his
conviction.

Uncommonly aware of the continuity of history, Schaff told them that America was "destined to be the Phenix grave . . . of all European churches and sects, of Protestantism and Romanism." For there, under religious freedom and separation of church and state, these groups contend as equals and no one is strong enough to dominate. He urged them to see the religious situation in America as a "motley sampler of all church history." There "all the powers of Europe, good and bad, are . . . fermenting together under new and peculiar conditions." And while to be sure everything "is yet in a chaotic transition state," yet "organizing energies are already present, and the spirit of God broods over them, to speak in time the almighty word: 'Let there be light!' and to call forth from the chaos a beautiful creation."

I have quoted Schaff not merely to enlist the defenseless dead in support of my views—which, like most historians, I am constantly tempted to do—but because in my opinion he correctly sensed the uniqueness of the American religious scene and suggested the motifs to be followed in interpreting its significance. The motifs are that the history of the Christian Church is an unbroken continuum, that the fragmentation in America is due primarily to the transplantation of all the churches and sects of Europe, that the religious freedom there practiced and the "frontier" situation placed the church under new and peculiar conditions, and that out of the ferment and conflict which give the appearance of chaos, "something wholly new will gradually arise."

These are the motifs that run through the following essays. In them I have tried to outline the shape of the "something wholly new" that is emerging and to trace its origins. How well I have succeeded in adumbrating its form and whether it is beautiful, I leave for others to decide.

Because the United States is a motley sampler of the results of all of church history, it confronts the historian with a vast jigsaw puzzle of events. Many of them seem to fit into more than one context, others fail to fit nicely into any rational scheme at all. There is no generalization about religious developments in

America that cannot be followed by a valid "yes, but" based on an outcast fact. It is a field wherein a measure of ignorance of such facts may be bliss indeed, enabling the interpreter to formulate clear and bold generalizations. By the same token it is a fearfully baffling field to anyone whose disciplined drive to achieve clarity is balanced by an equally strong aversion to oversimplification. A. N. Whitehead's phrase makes an appropriate motto for the historian of religion in America: "Seek simplicity and distrust it."

As history these essays are, in Herbert Butterfield's apt expression, interim reports that were issued periodically by one devoted to the exploration of the complex terrain of American church history. Each was originally designed to stand alone, but into each is woven the same central motifs. For this reason considerable minor and major editorial surgery was necessary to make them presentable for publication together. I found it practically impossible to perform such delicate operations on my own brain children. Therefore I am immeasurably indebted to Mrs. Joyce Appleby who appeared at just the right time and with unusual skill, patience, and ruthlessness not only performed the operations for me, but with a charming combination of persuasion and coercion made me like what might have been a painful process.

The central themes of my interpretation are carried in essays II, VII, VIII, and IX. These were originally given as Charles R. Walgreen Foundation Lectures in 1954 at the University of Chicago.

I have never intended a detailed "story of religion in America," largely because in all my teaching and writing I have assumed the ready availability of Professor William Warren Sweet's encyclopedic works. I gratefully acknowledge him as the Master who tutored me both when I was his student and his colleague at the University of Chicago. Like all good Masters he expected his students to accept his work critically and go beyond him if they could. In due time I expressed my growing independence from his basic interpretations in a critical evaluation of his work —an effort which he acknowledged with appreciation.[2]

The remaining five essays enlarge upon particular aspects of the main themes. Brief comment on them may be helpful. The significance of religious freedom and the relationship between Christianity and American democracy are basic to the interpretation of religious developments in America. These themes run through all the essays, but are dealt with most directly in essays IV and V. The first was intended primarily to suggest some of the still unresolved problems religious freedom created for the churches. In essay V I have probed the relationship between Christianity and democracy somewhat obliquely through an analysis of the thought of Abraham Lincoln. My hope was, and is, that these two might raise questions that others would explore further.

The sixth essay has not been previously published. It is a schematic presentation of a constellation of images that seem to have been almost universally shared during the period between the Revolution and the Civil War by thinkers representative of many different theological and philosophical positions. The constellation suggests the form of the forms of thought then widely prevalent.

With these explanations and reflections I send the essays out with the covering comment, which is perhaps a warning, of A. N. Whitehead, that "we must not expect simple answers to far-reaching questions. However far our gaze penetrates, there are always heights beyond which block our vision."

The community of congenial souls in which the professor lives and moves and has his being transcends by far the collegiate fellowship of his particular academic household, and because his indebtedness is coextensive with that community, it cannot adequately be expressed. He is the beneficiary even of those with whom he differs. Indeed, he may owe more to one who has etched his faults with acid than to the ninety-and-nine who have merely said, "I enjoyed your article."

The test of membership in this community is not intellectual agreement but commitment to the serious and disciplined conversation about affairs that matter. It is a community of works, and in it the only immortality to be hoped for is the perpetuation of one's ideas in work that endures. Although closely allied with the academic institutions in our society, it is only tangentially related to them in essence. In fact the academic life, which one perceptive professor aptly defined as a series of interruptions, is as likely to hinder as to help the kind of work that gives one a lasting place in the great conversation.

In this respect I consider myself singularly fortunate. For in the two schools wherein I have thus far labored, both professorial colleagues and administrators (many times the same people), ever mindful of that larger community to which their local academy belongs, have nurtured my particular work with sympathetic but critical encouragement as well as practical aid. The same can be said in a special way about the generations of students who, forgiving my teaching sins both of commission and omission, have responded to my efforts by applying themselves diligently to the work, often seeing and developing implications in my ideas that were beyond my imagination. Whatever the limitations and shortcomings to be found in the following essays may be, the reasons for them lie not in these my stars but in myself. Conversely, I hope to remain human enough to relish commendation for whatever in them my peers judge to be good.

Sidney E. Mead

Southern California School of Theology
Claremont, California
January, 1963

The Lively Experiment

The Shaping of Christianity in America

I

The American People: Their Space, Time, and Religion

They have all been uprooted from their several soils and ancestries and plunged together into one vortex, whirling irresistibly in a space otherwise quite empty.[1]

– I –

When the great tides of war between Britain and France for empire in America receded, many men who had fought the battles were left behind. Among them, none was more articulate than the Frenchman, J. Hector St. John de Crèvecoeur, who settled on a farm in western New York and soon became an ardent American. In his *Letters from an American Farmer*, first published in 1782, he asked the question that has haunted generations of thoughtful men since his time, "What then is the American, this new man?" and answered,

He is either an European or the descendant of an European. . . . who leaving behind him all his ancient prejudices and manners, receives new ones from the new mode of life he has embraced, the new government he obeys, and the new rank he holds.[2]

Crèvecoeur saw that this American was a "new man," but he also saw that his "newness" was a consequence of the new land, the new space, working its subtle magic in the heart and mind of the "old" man transplanted from abroad. He was among the first of those who have tried to unravel the deeper significance of the obvious fact that Americans, whatever else they may be, are, in origin, emigrants all—immigrants all—living in a spacious New World.

In the perspective of the history of Christendom, perhaps the most striking peculiarity about the settlements that eventually became the United States was the mixture of peoples. It is not the story of the clash of conquerors and a native population, eventuating very gradually in amalgamation and a new culture with twin roots, as was, for example, the Norman conquest of England or even the Spanish conquest of South and Central America. Rather, it is the story of the clash of many well-defined transplanted European cultural and religious groups—English Roman Catholics, Anglicans, Presbyterians, Congregationalists, Baptists, and Quakers; of German Lutherans, Reformed, and the "sectaries," and a host of others.

The Reformation had broken the once tangibly unified Christendom into the warring, absolutistic, rival faiths of the sixteenth and seventeenth centuries. By the time that Dutch and English planting had begun in the first quarter of the seventeenth century, the fragments were somewhat stabilized in Europe; and by the middle of the century the divisions had been grudgingly recognized and made official by the Peace of Westphalia of 1648. Confessional stabilization was achieved primarily on a territorial basis, with Anglicanism dominant in England, Lutheranism in most of Germany and the Scandinavian countries, the Reformed groups in Switzerland, Scotland, and the Low Countries, and Roman Catholicism in Spain and France. Each of these groups claimed within its territory religious absolutism. All the dominant groups believed in and demanded religious uniformity within their civil commonwealth enforced by the civil power. In this situation religious fervor combined with patriotism to tinge the relationships between rival groups and individuals with suspicion, fear, and hatred, evidenced by accentuated definitions of "orthodoxy" and "heresy," with consequent persecution of dissenters within, and open wars of extermination directed toward those without.

The remarkable thing about the English settlements in America is that there, in the brief period between 1607 and 1787, these traditionally antagonistic groups of people learned to dwell together side by side in relative peace. First, they learned to tolerate one another, and eventually they began to think of freedom for all as an inherent or natural right. This is the story of how the outcast groups—Jews, Roman Catholics, Baptist, Quakers, and òthers—gained first the privilege to exist, then toleration of their public expressions under restrictions imposed by the established churches, then complete equality and freedom under the civil law. Religiously, then, what was unique about this American—this "new man" after 1787—was his practice of religious freedom.

What worked this sudden transformation, this revolution in stubbornly rooted religious ideas and attitudes? The answer is difficult and complex. Of course, the seminal ideas of such freedom had long been present in Europe and were transplanted with some of the earliest comers—as witness the halting steps taken along this road by the Baltimores in Maryland and the surer steps of Roger Williams and his outcasts in Rhode Island or the confident stride of William Penn and his Quakers in Pennsylvania. In the beginning, none of the dominant and powerful groups in the colonies, whether Congregationalists in New England, Dutch Reformed in New Amsterdam, or Anglicans in the South, intended to place their feet on this particular road, and their opposition to those who did was long, hard, and bitter. Nevertheless, religious freedom came, although no one really planned it. It came, not because any dominant or even respectable religious group really wanted it, but, as one great church historian has put it, because, when the Constitutional Convention met in 1787, "Congress was shut up to this course by the previous history of the American Colonies and the actual condition of things at the time of the formation of the national government."[3]

The previous history of the American colonies had been brief, very brief, for the accomplishment of such a momentous revolution in Christian thinking and practice. What had been accepted as an axiom by all respectable Christian thinkers for about fourteen hundred years and transplanted to America as the guiding intention of the dominant groups was almost completely overthrown in the short span of one hundred and eighty years. The great experiment of religious freedom on a national scale, which Protestants in America now sometimes defend as the traditional way of doing things, has actually been tried for less than two hundred years. This alone is enough to suggest that perhaps time was not the most significant element in the development of the American way.

– II –

The time of these American people as "American" has been short. Whatever maturity they may have, it is not the maturity of hoary age, mellowed by long experience and made wise and patient by sheer accumulation. Once the first beachheads were gained at Plymouth and Jamestown and New Amsterdam, after tremendous struggle and suffering, these people, these emigrants, were set in motion and swept relentlessly on. The Pilgrims during that first terrible winter soon discovered what later generations of Americans came to know almost instinctively, that

> There is no time to grieve now, there is no time.
> There is only time for the labor in the cold.[4]

Francis Parkman, the cultivated New Englander, lured on to suffer the primitive vicissitudes of the Oregon Trail by his consuming passion to study the Indians in their native habitat, recorded in epigrammatic lines one great truth about his fellow Americans. Hunting for food one day, he shot an antelope:

When I stood by his side, the antelope turned his expiring eye upward. It was like a beautiful woman's dark and bright. "Fortunate that I am in a hurry," thought I; "I might be troubled with remorse, if I had time for it."[5]

In all the dark pages of American history, none is darker than that on which is written the story of the Indians. And that page, too, if not made bright, is at least grasped with tragic understanding when read in the context of time. Bernard DeVoto, whose historical writings were all informed by poetical insight, writing of the Indians in their last great preserve in the vast land "across the wide Missouri," stresses this point. "Perhaps," he says, "the Indians might have been adapted to the nineteenth-century order and might have saved enough roots from their own order to grow in dignity and health in a changed world—if there had been time."[6] But once the fur trader and the farmer, the missionary and the schoolteacher, came, living out the inexorable myth of "manifest destiny," there was no time at all. For the Indian, no time to adapt—but even more tragically, for the white man no time for remorse, but only time for the labor in the cold and in the heat and in the vast places.

There was remorse, of course, and loneliness and terror—especially among the women—and it was expressed in the infinitely sad folk songs and gospel hymns of the pioneers—the songs that would break the hearts even of modern sophisticates, had they not learned to immunize themselves against understanding this aspect of American history by a neat and comfortable sentimentality. But always this was a minor refrain, drowned in the great crashing music of the outward events that mark in history the conquering of a continent and the building of a great nation.

Americans have never had time to spare.

What they did have during all their formative years was space —organic, pragmatic space—the space of action. And perhaps this made the real difference in the formation of "this new man." From time immemorial the peoples of the Orient, of the Near East, and of Europe have been a people hemmed in, confined within the spatial boundaries set by geography and by the closely related boundaries set by tradition and custom. Within such boundaries and impressed by the regular passing of one generation after another within the confines of familiar places, they tended to find what freedom they could for the human mind and spirit within the context of time—time as duration, as the endless flow and flux of events which might be abstractly conceived in terms of great cyclic revolutions endlessly repeating, or, in Christian times and lands, in terms of a beginning in creation, a center in Jesus the Christ, and an end in judgment.

But when the first white men from Europe set foot on the new continent with the intention to remain as settlers, this relative significance of time and space was reversed. Stephen Vincent Benét says of the Pilgrims—in this sense the prototype of all who followed upon their heels—

> They were all alone as few we know are alone.
> They made a small, bustling noise in an empty land.[7]

And perhaps that made the difference. Gone was the traditional sense of confinement in space, for space relative to people that mattered was practically unlimited.[8] Thus the first emigrants experienced a new birth of freedom—the possibility of unconfined movement in space—while concurrently the time ties were tattered or broken by the breaking of the continuity of the regular passing of one generation after another in one place. The present immersion of these people, increasingly cut off from traditional reminders of the past, in the struggle for survival tended but to accentuate the hope for a brighter future which was woven into their dream of destiny.

It is not too much to say that in America space has played the part that time has played in the older cultures of the world.

There was, of course, the vast geographical, pragmatic space —enough to satisfy the most elemental urge for sheer movement, luring men on by the promise of the primitive thrill of looking at scenes that no white man had ever looked upon before. There were visions of new Edens wherein men, emerging with regained innocence from baptism in infinite space, might begin all over again. Social space, the theoretical average distance between individuals, was also immense. And this American, this "new man," felt new, and was new, in part because of the plain possibility of escaping the physical proximity of his fellow men if and when he wished. The binding ties of habit, custom, and tradition were largely broken, for their formative influence on the individual depends finally upon his inability to escape the society of his peers. The American could always believe, however much the actual situation in which he found himself might contradict the belief, that he could, if he wished, move on in space. He could ignore the traditional boundaries of habit, class, custom, and law and begin anew, unfettered by these ancient restraints.

Horatio Alger enshrined the plausible dream of every poor barefoot boy that he might ascend from rags to riches, from log cabin to White House, from a humble peddler of groceries or shoestrings to a mighty tycoon of oil or steel or lumber. The bounties of the virgin space offered to these dreamers the possibility of support, of the maintenance of independent existence. They nurtured within their breasts a kind of personal freedom and dignity that enabled them to confront all traditional institutions with tolerance, with amusement, with anger, with impatience, but never with submissiveness. Under the freedom offered by space, strict conformity became the mark of the weakling, the person too inept to move "west" and dig with firm hands for the "Acres of Diamonds" buried there.[9] Ralph Waldo Emerson, the gentle and provincial New Englander, was never more ruggedly and broadly American than when he coined the phrase, "Whoso would be a man must be a non-conformist."

– III –

Americans during their formative years were a people in movement through space—a people exploring the obvious highways and the many unexplored and devious byways of practically unlimited geographical and social space. The quality of their minds and hearts and spirits was formed in that great crucible—and in a very short time.

Their great and obvious achievement was the mastery of a vast, stubborn, and ofttimes brutal continent. This is the "epic of America," written with cosmic quill dipped in the blood, sweat, and tears of innumerable nameless little men and women and a few half-real, half-legendary heroes, people who struggled ever westward, building their own temples of logs and sod, making and singing their own songs to the accompaniment of rhythmic hoofbeats, creaking oarlocks, and the grinding rumble of the great wagons. This is the mighty saga of the outward acts, told and retold until it has overshadowed and suppressed the equally vital, but more somber, story of the inner experience. Americans have so presented to view and celebrated the external and material side of their pilgrims' progress that they have tended to conceal even from themselves the inner, spiritual pilgrimage, with its more subtle dimensions and profound depths.

For these pioneers—these little people pitted against space—were not, of course, all of one kind. There were pioneers and pioneers—there were eager beavers, there were reluctant pioneers, there were the settlers.

The eager beavers were the doers, the lusty extroverts, to whom the mere existence of unoccupied land to the west was a perennial challenge to move on, to trap and hunt in the virgin wilderness, to dig for precious metals in wild mountain valleys, or to set crude plows in unbroken earth. They could forget the past and the "east" with its settled ways and largely overlook the pleasures as well as the miseries of the present, as they dwelt in the golden promise of the untried space to the west. They lived on movement and newness, largely on the surface of things and largely without nostalgia for the home left behind.

But all the pioneers were not so. In the great surging tide of movement created by the eager beavers, there were always the reluctant pioneers—those who were swept on and on with the stream, but ever fearfully, with dragging feet and eyes turned back toward "home," where the heart remained among the settled, cultured ways of the "east." These felt lost in the limitless spaces, overwhelmed and terrorized by brute nature given voice and arms by wild animals and savage Indians. They were fearfully eroded by the endless round of menial toil. In them passionate memories of home easily mingled with the hope for a heaven in which the loneliness, the terror, and the toil would be assuaged by the God who would stoop to wipe away every tear from the tired eyes of those wanderers who laid the burden down. Mary Walker, one of the first women to go out over the Oregon Trail, epitomized in her diary one night all the sad and often forgotten footnotes to the boisterous saga told by the eager beavers: "I cried to think how comfortable father's hogs were" back home in New England.[10] The hearts of the reluctant ones were not in the "west."

And there were, of course, the settlers—those who followed upon the heels of the eager beavers and their ever-reluctant companions, but whose stamina, or courage, or resources, or whatever it was, carried them only to settlements. These were the true builders and stabilizers. Perhaps not fully knowing what they did or why, they stayed put, and sometimes with a kind of plodding heroism, sometimes perhaps in the quiet desperation so scorned by Henry Thoreau, who hardly ventured west of the Hudson, they rebuilt what they could of the old and remembered in the new place. The new structure never looked quite like the old, but it was their own, and it was continuous with the past and the "east," and it was the surest hope for the future. These, then, were the true conservatives, the salt of the earth, and the backbone of the new nation—the forgotten men who made the most of the space immediately around them.

Here are three authentic American types, and in the great symphony of the Republic their respective themes recur again and again, now one, now another, dominant, but most true when they are harmoniously mingled. In the probing literature of the land they appear many times, but perhaps nowhere more clearly than in Hamlin Garland's story of *A Son of the Middle Border* and in Ole Rölvaag's *Giants in the Earth*. Rölvaag's tragic tale contrasts Per Hansa, "the natural pioneer who sees the golden light of promise flooding the wind-swept plains, and Beret, child of an old folk civilization who hungers for the home ways and in whose heart the terror of loneliness gathers."[11] In Garland's story, the types are seen in almost pure form. There is the father, the eager beaver, veteran of the Civil War, possessed of a tract of the good earth in the coulee country of Wisconsin, surrounded by family, relatives, and friends, and immersed in the institutions of a growing society, yet consumed by a relentless urge to move on and on—to Iowa, to the Dakotas, to Montana. Ever the wife and mother went with him, sadly, reluctantly, torn from her roots in Wisconsin where her spirit remained in memory among the familiar scenes. Hamlin escaped to the east, and from "the End of the Sunset Trail" he brought his parents back home again to Wisconsin in their declining years. This return meant to his mother that "her wanderings were over, her heart at peace," but for his father, who still wanted to "fight it out . . . farther west," it was a retreat, the acknowledgment of outward defeat and inner frustration. Hamlin, the child of both, tasted through them the strange mingling of fulfillment and frustration that has characterized so many of the achievements of the children of the pioneers. In him as "love of the wilderness was increasing year by year . . . all desire to plow the wild land was gone." His ideal was a small house—"New England in type" —and "in a village." But he realized that "never again would we hear those wistful, meaningful melodies" that spoke of the time when "all the west was a land of hope."[12]

This is one great parable of the American people that can be endlessly applied for the understanding of themselves. A Henry Ford, who is said to have proclaimed that history was "bunk," is Per Hansa and Hamlin Garland's father in mechanized modern dress. Henry James and T. S. Eliot are Beret and Garland's mother, gifted with articulateness and living out the myth of going home again. Sinclair Lewis is the child of both torn apart by his equal appreciation for the peace and fulfillment and the defeat and frustration that he found in "Babbitt" and those who lived on "Main Street."

The three types found grass-roots religious expression in the gospel songs that sprang up out of the continuous movement through space, the songs that were too simple, too close to the springs of piety, to conceal the emotions surging in the hearts of the common people. These are the songs sung by the flickering light of fires at the great camp meetings and periodic revival meetings in churches large and small all over the land.

The eager beavers and their descendants could translate much of the resistless urge for movement that possessed them into an accepted idiom of their revivalistic Protestantism as, perhaps clapping their hands and stamping their itching feet, they sang

> I'm pressing on the upward way,
> New heights I'm gaining every day.
> Still shouting as I onward bound,
> Lord, plant my feet on higher ground.

Meanwhile all the deep, sad yearnings known to the reluctant pioneers welled up to the surface, and still wells up in the invitation song,

> I've wandered far away from God,
> Now I'm coming home.
> The paths of sin too long I've trod,
> Now I'm coming home.
> I'm coming home, coming home,
> Never more to roam.
> Open wide thine arms of love,
> Lord, I'm coming home.

And the sober, more plodding settlers, concentrating on what was immediately before them, might find expression in

> Work, for the night is coming,
> Work through the sunny noon;
> Fill brightest hours with labor,
> Rest comes sure and soon;
> Give every flying minute,
> Something to keep in store;
> Work, for the night is coming,
> When man works no more.

He who would understand America must understand that through all the formative years, space has overshadowed time—

has taken precedence over time in the formation of all the ideals most cherished by the American mind and spirit.

Among these ideals, none is more dear than "freedom," and the simple fact is that this concept has always had for Americans a primary dimension of space. The pioneer felt "free" so long as he felt that he could move on when he could see the smoke from a neighbor's cabin or hear the sound of his neighbor's rifle. His descendant, the modern city dweller, feels "free" so long as he feels that he can move away from the undesirable location or neighbors to the suburbs, to the "country home in Connecticut." The trailer-house hitched to an automobile is as fitting a symbol of the Americans' concept of freedom today as once were the saddlebags, the rifle, and the ax.[13] The Civil War, the center of American history, can be seen as an attempt to exercise this freedom of flight from an undesirable alliance that had almost as much appeal in the North as in the South. One evidence of the genius of the gaunt, brooding man in the White House was his seeing that this was an inadequate conception of freedom. He reminded the nation that the mystic chords of memory that bound the Union together could not be cut by the simple expedient of dividing the country along a geographical line.

Nevertheless, and despite this insight, the concept of freedom as freedom to move in space has remained dominant. The mill-run of Americans have seldom been notably tolerant when confined in limited space with those they disliked for any reason. No doubt this helps to account for some of the hysteria of the present—a hysteria generated in the still dominant eager-beaver mind by the recognition pressed upon it by inexorable forces that such freedom is less and less possible in the increasingly crowded One World of the modern age. The situation is complicated, of course, by that ingrained ambivalence of attitude toward such freedom of space that we have been talking about— on the one hand, the eager beavers' acceptance and glorification of it and, on the other hand, the reluctant pioneers' fear of such freedom and deep yearning for stable, settled ways. Here is the basis for the surge of feeling that we must keep things as they are and have been. And hence the peculiarly confusing phenomenon of an attempt to bolster and preserve the *status quo* on the basis of a philosophy of *laissez faire*.

Perhaps, then, the real hope lies in the thus far most inarticulate ones—the settlers, who deep within themselves have never lost the sense that somehow human freedom must work itself out within the context of stable, traditional patterns—a hope for freedom based on the thought that, while space on this earth is obviously limited, time is less so and may indeed be infinite.

– IV –

And now to pick up again the theme of religious freedom within the context of this picture of the Americans' time and space. There really was not much time in America for the traditionally antagonistic religious groups to learn to live together in peace. But there was space, and no one could deny that one part of the space appeared to be about as desirable as any other. John Cotton, who could always be depended upon to make smooth the angular ways of the Puritans, professed to be somewhat puzzled by the agitation caused by the banishment of Roger Williams:

The Jurisdiction (whence a man is banished) is but small, and the Countrey round about it, large and fruitful: where a man may make his choice of variety of more pleasant, and profitable seats, then he leaveth behind him. In which respect, Banishment in this countrey, is not counted so much a confinement, as an enlargement.[14]

Other early spokesmen for the powerful groups that intended to perpetuate religious uniformity within their territory offered dissenters this freedom of space. Nathaniel Ward proclaimed for Massachusetts Bay that "all Familists, Antinomians, Anabaptists, and other Enthusiasts, shall have free liberty to keep away from us, and such as will come to be gone as fast as they can, the sooner the better."[15] This sentiment was generalized and plowed into the American mind. "Billy" Sunday, whose effusions reflected us uncritically as a mirror so much of America, but echoed Ward in saying of some immigrants, "If they don't like it here, let 'em go back to the land where they were kenneled." Later the same sentiment was expressed by nicer people in the song,

> If you don't like your Uncle Sammy
> Just go back to your home o'er the sea.

But, from the beginning, the subtle magic of space began to work upon the tight little islands of the transplanted authoritarians themselves, eroding their most ingeniously contrived and zealously guarded barriers of creed and logic and doctrine, until, by the time of Crèvecoeur, it was no more than the repetition of a platitude to say that "zeal in Europe is confined; here it evaporates in the great distance it has to travel; there it is a grain of powder inclosed, here it burns away in the open air, and consumes without effect."[16]

The platitude expressed a truth, but it did not include all the truth, for both transplanted and indigenous zeal continued to burn, even in the open air, and not without effect. The Bay Puritans, in the attempt to protect their own religious absolutism, might banish such dissidents as Anne Hutchinson, Roger Williams, the Quakers, and the Baptists. But they could neither keep them from establishing themselves in neighboring colonies nor hide the attractive example of their freedom from the citizens of Massachusetts. They did not anticipate that the good space about them might provide a secure home for all dissenters whose zeal, far from being evaporated, was augmented by the knowledge thus forced upon them that even the long arms of civil and ecclesiastical authority could not encompass the vast space of the new land. Although four stubborn Quakers were effectively and permanently suppressed in Boston with the hangman's noose, the vast majority of dissenters in America soon learned to escape the deadly vertical pressures of intrenched authority by the simple expedient of moving horizontally in the free space.

The story of America is the story of uprooted emigrant and immigrant people, ever moving rapidly onward through space so vast that space came to take precedence over time in the formation of their most cherished ideals, chief of which has been the ideal of freedom. But since the freedom of space did not appeal to all in the same way, there was created a strange mingling of attitudes toward the predominant conception of freedom, suggested by the three types of pioneers. These three attitudes are seen in relief today as Americans become increasingly aware that their space is almost filled up and hence that their predominant conception of freedom is somehow askew and inadequate.

The "story of religion in America" must be reinterpreted in this general context and both its most outstanding accomplishment—religious freedom—and its outstanding failure—theological structure—re-examined in the light of these insights.

II

From Coercion to Persuasion: Another Look at the Rise of Religious Liberty and the Emergence of Denominationalism

By the time English colonization got underway in the seventeenth century, the Reformation movement had shattered the once tangible unity of European Christendom. The spiritual reformation of the church was concurrent with the rising self-consciousness of the emerging nations. Quite naturally the reformation of the church found diverse expressions in the several countries—Lutheranism in the realms of the German princes and in the Scandinavian countries, Anglicanism in England, Reformed in Geneva and Scotland.

In general these right-wing Protestant groups agreed with Roman Catholics on the necessity for enforcing religious uniformity in doctrine and practice within a civil commonwealth. This view of many centuries' standing in Christendom the new churches accepted without question.

Meanwhile, in the social crevices created by universal upheaval, certain sects or left-wing groups were emerging as blades of grass spring up through the cracks once a cement sidewalk is broken. Throughout Europe, Catholics and Protestants alike tried to suppress these groups by force, branding them as heretics and schismatics who constituted a threat to the whole structure of Christian civilization.

All of the first settlements on that part of the continent that was to become the United States were made under the religious aegis of right-wing groups with the exception of Plymouth where a handful of separatists "made a small, bustling noise in an empty land." But Anglicans who were making a bigger noise on the James, as were Dutch Reformed on the Hudson, Swedes on Delaware, and Puritan Congregationalists on the Charles, all assumed that the pattern of religious uniformity would of necessity be transplanted and perpetuated in the colonies. And all took positive steps to insure this—even the Pilgrims. For as Plymouth colony prospered it made support of the church compulsory, demanded that voters be certified as "orthodox in the fundamentals of religion," and passed laws against Quakers and other heretics.[1]

The first Charter of Virginia of 1606 provided that "the true word and service of God and Christian faith be preached, planted, and used . . . according to the doctrine, rights, and religion now professed and established within our realm of England," and from the beginning laws provided for the maintenance of the church and clergy and for conformity.

Orthodox ministers of the Dutch church came early to New Netherlands, and the new charter of freedoms and exemptions of 1640 stated that

no other religion shall be publicly admitted in New Netherlands except the Reformed, as it is at present preached and practiced by public authority in the United Netherlands; and for this purpose the Company shall provide and maintain good and suitable preachers, schoolmasters, and Comforters of the sick.

When John Prinz was sent as Governor to the struggling Swedish colony in 1643 he was specifically instructed to

labor and watch that he render in all things to Almighty God the true worship which is his due . . . and to take good measures that the divine service is performed according to the true confession of Augsburg, the Council of Upsala, and the ceremonies of the Swedish church . . .

After a brief stay he was happy to report that

Divine service is performed here in the good old Swedish tongue, our priest clothed in the vestments of the Mass on high festivals, solemn prayer-days, Sundays, and Apostles' days, precisely as in old Sweden, and differing in every respect from that of the sects around us.[2]

That the New England Puritans' experiment in the Bible Commonwealth required uniformity hardly needs documentation. "There is no Rule given by God for any State to give an Affirmative Toleration to any false Religion, or Opinion whatsoever; they must connive in some cases, but may not concede in any," was the dictum of their self-appointed spokesman, Nathaniel Ward. Although the forthright clarity of this lawyer-minister disguised as a "Simple Cobler" was not typical of the more discreet apologists for the New England way, nevertheless Ward's sentiment was one of the stones in the foundation of their "due forme of Government both ciuell & ecclesiastical."

Yet in spite of such beginnings the intention to perpetuate uniformity in the several Protestant colonies that were gathered under the broad wings and "salutary neglect" of mother England during the seventeenth and eighteenth centuries was everywhere frustrated. The tradition of thirteen-centuries' standing was given up in the relatively brief time of one hundred and eighty years. By around the middle of the eighteenth century toleration was universally, however reluctantly, accepted in all the English colonies. Within fifty years complete religious freedom was declared to be the policy of the new nation formed from these colonies.

The importance of this change can hardly be overestimated. Professor W. E. Garrison has rightly called it one of "the two most profound revolutions which have occurred in the entire history of the church . . . on the administrative side"—and so it was.

– I –

There have been many studies of the rise of religious freedom in America. They range all the way from the sentimental to the cynical with a large number of very substantial works by careful scholars in between. There seems to be fairly wide agreement with Professor Philip Schaff's thesis that the Constitutional Convention "was shut up to this course" by the previous history of the colonies and the situation existing at the time. In this essay I do not intend a detailed historical explanation of this "profound revolution," but wish only to raise two questions: What was the situation in 1787? and How had it come to be?

In order to answer the second question two factors have to be weighed and balanced: that of the positive ideological thrust for such freedom made, for example, by the Baptists as a group, and by individual leaders in most of the other churches, and that of practical necessity. The latter position is ably represented by Perry Miller, who argues that Protestants by and large "did not [willingly] contribute to religious liberty, they stumbled into it, they were compelled into it, they accepted it at last because they had to, or because they saw its strategic value."[3]

It is my impression that Protestant writers have commonly stressed the first factor, usually suggesting that religious freedom was a natural concomitant of the Reformation. If in this essay I stress the second factor, it is primarily to bring into the discussion what I hope will be a corrective emphasis.

This emphasis necessarily reduces the historical importance Protestants have placed upon the positive, self-conscious, and articulated aspiration for religious freedom expressed in our popular folklore through such gems as Felicia Heman's poem on the landing of the Pilgrims. It does not deny the existence of important seminal ideas among left-wingers and other outcasts such as the Roman Catholics who established Maryland or even among the respectable Puritans and Presbyterians. Nor does it underestimate the long-term symbolic value of the steps taken along this road by the Baltimores, by Roger Williams and that motley collection of the banished in Rhode Island, and by William Penn and his Quakers in the Jerseys and Pennsylvania. Still it should be kept in mind that Protestants connived in the freedom extended to all by Roman Catholics in Maryland only so long as was necessary for them to do so. Rhode Island was the scandal of respectable Massachusetts precisely because of its freedom and was commonly referred to by the Bay dignitaries as the sewer and loathsome receptacle of the land. They did not cleanse it because they could not. And by the time Penn launched his experiment with freedom in Pennsylvania, coerced uniformity had already broken down in the neighboring colonies, and England herself, having experimented extensively with toleration between 1648 and 1660 and unable to forget it during the Restoration, was trembling on the verge of toleration.

Accepting, then, the view that the original intention of the dominant and really powerful groups was to perpetuate the pattern of religious uniformity, I shall argue that this intention was frustrated by the unusual problems posed by the vast space with which the Planters had to deal, by a complex web of self-interest in which they were enmeshed, and by the practical necessity to connive at religious variety which both space and self-interest imposed. Finally, too, pressures from the motherland contributed to the process leading to religious freedom.

The web of self-interest was complex indeed, the strongest strands being Protestant, national, and personal. At a time when in England Protestant was synonymous with patriot, and the first feeble English settlements were encircled by the strong arms of French and Spanish Catholicism, whose fingers touched on the Mississippi, it is small wonder that all the early writings and charters stressed the planting of *Protestant* outposts of empire, and that a sentiment came to prevail that almost any kind of Protestantism was preferable to Catholicism. Perhaps this is why Dutch and English policy differed radically from French, in that the Protestant countries after a few random gestures such as the provision in the second Virginia Charter of 1609 that "none be permitted to pass in any Voyage . . . to be made into said Country but such as first shall have taken the Oath of Supremacy," let their dissenters go. Civil and ecclesiastical pressures ranging from slight disabilities to active persecution thus added an external push from the rear to the lure of land and of economic and social betterment operating in the colonists' minds. And this, coupled in many of them with a religious fervor that was always in danger of crossing the boundary into self-righteousness, pushed them out with the intention to become permanent settlers, to possess the land, and perchance to be an example for all mankind—as witness the Bay Puritans.

It is notable also that from the beginning the one outstanding Roman Catholic proprietor had to tolerate a majority of Protestants in his colony, and that eventually the heirs of the first Baltimore probably retained their lands and prerogatives only by becoming Protestants.

National self-interest mated easily with Protestant interests and spawned a desire for strong and profitable colonies that tended to overcome squeamishness about the religious complexion of the settlers. When Peter Stuyvesant came to New Netherlands in 1647 as Director General, he immediately took steps to put the religious house in order by limiting the sale of liquor on Sundays, instituting preaching twice rather than the former once a day, and compelling attendance thereon. When Lutherans, Jews, and Quakers arrived he tried to suppress them, finally shipping one notorious Quaker back to Holland. The Directors' reaction to this move is eloquent testimony to the mind that prevailed among them. They wrote in April 1663 that

although it is our cordial desire that similar and other sectarians might not be found there, yet as the contrary seems to be the fact, we doubt very much if vigorous proceedings against them ought not to be discontinued, except you intend to check and destroy your population; which, however, in the youth of your existence ought rather to be encouraged by all possible means: Wherefore, it is our opinion, that some connivance would be useful; that the consciences of men, at least, ought ever to remain free and unshackled. Let everyone be unmolested, as long as he is modest; as long as his conduct in a political sense is irreproachable; as long as he does not disturb others, or oppose the government. This maxim of moderation has always been the guide of the magistrates of this city, and the consequence has been that, from every land, people have flocked to this asylum. Tread then in their steps, and, we doubt not, you will be blessed.[4]

So on another occasion Stuyvesant argues that "to give liberty to the Jews will be very detrimental . . . because the Christians there will not be able at the same time to do business." And besides, "giving them liberty, we cannot refuse the Lutherans and Papists."[5]

At the time he was backed by the doughty Reformed minister, Megapolensis, who thought the situation was already bad enough since there were "Papists, Mennonites and Lutherans amongst the Dutch, also many Puritans or Independents, and various other servants of Baal among the English under this government," all of whom "conceal themselves under the name of Christians." Nevertheless, the desire of the Directors not to "check and destroy" the population overruled the desire of both magistrate and clergy for a semblance of religious uniformity and Jews had to be granted permission to reside and traffic in New Netherlands only "provided they shall not become a charge upon the deaconry or the Company."[6]

– II –

Finally, from the beginning the ruling geniuses of the new age of expansion managed to mingle strong personal self-interest with the more abstract Protestant and national goals by making trading companies and proprietaryships the instruments of planting. Dutch, Swedish, and English companies organized the plantings in Virginia, Plymouth, New Netherlands, Massachusetts Bay, and Delaware, while proprietors were instrumental in the founding of Maryland, New Hampshire, New Jersey, the Carolinas, Pennsylvania, and Georgia. It might further be argued that William Coddington and his commercial-minded cohorts were the real backbone of Rhode Island, while obviously Theophilus Eaton, the merchant, was hand in hand with John Davenport, the minister, in the founding of the ultratheocratic New Haven.

By 1685, says Greene, more territory along the seaboard than New England and Virginia combined was under proprietary control, and there "governmental policies in relation to religion were radically different from those prevailing either in New England or Virginia." From the viewpoint of the proprietors, he continues, "it was obviously not good business to set up religious tests to exclude otherwise desirable immigrants." "The proprietors tried to attract settlers," Greene explained, "by promising, if not full religious equality, at least greater tolerance than was allowed elsewhere."[7]

But if self-interest dictated in more or less subtle and devious ways a kind of connivance with religious diversity that helped to spell out toleration in the colonies, the efforts even of the most authoritarian groups to enforce uniformity on principle was dissipated in the vast spaces of the new land.

The Anglicans tried it in Virginia, even resorting to the savage "Lavves Diuine, Morall and Martiall &c." published in 1612 which threatened the death penalty for speaking "impiously or maliciously against the . . . Trinitie," or "against the knowne Articles of the Christian faith," or for saying or doing anything which might "tend to the derision or despight of Gods Holy Word," and threatened loss of the "dayes allowance," whipping, "a bodkin thrust through his tongue," six months in the "gallies," or other punishments for failing, among other things, in respect for the clergy, for not attending divine services twice daily, for breaking the "Sabboth by any gaming, publique or private, or refusing religious instruction."[8]

No one supposes that such laws were enforced during the horrendous years between 1607 and 1624 when thirteen thousand of the fourteen thousand people sent over died from exposure, disease, starvation, and the weapons of the savages. Meanwhile the economic awards in the cultivation of tobacco had been discovered and this scattered the families to plantations along the rivers. Even honest clergymen began to despair of conducting the routine affairs of the English church in parishes that might be one hundred miles in length. In 1661 an acute observer argues in *Virginia's Cure* . . . that the chief difficulty was due to the "scattered Planting" for which there was "no other Remedy . . . but by reducing her Planters into towns." His proposal to build towns in every county, and then to make the

Planters bring their families and servants to these centers on
weekends for catechetical instruction and church attendance was
obviously the counsel of despairing, albeit ardent, churchmen
who were beginning to realize that the snug parish life of settled England could not be duplicated in the wilderness.[9]

The Puritan theocrats on the Charles soon had one important
aspect of the meaning of the great space available thrust upon
them. They discovered that while they might protect their own
religious uniformity by banishing all dissenters, they could
neither keep the banished from settling in neighboring Rhode
Island where "Justice did at greatest offenders wink,"[10] nor
prevent every wind from the south carrying their contagious
ideas back to the Puritan stronghold. They did not foresee that
the same inscrutable Providence that gave Puritans the opportunity to build their kind of Bible commonwealth on Massachusetts
soil would offer dissenters the equal opportunity to build whatever kind of commonwealth they wished on Rhode Island soil.

Meanwhile the zeal of the dissenters, far from being dissipated
by banishment, was truly enlarged by the knowledge thus
forced upon them that even the long arms of civil and ecclesiastical authority could not encompass the vast spaces of the new
land. In rather short order, belief in the effectiveness of suppression by force and the will to use it to maintain religious uniformity were undermined by the obvious futility of trying to
land solid blows on the subversive men and women who were
seldom there when the blows fell. Samuel Gorton, compelled to
attend church in the Bay, wrote that the sermonic fare seemed
adapted to the digestive capacities of the ostrich. But in spite of
such capacities, the residents were unable to stomach the savage
proceedings against the Quakers, and finally even the magistrates
and ministers had to connive in their existence.[11]

There was of course another aspect of space—the distance
from the motherland, which, relative to existing means of movement and communications, was immense. The Puritans began
with the idea that

God hath provided this place to be a refuge for many whome he meanes to save out of the generall callamity, and seeinge the Church hath noe place to flie into but the wildernesse, what better worke can there be, then to goe and provide tabernacles and foode for her against she comes thether.[12]

They early sensed the protection inherent in the great distance. Their ingenious idea of taking the Charter and the Company with them to New England is evidence of this. Thereafter they perfected a system of sanctified maneuvering within the time granted by distance that succeeded for three generations in frustrating the attempts of English courts and Crown to control them.

Distance also militated against effective control of the Church of England in the Southern colonies. From the beginning, oversight fell somewhat accidentally to the Bishop of London. During the last quarter of the seventeenth century, the Bishops sought to instrument their supervision of church activities in the colonies through representatives called Commissaries. But without resident Bishops, effective supervision proved to be impossible. The church languished under too many second-rate and even fraudulent clergymen. Increasingly the control passed to parochial vestries composed of local laymen.

Turmoil in Britain at times reinforced distance in frustrating effective ecclesiastical control of the colonies. In 1638, after a series of reports and proclamations beginning in 1632, Archbishop Laud made arrangements to send a bishop to New England with sufficient troops to enforce conformity and obedience if necessary. The outbreak of troubles in Scotland sidetracked this interesting project, however, and "no records of any official connection between the Anglican episcopate and the colonies during the period 1638-1663" exist.[13]

Meanwhile through revolution, Protectorate, and Restoration, England was moving toward its rendezvous with the kind of toleration made manifest in the famous Act of 1689. Already in 1652 Dr. John Clarke had published in London his *Ill Newes from*

Newe England or a Narrative of New England's Persecution, protesting the fining and whipping of three Baptists in Massachusetts under the aegis of a law passed in 1644. His telling thesis was that in matters of religious tolerance, "while Old England is becoming new, New England is become Old."[14]

From about that time the mother country took definite steps to curb persecution in the colonies. When the King was reminded by Edward Burroughs that the execution of Quakers in Boston meant that there was *"a Vein of innocent Blood opened in his Dominions, which, if it were not stopt would overrun all,"* he declared, *"But I will stop that Vein,"* and he did. A Mandamus was granted and carried to New England by Samuel Shattock, a resident of Salem who had been banished on pain of death. Shattock and his fellow Quakers made the most of the occasion, which resulted in a suspension of the laws against the Quakers as such in November, 1661.[15]

Meanwhile, John Clarke's *Ill Newes from New England* . . . had resulted in a protest to the Governor of Massachusetts from ten Congregational ministers in London, who, seeking for more toleration in England, were embarrassed by this show of intolerance on the part of their New England brethren. Sir Richard Saltonstall added his protest in a letter to Cotton and Wilson of Boston's First Church. The Puritans' reply that it was better to have "hypocrites than profane persons" in their churches sounded outmoded.[16]

In 1663 the Crown, in giving its consent to Rhode Island's "lively experiment" with "full liberty in religious concernm[ts]" in the new Charter,[17] gave official sanction to the scandal of Massachusetts Bay and forestalled all future attempts on the part of the Bay Puritans to impose their kind of theocratic order on the neighboring chaos.

The most spectacular case of royal interference that worked for the broadening of colonial toleration was the revocation of the Massachusetts Bay Charter in 1684 and the coming of Sir Edmund Andros as the Royal Governor in 1686. Andros brought an Anglican chaplain with him. Seeking a place for Anglican Services, he tried to persuade the Puritan ministers to provide a church. When this proved unsuccessful, he took over one of their meetinghouses by force and had the English services conducted therein while King's Chapel was being built. The new charter of 1691, in which the New Englanders themselves had a part through the person and work of Increase Mather, wrote "the end" to the Puritan chapter on the preservation of uniformity in the new land.

– III –

Thus the new century found the original intention to perpetuate religious uniformity almost universally frustrated by the strange rope of circumstances woven from various kinds of self-interest and the problems posed by the great space. Effective interference from the motherland in the interests of broader toleration served only to hasten the process. When the two Mathers, father and son, took part in the ordination of a Baptist minister in Boston in 1718, a new day was indeed dawning. But it is probably not to be wondered at that most of them adhered to the inherited standards and conceptions of the church with religious fervor sometimes bordering on desperation. It took the prolonged upheavals associated with the great revivals to break the dwindling hold of the old patterns and give the new an opportunity to grow, and, in the process, to scramble both inextricably with others emerging out of the immediate situation.

Once it was seen that uniformity was impracticable, two possible paths lay open before the churches: toleration, with a favored or established church and dissenting sects—the path actually taken in England—or freedom, with complete equality of all religious groups before the civil law. Favoring the first solution was the fact that transplanted offshoots of Europe's state churches were clearly dominant in all but two of the colonies, and indeed remained so until after the Revolution. Nine of the colonies actually maintained establishments—Congregationalism in New

England, Anglicanism in the South and, nominally, in part of New York. Presbyterians in the South and Anglicans in New England were willing to acknowledge the prerogatives of establishments by assuming the role of dissenters. On the eve of the great revivals, then, these dominant churches had not as yet rejected the principle of religious uniformity but were compelled to recognize the fact of religious variety.

Meanwhile in Rhode Island and the stronger middle colonies religious freedom prevailed—in New York practically, ambiguously, and largely because of necessity, in Rhode Island and Pennsylvania actually and more clearly on principle and experience. As intimated above, the factors that had confounded the uniformitarian intentions of the churches originally established in the new land had also encouraged the numerical growth, geographical expansion, and bumptious self-confidence of the dissenting and free groups in all the colonies. However, they were as yet largely unconscious of their real strength which was to lay in their success with persuasion alone for recruiting members and maintaining their institutions in competition with other groups. An entry in Henry M. Muhlenburg's *Journal*, November 28, 1742, suggests how rapidly a minister, transplanted from a European state church, might size up the realities of the new situation in America and come to terms with them. Sent over to bring some order into the scrambled Lutheran affairs, he immediately ran into a squabble in one of the churches, and recorded:

The deacons and elders are unable to do anything about it, for in religious and church matters, each has the right to do what he pleases. The government has nothing to do with it and will not concern itself with such matters. Everything depends on the vote of the majority. A preacher must fight his way through with the sword of the Spirit alone and depend upon faith in the living God and His promises, if he wants to be a preacher and proclaim the truth in America.[18]

Such espousal of voluntaryism by these American offsprings of Europe's right-wing state churches meant that they accepted one aspect that had been common to the left-wing sectarian groups of Europe from their beginnings. But this was a triumph of a left-wing influence in America, as it is sometimes held, in a guilt-by-association sense only.

Much more important for the future than left-wing influence was the movement called Pietism. Originating in the European right-wing state churches during the last quarter of the seventeenth century, its leaders were seeking for more palatable spiritual food for the hungry souls of the common folk than current Protestant scholasticism and formalism afforded. Conceived and projected as a movement *within* churches aimed at the revitalization of the personal religious life of the members and a restoration of Christian unity, Pietism did tend to develop its own patterns of doctrine and polity. While assuming the validity and continuance of traditional standards and practices, Pietists tended to make personal religious experience more important than assent to correctly formulated belief and the observance of ecclesiastical forms. Here was an intimation that the essence of a church was the voluntary association of individuals who had had the experience.

Stress on the intuitive religion of the heart "strangely warmed" by "faith in Christ," as John Wesley was later to put it, became a possible seedbed for the dreaded religious "enthusiasm." However, in Europe the movement was always somewhat constrained by the sheer existence and accepted forms of the powerful state churches.

But, sprouting indigenously in America, or transplanted thereto by such leaders as Freylinghuysen, Muhlenberg, Zinzendorf, and the great Whitefield, where such constraining ecclesiastical forms were already weakened, Pietism, cross-fertilized by other movements, grew rankly and blossomed into the spectacular phenomena associated with the Great Awakenings. It swept the colonies from the 1720s to the Revolution, transforming the religious complexion of the land as it went.

Jonathan Edwards' experience in Northampton indicates how short was the step from preaching even the most traditional doctrines out of a heart "strangely warmed," to the outbreak of a surprising revival in the church that soon led to "strange enthusiastic delusions" which threatened to disrupt established parish customs.[19] To a modern student the emotional upheavals created by George Whitefield's preaching seem to be out of proportion to that noted evangelist's reputed powers that so impressed Benjamin Franklin.

Back of this was the peculiar religious situation that had been developing in the colonies for a century. Concurrent with the fracturing of uniformity had come the obvious decline of vital religion which concerned clergymen throughout the colonies during the twilight years of the seventeenth century and often turned their sermons into lamentations. The churches were not reaching the masses of the people, and they now confronted a greater proportion of unchurched adults than existed in any other Christian country. This grim statistic reflected the breakdown of the traditional pattern of church membership by birth into a commonwealth and baptism into a church that was coextensive with it, as well as the passing of support induced by coercion, at a time when no new, effective, and acceptable method for recruiting and holding members had emerged.

There was also the general cultural attrition associated with living on the frontier of western civilization where so much of the vital energy of the prosperous went into practical affairs—usually related to immediate profits—and of the poor in the even more engrossing problem of survival. The end of the seventeenth century has been called with reason the lowest ebb tide of the cultural amenities in America. Here was fertile soil for the growth of the kind of fearful and superstitious religiosity later so vividly pictured by Crèvecoeur in the twelfth of his *Letters from an American Farmer*. Hence, to change the figure, at the very time when the tried old dams of civil and ecclesiastical law and custom were crumbling, there was building up behind them a religious yearning waiting to be released in floods of religious enthusiasm. And the revivals came, doing just that.

Most of the early revivalists were pietistically inclined ministers who more or less unwittingly stumbled upon this technique.

It so perfectly met the immediate needs of the churches that it seemed a direct answer to their prayers and a sign of the divine approbation of their doctrines.[20] The revivalists were obviously successful in carrying the gospel to the masses of indifferent people, in recruiting members from among the large body of the unchurched, and in filling the pews with convinced and committed Christians. The revivals demonstrated the spectacular effectiveness of persuasion alone to churches rapidly being shorn of coercive power.

In the context of our general interpretation it is important to note two things. The first is that the revivals took place largely within the entrenched and dominant churches of right-wing tradition. The second is that everywhere, whether among Dutch Reformed and Presbyterians in the middle colonies, Congregationalists in New England or Anglicans in the South, head-on clashes developed between the pietistic revivalists and the powerful defenders of the traditional authoritarian Protestant patterns of doctrine and polity. For the latter correctly sensed that the revivalists stressed religious experience and results—namely conversions—more than correctness of belief, adherence to creedal statements, and proper observance of traditional forms. They knew that in the long run this emphasis might undermine all standards.

When the revivals broke out, traditionalists were largely in control in all these churches. Their attitude is fairly reflected in the Old Side Presbyterian condemnation of the revivalists for

preaching the terrors of the law in such a manner, and dialect as has no precedent in the Word of God . . . and so industriously working on the passions and affections of weak minds, as to cause them to cry out in a hideous manner, and fall down in convulsion-like fits, to the marring of the profiting both of themselves and others, who are so taken up in seeing and hearing these odd symptons, that they cannot attend to or hear what the preacher says; and then, after all, boasting of these things as the work of God, which we are persuaded do proceed from an inferior or worse cause.[21]

As for the greatest of the revivalists, George Whitefield, the Rev. John Thompson wrote that he was almost fully persuaded that Whitefield was either "a downright Deceiver, or else under a dreadful Delusion," and condemned his publications as "nothing but mere confused inconsistent religious jargon, contrived to amuse and delude the simple."[22]

Men like Thompson felt a strong sense of responsibility for order and decency in the churches. Still powerful in every colony they used all available civil and ecclesiastical weapons against the revivialists.

The revivalists defended themselves primarily on the basic ground that personal religious experience was the important thing. They thought of course that the traditionalists neglected it. Gilbert Tennent struck their keynote in his sermon of March 8, 1740, which he called "The Danger of an Unconverted Ministry." Such ministers, he asserted, are "Pharisee-teachers, having no experience of a special work of the Holy Ghost, upon their own souls." They are merely "carnal," and have

discover'd themselves too plainly to be so in the Course of their lives; some by Ignorance of the Things of God, and Errors about them, bantering and ridiculing of them; some by vicious Practices, some both Ways, all by a furious Opposition to the Work of God in the Land; and what need have we of further Witnesses?

Of course, he added, "God, as an absolute Sovereign, may use what Means he pleases to accomplish his Work by," *but* "we only assert this, that Success by unconverted Ministers Preaching is very improbable, and very seldom happens, so far as we can gather."[23]

Here was the revivalists' most telling argument—they were obviously more successful than their traditionalist brethren. The experience of the Presbyterian churches divided into traditional and revivalist groups between 1745 and 1758 amounted to a demonstration. At the time of the separation the Old Side party numbered twenty-five ministers, at its close only twenty-two. Meanwhile the New Side revivalist party which began with twenty-two ministers, had seventy-two in 1758 with churches and members proportionately in keeping with these figures. The success of the revivalists could be made very tangible and nicely measured merely by counting ministers, churches, and converts. Thereafter the emphasis upon success in numbers was to play havoc with all tradition-rooted standards of doctrine and polity in the American churches. One hundred and fifty years later Dwight L. Moody was to declare that it makes no difference how you got a man to God, just so you got him there. Moody's outlook was a natural culmination of the emphasis originating with his eighteenth-century forebears.

At this point it is worthwhile to note specifically that the battle was not one between tolerant left-wing sectarian revivalists riding the wave of the democratic future, and anachronistic rightwing churchmen stubbornly defending the past and their own present prerogatives. It is important to stress this, because even Professor William Warren Sweet, dean of the historians of Christianity in America, gave the prestige of his name to the thesis that "it was the triumph of left-wing Protestantism in eighteenth century colonial America which underlay the final achievement of the separation of church and state."[24] This thesis has difficulties, chief of which is the plain fact that the left-wing, whether defined institutionally or ideologically, never "triumphed" during the colonial period in America.[25] Colonial revivalism was largely a right-wing church affair.

To be sure the pietistic revivalists everywhere belabored what Tennent had called "The Danger of an Unconverted Ministry," and Jonathan Edwards was dismissed from his Northampton church in 1750 primarily for insisting, in that stronghold of rightwing sentiment locally known as "Stoddardeanism," that a conversion experience was the prime requisite for full communion in a Christian church—something he had perhaps learned in the revivals. The revivalists—harassed by traditionalists—naturally developed a kind of anticlericalism and antiecclesiasticism that helped to blur the lines between them and those of more authentic left-wing origin. Compounding this confusion between the revivalists and authentic left wingers was the fact that ever since the time of Munster, every departure from accepted order in the Protestant churches was apt to conjure up visions of an imminent upsurge of familism, antinomianism, anabaptism, and enthusiasm. These were terms that the traditionalists used freely but loosely during the heat of the controversies over revivalism.

Actually all the outstanding revivalists belonged to churches of right-wing tradition, and it might cogently be argued that what growth accrued to left-wing groups as a result of the revivals came largely through their ability to reap where others had sown. Thus, for example, the Baptists in New England apparently took little part in the Awakenings there, looking upon them as a movement within the churches of their Congregational oppressors.[26] But when conflict led to a separatist movement, and Separate Congregationalists were treated even more harshly than Baptists by their erstwhile Congregational brethren, many separatists became Baptists.

Once this point is clear, we see that during the clash between traditionalists and revivalists, the latter were thrown willy-nilly—but somewhat incidentally—on the side of greater toleration and freedom. It was not that they developed clearly formulated theories about religious freedom. In fact the striking thing about the whole pietistic movement, as A. N. Whitehead pointed out, was that it "was singularly devoid of new ideas." Rather it appears that the revivalists were prompted by a practical desire for freedom from the immediate restraints imposed by the dominant churchmen. They fought for the right to promote their own point of view in their own way unmolested by traditional civil and ecclesiastical customs and laws.

Simultaneously the rationalist permeation of the intellectual world during the eighteenth century led to a situation where any man or group that appeared to be fighting for wider toleration of religious differences would attract the sympathetic attention of "enlightened" men in positions of social and political leadership. Furthermore, these men, unlike the pietists, were interested in giving religious freedom rational, theoretical justification.

However much they might abhor "enthusiasm," they could take a sympathetic view of the practical moral application of the revivalists's gospel and the concomitant pietistic appeal to the teachings and simple religion of Jesus. As these rationalists observed the controversies in and between the religious "sects" occasioned by the revivals, along with the attempts of entrenched traditionalists to preserve order through the use of power, their sympathies were with the revivalists who appeared to be on the side of freedom.

Hence came that apparently strange coalition of rationalists with pietistic-revivalistic sectarians during the last quarter of the eighteenth century. Together, they provided much of the propelling energy behind the final thrust for the religious freedom that was written into the constitution of the new nation. This coalition seems less strange if we keep in mind that at the time, religious freedom was for both more a practical and legal problem than a theoretical one. They agreed on the practical goal.

– IV –

Now to hark back to my guiding questions. Having suggested how it had come to be, we may briefly describe the situation in 1787 that necessitated the declaration for religious freedom in the new nation.

First, the churches of right-wing background were still dominant in every area. But no one of them, and no possible combination of them, was in a position to make a successful bid for a national establishment even if those of the Calvinistic tradition were numerous and powerful enough to give Jefferson reason to fear the possibility.[27] Meanwhile the sweep of pietistic sentiments through these right-wing churches during the revivals had undermined much of their desire for establishment. On the question of religious freedom for all, there were many shades of opinion in these churches, but all were practically unanimous on one point: each wanted freedom for itself. And by this time it had become clear that the only way to get it for themselves was to grant it to all others.

Second, the situation had actually made all previous distinctions between established churches and sects, between right- and left-wing groups, practically meaningless. In the South all but the Anglican Church were dissenting sects, as in New England were all but Congregational churches. In this respect, there was no difference between historically right-wing groups such as Presbyterians, Lutherans, and Anglicans, and historically left-wing groups such as Quakers and Baptists. The latter, of course, had traditionally held for religious freedom on principle, while the former had recently come to accept it of necessity. But since the immediate problem of such freedom was practical and legal, all worked together for it—each for his own complete freedom to publish his own point of view in his own way.

Hence the true picture is not that of the "triumph" in America of right-wing or left-wing, of churches or sects, but rather a mingling through frustration, controversy, confusion, and compromise of all the diverse ecclesiastical patterns transplanted from Europe, with other patterns improvised on the spot. The result was a complex pattern of religious thought and institutional life that was peculiarly "American," and is probably best described as "denominationalism."

Most of the effectively powerful intellectual, social, and political leaders were rationalists, and these men made sense theoretically out of the actual, practical situation which demanded religious freedom. They gave it tangible form and legal structure. This the churches, each intent on its own freedom, accepted in practice but without reconciling themselves to it intellectually by developing theoretical defenses of religious freedom that were legitimately rooted in their professed theological positions. And they never have. Anson Phelps Stokes' massive three-volume work on *Church and State in the United States,* proceeding over the historical evidence like a vacuum cleaner over a rug, is notable for the paucity of positive Protestant pronouncements on religious freedom that it sweeps up.

The religious groups that were everywhere dominant in America throughout the colonial period seem to have placed their feet unwittingly on the road to religious freedom. Rather than following the cloud and pillar of articulated aspiration in that direction they granted it (insofar as any can be said to have "granted" it) not as the kind of cheerful givers their Lord is said to love, but grudgingly and of necessity.

Meanwhile, by the time that the original intention to preserve religious uniformity was seen to be impossible of fulfillment in the new land, there had been incubated, largely within the dissenting groups (which were not necessarily left wing), ideas, theories, and practices that pointed the way toward a new kind of "church" consistent with the practice of religious freedom. During the colonial upheavals of the Great Awakenings, these dissenters' patterns of thought and practice infiltrated the dominant churches, and through the misty atmosphere of confusion and compromise, there began that historical merging of the traditional European patterns of "church" and "sect," "right" and "left" wings into a new kind of organization combining features of both plus features growing out of the immediate situation. The resulting organizational form was unlike anything that had preceded it in Christendom, and for purposes of distinctive clarity it is best known as the "denomination."

III

American Protestantism During the Revolutionary Epoch

It is commonly accepted that the two live movements in European and American Christianity during the eighteenth century were rationalism and pietism. Both were rooted in the seventeenth century. And commonly their differences, which were real, are stressed to the point of making them appear to have been completely separate and even mutually exclusive developments. This obscures the fact that in origin they were but obverse sides of a single movement which gathered enough power and momentum during the eighteenth century to sweep in religious freedom and separation of church and state over the opposition of traditional orthodoxy in the churches.

Only *after* this momentous achievement[1] did pietism discover its latent incompatibility with rationalism and arrange a hasty divorce in order to remarry traditional orthodoxy. American denominational Protestantism is the offspring of this second marriage living in the house of religious freedom which was built during the first marriage. The child has always accepted and defended the house with fervor, if not always with intelligence. But it has commonly exhibited great reluctance to own up to its rationalist architect and builder.[2]

This parable suggests the motifs that guide the following interpretation of religious developments during the Revolutionary epoch (roughly 1775 to 1800). It is to this period that we must turn if we are to understand some of the peculiar characteristics of the American religious scene.

– I –

The sixteenth and seventeenth centuries saw the hardening of a Protestant scholasticism which cramped the style of the learned and a growing formalism in the churches which provided but dry food for the hungry souls of common people. Meanwhile Christendom was fragmented into absolutist rival faiths, and devastated by the religious wars among them.[3] As a consequence there developed a sheer weariness with divisions, a repugnance toward wars of extermination, and a widespread positive desire for peace and unity. Underneath it all was the growing suspicion that formal theological and liturgical differences were probably not of ultimate importance and perhaps not even important enough to fight over. It is understandable that in this situation "a small number of divines and laymen . . . tried to introduce 'sweet reasonableness' into theological discussion," while others thought they had found a way more excellent than that provided by scholasticism "in the intuitive religion of the heart, and in the simplest and most primitive forms of faith, more or less independent of external ordinances and a 'form of words.' "[4] Originally these two movements were complimentary.

Rationalist and pietist were alike in that both managed to shrug off the theological questions that had divided their most Christian fathers. Each suggested and sometimes practiced his own way of unity. The rationalist, as befitted the learned, found that "the essentials of every religion" could be reduced to a set of intellectual propositions regarding God, immortality, and the life of virtue. As Benjamin Franklin put it, these being

found in all the religions we had in our country, I respected them all, tho' with different degrees of respect, as I found them more or less mix'd with other articles, which, without any tendency to inspire, promote or conform morality, serv'd principally to divide us, and make us unfriendly to one another.

Back of this genial but discriminating respect for all was the "opinion that the worst had some good effects."[5] What "good effects" these men had in mind, Thomas Jefferson made clear. Surveying his "sister states of Pennsylvania and New York" in 1781 or 1782, he noted that there were religions "of various kinds, indeed, but all good enough; [because] all sufficient to preserve peace and order."[6] This, he thought, amounted to a practical demonstration that uniformity of religious belief and practice in a civil commonwealth was not essential to the public welfare, as had been assumed in Christendom for many centuries.

The pietist leader, on the other hand, might be as learned in his generation as any rationalist. But his concern was for the spiritually hungry members in the churches who perhaps respected but could not find nourishment in formal creeds, massive theologies, or bare intellectual propositions. All, however, could understand John Wesley's "heart strangely warmed" with "trust in Christ," and pietists found peace and a basis for unity in such personal religious experience. This they preached, spreading "scriptural religion throughout the land, among people of every denomination; leaving every one to hold his own opinions, and to follow his own mode of worship."[7] So John Wesley could rhapsodize:

Methodists do not impose in order to their admission, any opinions whatever. Let them hold particular or general redemption, absolute or conditional decrees; let them be churchmen or dissenters, Presbyterians or Independents, it is no obstacle. Let them choose one mode of baptism or another, it is no bar to their admission. The Presbyterian may be a Presbyterian still; the Independent and Anabaptist use his own worship still. So may the Quaker; and none will contend with him about it. They think and let think. One condition, and only one is required—a real desire to save the soul. Where this is, it is enough; they desire no more; they lay stress upon nothing else; they only ask, "Is thy heart herein as my heart? If it be, give me thy hand."[8]

Thus rationalists appealed to the head, and concluded that all the multifarious differences over which Christian churchmen fought were matters of nonessential opinion. At the same time pietists appealed to the heart and concluded that the differences over which Christians had battled and bled for a millennium were immaterial between those of like heart. However, it is important to keep in mind that while similar in their reaction against traditionalism and formalism, rationalists and pietists represented basically different religious outlooks. And each in its own way was capable of setting men adrift by breaking their sense of continuity with the Christian past while scattering the content of the faith.

– II –

The situation in America during the eighteenth century was such as to minimize the differences between rationalists and pietists, and even to accentuate their positive agreements. In the first place the American colonial rationalists, although numerous, were not fomenters of religious controversy, being "willing to leave the question of divine revelation alone,"[9] in a genial respect for the unenlightened. While Deistic thinking permeated the air the intellectual world breathed,[10] mature Deists were apparently mild, urbane, and outwardly conforming. The prime example is Philadelphia's suave and impeccable Franklin, who "regularly paid my annual subscription for the support of the only Presbyterian minister or meeting we had,"[11] who urged his daughter to "go constantly to church, whoever preaches,"[12] and who punctiliously, as new meetinghouses were erected in Philadelphia, contributed his "mite for such purpose, whatever might be the sect."[13] Jefferson, while pressing the Act for Religious Freedom in Virginia in 1777, exhibited the same spirit by writing and sponsoring subscription lists for the support of the clergy who were to be cut off from state support.[14]

In the second place, beginning during the third decade of the century, and under the impetus given by both native and imported leaders, great revivals swept the colonies from New England to Georgia. Everywhere they brought controversy as stanch defenders of the old order, the traditionalists, rose to defend their churches against the disintegrating inroads of rampant "enthusiasm." Whether among Congregationalists in New England, or Presbyterians in the middle colonies, or Anglicans in the South, the substance of the controversy was the same—a clash between the revivalists and the right-wing[15] supporters of the traditional forms of clerical and ecclesiastical authoritarianism that had been transplanted from Europe.

The hold of these forms had already been weakened by the inroads of transplanted left-wing sectarian groups which by this time were firmly entrenched in Rhode Island and the middle colonies and had gained a measure of tolerance in the other colonies. During the revivals the number of these sectarian groups was increased by schisms in the right-wing churches like that of the Separate Congregationalists in New England. Their membership was growing, and they spread widely through all the colonies. This expansion brought the sectarian groups into sharp conflict with the dominant or Established churches in every colony.[16] These churches, although harassed and torn internally by the conflicts between revivalists and traditionalists, brought every possible weapon to bear against the sectarians and schismatics.[17] Under such widespread persecution from the entrenched churches, the anticlerical and antiecclesiastical sentiments characteristic of left-wing groups developed into a vigorous, positive thrust for complete religious freedom.

Meanwhile the rationalist permeation of the intellectual and cultured classes meant that many men in positions of social and political leadership were Deists. These men, however much they might abhor "enthusiasm," were appreciative of the practical moral application of the revivalists' gospel, especially since it was based upon an appeal to the teachings and simple religion of Jesus. Rationalist and sectarian-pietist were agreed that religion was a matter between the individual and his God without institutional mediation. It followed from this position that the church was a voluntary organization of like-minded and like-hearted individuals. They were also united in opposition to the clerical and ecclesiastical authoritarianism of the right-wing churches.[18] This they attempted to undermine by appealing to the pure moral teachings of Jesus or the New Testament church and strongly denying the binding power of all traditions developed thereafter.

Small wonder, then, that the sympathies of the Deistic political leaders, as they observed the controversies in and between the religious sects that were caused by the revivals, were with the sectarian-pietists from the beginning. Often they became their spokesmen and defenders in the legislatures—as, for example, James Madison and Thomas Jefferson in Virginia.[19]

The struggles for religious freedom during the last quarter of the eighteenth century provided the kind of practical issue upon which rationalists and sectarian-pietists could and did unite, in spite of underlying theological differences. The positive thrust for the separation of church and state and the making of all religious groups equal before the civil law came from the sectarian-pietists both within and without the right-wing churches, and from the rationalistic social and political leaders. It was indeed

the leadership of such Lockian disciples as Jefferson and Madison, backed by an overwhelming left-wing Protestant public opinion, that was responsible for writing the clauses guaranteeing religious freedom into the new state constitutions and finally into the fundamental law of the land.[20]

This way of looking at the complex alignment of forces during the eighteenth century which resulted in the declaration for national religious freedom prepares us to understand the religious developments that followed. It is obvious that the very success of the rationalist-pietist alliance in effecting religious freedom removed the primary bond that held them together. Conditions which then brought theological issues to the fore resulted in a realignment of pietists with traditionalists against rationalists.[21]

– III –

Thus far we have stressed the likenesses and agreements of rationalists and sectarian-pietists which made it possible for them to work together while the pressing issue was practical and political. In order to understand the realignment that took place during the Revolutionary Epoch their differences must now be noted.

First was the sociological difference. Rationalism belonged to the classes, to the aristocracy of birth, breeding, and wealth, with its tradition of paternalistic social responsibility, of learning and of concern for fundamental intellectual problems. These aristocrats, although feeling themselves superior to the "enthusiastic" religion of the common man, were nevertheless apt to frown upon the dissemination of their own religious views among the masses because of the possibly bad effect on morals. Benjamin Franklin spoke for them in typical fashion in a letter believed by some to have been addressed to Thomas Paine.[22]

. . . think how great a portion of mankind consists of weak and ignorant men and women, and of inexperienced, inconsiderate youth of both sexes, who have need of the motives of religion to restrain them from vice, to support their virtue, and retain them in the practice of it till it becomes *habitual*, which is the great point for its security.[23]

And Herbert M. Morais concluded that much of the later "vilification of Paine was due to the fact that he was guilty of carrying heresy to the people" and hence was a traitor to his class.[24]

It is obvious that any position which was secure only within an aristocratic setting had a very questionable future in store for itself during a period when the outstanding trend was toward equalitarianism. Jefferson's democratic party lost its aristocratic leadership by the time of Jackson, and apparently had even lost Jefferson's concept of a responsible "natural aristocracy" of "virtue and talents."[25] The ethos that had sheltered Deism during the eighteenth century disintegrated, and Deistic thinking carried to the people in the popularized version of Thomas Paine's *Age of Reason* was soon found wanting.

More important than the sociological was the theological difference—the issue between those who defended the necessity for a particular revelation in the Scriptures and those who argued for the sufficiency of human reason alone to interpret the universal revelation of God in the Creation. Many conservative, rational Christians during the eighteenth century assumed a compromise position, holding that "the authoritative basis of natural religion did not rest in reason alone but also depended upon the Christian revelation."[26] Those who rejected the idea of a peculiar revelation commonly did not press the point publicly. Benjamin Franklin, just a month before he died in 1790, when asked by Ezra Stiles the test question about his belief in the divinity of Jesus, replied in a way completely to avoid the issue:

I have, with most of the Dissenters in England, some Doubts as to his Divinity; tho' it is a question I do not dogmatize upon, having never studied it, and think it needless to busy myself with it now, when I expect soon an Opportunity of knowing the Truth with less Trouble.

However, he added with disarming candor,

I see no harm . . . in its being believed, if that Belief has the good Consequence, as probably it has, of making his Doctrines more respected and better observed; especially as I do not perceive, that the Supreme takes it amiss, by distinguishing the Unbelievers in his Government of the World with any peculiar Marks of his Displeasure.[27]

Even an ardent champion of orthodoxy would have to have time on his hands in order to pick a quarrel with such a genial wit who contributed regularly to one church and gave his mite to all.

Looking back on the period, however, it seems obvious that once the practical political goal of religious freedom was achieved, it would take only a situation accentuating the differences between rationalists and pietists to bring them into open conflict. Even so, the break developed only when rationalistic religious thinking assumed real or imagined social and political implications. This happened when an interpretation of the French Revolution led to the conclusion that there was a direct cause-and-effect relationship between "infidel" thinking and the later phases of the revolution; and when, during the rise of the Jeffersonian party, the religious views of Jefferson and other leaders of the party could be labeled "French" with enough popular plausibility to make the label stick.

The rise of the Jeffersonian party in America coincided with the events of the French Revolution. America was still oriented to Europe, and the struggles in the Old World were reflected in the new. Within the very first Cabinet of the new government the names of Hamilton and Jefferson symbolized sympathies with England and with France—at least, and this was sufficient, so it was widely supposed.[28]

Jefferson and his cohorts were not, of course, theologians or religious leaders. They were political reformers with typical eighteenth-century theories about the nature of man and the social and political institutions most suited to him as a rational being. Basic was the notion that man's present deplorable situation was largely due to the enslavement of his natural reason in the interests of selfish and privileged individuals and groups in the society. Jefferson merely echoed the opinion of his group when he said,

My opinion is that there would never have been an infidel, if there had never been a priest. The artificial structure they have built on the purest of all moral systems, for the purpose of deriving from it pence and power, revolt those who think for themselves, and who read in that system only what is really there.[29]

Rationalists like Jefferson concluded that reform depended upon the freeing of man's natural reason from such enslavement —largely by opening all the channels of communication through freedom of speech, freedom of the press, freedom to assemble and petition, so that every opinion could have a hearing. Errors, they believed, would cease "to be dangerous when it is permitted freely to contradict them."[30] This is the theory that lies back of the great zeal for freedom developed during the eighteenth century.

In France, to which all eyes were directed, this reforming thrust found directly across its path the twin institutions of monarchy and church. And of the two, the latter came to be regarded as the more culpable because it seemed to the reformers that it was the church that really operated the machinery for the enslavement of the minds of the people. The principles of Jesus, said Jefferson, "were departed from by those who professed to be his special servants, and perverted into an engine for enslaving mankind, and aggrandizing their oppressors in church and state." These men, he continued, warped "the purest system of morals ever before preached to man . . . into a mere contrivance to filch wealth and power to themselves."[31] Thomas Paine, a more excellent and less cautious pamphleteer, put it more briefly and bluntly:

All national institutions of churches—whether Jewish, Christian, or Turkish—appear to me no other than human inventions, set up to terrify and enslave mankind and monopolize power and profit.[32]

Hence the church came under attack as the first institution that must be broken in the interests of freedom and reform. There were two obvious ways to undermine its control over the minds of the people.

The first was to attack the existing churches as institutions reared not upon the "pure religion of Jesus" but upon the historical corruptions of that pure religion. A prime example of this sort of attack is Joseph Priestley's two-volume *History of the Corruptions of Christianity*, first published in 1782. Priestley conceived the work as "researches into the origin and progress" of the corruptions of Christianity, in such manner as "will tend to give all the friends of pure Christianity the fullest satisfaction that they reflect no discredit on the revelation itself."[33] In the interests of the true Christian faith, he thought, it was necessary "to exhibit a view of the dreadful corruptions which have debased its spirit, and almost annihilated all the happy effects which it was eminently calculated to produce."[34]

This attack on the existing churches, even though launched by a rationalistic Unitarian, was in essence the same kind of attack

that was dear to the hearts of anticlerical and antiecclesiastical
sectarian-pietists. Its wide appeal in America was possible in part
because it did not push the crucial issue regarding revelation
versus reason to the front. The rationalist political leaders were
also attracted by this line of thought. Thomas Jefferson is said to
have read Priestley's history through once a year, and to have
recommended it for students at the University of Virginia as the
work most likely to wean them from sectarian narrowness. His
own attempt while President, and later, to distill from the Four
Gospels "the Philosophy of Jesus of Nazareth . . . for the use of
the Indians, unembarrassed with matters of fact or faith beyond
the level of their comprehension," was his positive contribution
in the form of a definition of the "pure religion of Jesus." "We
must," he said, "reduce our volume to the simple Evangelists:
select, even from them, the very words of Jesus." This, his added,
he had performed for his own use

by cutting verse by verse out of the printed book, and arranging the
matter which is evidently his and which is as easily distinguished as
diamonds in a dunghill.

This cluster of diamonds mined out of the dunghill constituted

the most sublime and benevolent code of morals which has ever been
offered to man . . . forty-six pages of pure and unsophisticated doctrines such as were professed and acted upon by the unlettered
Apostles, the Apostolic Fathers, and the Christians of the first century.[35]

Sectarian pietists could have little quarrel with this.

But this attack on the church, depending as it did upon the
ability to keep in mind the distinction between the pure religion
of Jesus and the religion of the existing churches, was too subtle
for use during the excitements of social and political upheaval.
Hence the more radical attack—always latent in deistic thinking[36]—upon the orthodox Christian view of revelation itself. It
was because it claimed to be the sole guardian and interpreter of

God's saving revelation to man that the church held its great power over the minds of the people—so the argument ran. Thomas Paine popularized this kind of attack in his famous *Age of Reason*. Said Paine,

Every national church or religion has established itself by pretending some special mission from God, communicated to certain individuals. The Jews have their Moses; the Christians their Jesus Christ, their apostles and saints; and the Turks their Mahomet—as if the way to God was not open to every man alike.[37]

The motivating thought in the mind of the author here is clear —if the people's belief in the idea of revelation as held by the orthodox could be completely undermined, the whole structure of the church would collapse[38] and the way be cleared for the true religion founded upon the true revelation of God in "CREATION." For, since

all corruptions . . . have been produced by admitting of what is called *revealed religion;* the most effectual means to prevent all such evils and impositions is, not to admit of any other revelation than that which is manifested in the book of creation, and to contemplate the creation as the only true and real word of God that ever did or ever will exist; and that everything else called the word of God is fable and imposition.[39]

Here, then, the real theological issue was raised and the direct claims of "natural" as over against "revealed" religion were laid bare. But as the exponents of natural religion had became explicit in their claims only when goaded into doing so to promote their reforms, the theological issue was inextricably bound up with the social and political issues and all but lost to sight.[40]

What could be clearly enough sensed by religious leaders of all groups, even by the most heart-happy pietists, was that the radical attack upon revelation undermined not only the traditionally authoritarian churches, Catholic and Protestant, but Christianity itself, as they conceived it. And this prospect could be made alarming not only to leaders in the several churches, including sectarian pietists, but also to many intellectuals who, while nominally, at least, Deists themselves, deplored the undermining of the people's simple faith.

At this juncture of events, as befitted the new republic, the battle became one for the allegiance of the masses of the people. Works like Ethan Allen's *Reason the Only Oracle of Man* (1784), and Paine's *Age of Reason* (1794) carried the issues to the people through popularization. And defenders of orthodox Christianity—men like Timothy Dwight—followed suit. Because most of them were revivalists they were eminently prepared to do so. Such popularized discussion conducted in the vernacular did not admit of subtle intellectual distinctions. The tendency on both sides greatly to oversimplify the issues became irresistible. Unless we keep this in mind we are not likely to understand the ensuing conflict. It was not a debate among intellectuals, but all-out ideological warfare—a battle for the mind of the people.

The striking revolutionary developments of the period provide the context. The European political situation lent itself to the interpretation that an Infidel International was deliberately fostering the overthrow of all religion and all government—that it had been successful in France and was pushing out from there. Jedediah Morse of the First Church of Charlestown, Massachusetts, became an outstanding spokesman for this view in his Fast Day sermon preached in Boston on May 9, 1798. He took his cue from a work published by Professor John Robison of the University of Edinburgh, the title of which is sufficiently explanatory of the contents:

> *Proofs of A Conspiracy Against All The Religions and Governments of Europe, Carried On In The Secret Meetings of Free Masons, Illuminati, and Reading Societies.*[41]

Morse claimed that branches of the Order were already established in America, and suggested that Paine's *Age of Reason* was one of its products. He held that the Democratic Societies were spreading the principles of illuminism through the land.

This simplified interpretation of the situation in America, although vehemently and soundly disputed by some, was of a nature to become widely accepted. It was picked up and broadly echoed through sermons and speeches until, as Vernon Stauffer concluded, "there was probably not a solitary Federalist leader in the United States who did not believe that French ministers and agents were in secret league with influential representatives of the Democratic party."[42]

Meanwhile the Federalists who, understandably enough, identified their continued well-being and control of the government with the continued well-being of the new nation, had in effect declared "war upon the ideas of the French Revolution" in the Sedition Act of 1798.[43] Such men easily recognized in the party led by Thomas Jefferson the American instrument of the Infidel International. Jefferson was known to have consorted with French Infidels during his five years in France. Always cautious in his public pronouncements on religion, he had revealed enough of his Deistic views to give popular plausibility to the notion that he was a thoroughgoing Infidel with diabolical designs on American institutions.[44] This view of Jefferson and his party seemed to be confirmed by the concurrent organization of radical Deistic Societies in several American cities, as well as the publication and circulation of several outspoken Deistic papers, and the attempt on the part of Deistic speakers—notably the renegade Baptist preacher, Elihu Palmer—to work up a definitely anti-church crusade among the people.[45]

It was in New England that the controversy became hottest, and the most effective anti-infidel party line was developed by colorful and able leaders. There the Congregational churches were established, and their clergy—Federalist almost to a man—were inclined to identify true religion with the Standing Order. Indeed, they constituted the chief bloc of opposition to the rising Jeffersonian party. The Jeffersonians, in turn, attacked this "political Congregationalism" which seemed to bear out the reformer's notion that the church was the mainstay of conservative and reactionary government. Disestablishment became one of the main objectives of the Jeffersonians as it was of the sects which suffered some restrictions and more humiliations under the Establishment.

Once disestablishment finally came, the realignment of sectarian-pietist with traditionalist against rationalist immediately took place. As Lyman Beecher noted, in retrospect, the defense of Establishment had led to a false alignment of religious forces. But once corrected "the occasion of animosity between us and the minor sects was removed, and infidels could no more make capital with them against us." Then indeed, those of the minor sects "began themselves to feel the dangers of infidelity, and to react against it, and this laid the basis of co-operation and union of spirit."[46] Thus the sectarian-pietist lamb snuggled up against the lion of traditionalism for protection against the infidel wolf. But there the metaphor breaks down, for the lion and the lamb produced offspring—the American Protestant denominations.

– IV –

The Revolutionary Epoch is the hinge upon which the history of Christianity in America really turns. During this period, forces and tendencies long gathering during the colonial era culminated in new expressions which came to such dominance that a fresh direction was given to the thought patterns and institutional life of the churches. The symbolic center of these new expressions is found in the declarations for religious freedom and separation of church and state, promoted, as we have seen, by that strange coalition of rationalist and pietist. With the realignment of pietist-sectarians and traditionalists against the rationalists, now viewed as Infidels,[47] came the second major development in this period, the birth of the new revivalism.

It is important to note that the theological issue which formed the basis of the union of traditionalist and sectarian-pietist in America—the issue, indeed, which constituted their real point of difference from the infidels—was all but lost sight of in the excited attack on infidelity. The most effective argument used against infidelity was moral and political, not theological. It was the "argument from tendency," the vivid assertion that infidel thinking led directly and necessarily to personal immorality and social chaos while Christianity was the only sure foundation for good morals and sound government, and that men must choose between these two. The success of this approach in gaining popular support in the attack on infidelity meant that the crucial issue between natural and revealed religion was seldom discussed on the theological level at all. Men like Timothy Dwight had a way of making what he called "infidelity" as vivid and repulsive for his generation as his grandfather, Jonathan Edwards, had made hell fire for a previous generation. Of such substance was much of the new revivalism shaped.

Although there was at the time a theological issue important enough to divide honest and able men, the nature of the controversy was such that it was not discussed on its own merits. Dwight's eminent men who were finally persuaded and began to insist that Christianity "was absolutely necessary to good Government, liberty and safety" were not necessarily convinced that revealed religion was true and natural religion was false. There is considerable evidence to indicate that they may have been convinced only that the choice was more expedient.[48]

The substance of the new revivalism, although clothed in less learning on the frontier than in New England, was the same the country over. The alignments that saw infidelity drowned in the great tidal wave of revivalism that swept the country early in the nineteenth century were formed during the Revolutionary Epoch. This new alignment was to condition the development of Protestantism in America for more than a century and to stamp it with characteristics that almost baffle analysis. But all are related to the fact that pietism came to dominate overwhelmingly in practically all the denominations.

This alignment of traditionalism and sectarian-pietism against rationalism gained a tremendous victory for Christianity in the popular arena, placing its marks and peculiar strengths and weaknesses upon all subsequent American Protestantism. Its strength produced "the Great Century [1814-1914]" celebrated by Professor Kenneth Scott Latourette in his massive "History of the Expansion of Christianity" series. Its weaknesses effectively scuttled much of the intellectual structure of Protestantism. When the tremendous growth and innumerable good works of American Protestantism are celebrated, it must also be noted that "no theologian or theology of first rank issued from the nineteenth-century Christianity of the United States."[49] Why? This analysis of the Revolutionary Epoch suggests that a primary reason may have been that Christianity won its first great battle with the forces of "infidelity" and evil in America with practically no appeal to a rigorous discussion of intellectual issues.

IV

Thomas Jefferson's "Fair Experiment"—Religious Freedom

Following the Revolutionary Epoch American Christians laid much unfinished intellectual business on the table as the free churches turned their attention to the practical problems confronting them. Organizations had to be perfected to meet the new conditions. Infidel currents of thought sweeping the people into an atheistic rapids had to be stemmed. A growing and rapidly moving population had to be won for Christ. The challenges were real.[1]

Revivalism, developed during the colonial period, emerged as the most effective technique for reaching the unchurched and turning the tide of infidelity. Revivalists, as will be noted in Chapter VII, tended to be intellectually uncritical and doctrinally amorphous. It has cogently been argued that the second great awakening "terminated the Puritan and inaugurated the Pietist or Methodist age of American church history."[2] In the long run the genuine passion for souls in the new evangelical denominations tended to overwhelm the traditionally and equally important passion for truth articulated in logical structures. In this situation, as Henry Steele Commager has said, "during the nineteenth century and well into the twentieth, religion prospered while theology went slowly bankrupt."[3]

The major piece of the churches' unfinished intellectual business to be examined in this essay is religious freedom. American

Protestantism has never developed any full-blown theoretical justification for its most distinctive practice. It was the rationalists who articulated the original defense at a time when religious coercion was not only accepted but deemed essential for the fulfillment of the churches' educational and spiritual role. But once they had religious freedom, the free churchmen rejected these erstwhile friends with great passion. Now, as we approach the two-hundredth anniversary of the Declaration of Independence, I think we must agree with the writer who on its one-hundredth anniversary argued that

we seem to have made no advance whatever in harmonizing [theoretically] the relations of religious sects among themselves, or in defining their common relation to the Civil power.[4]

– I –

The legal basis for the practice of separation of church and state in the United States is found in Article VI of the Constitution and the First Amendment. The first stipulates that "no religious test shall ever be required as a qualification to any office or public trust under the United States"; and the second, that "Congress shall make no law respecting an establishment of religion, or prohibiting the free exercise thereof; or abridging the freedom of speech or of the press; or the right of the people peaceably to assemble and to petition the Government for a redress of grievances."

Obviously these provisions applied only to the officers of the United States, and to acts of the Federal Congress. They in no wise directly affected the church establishments in those states where they existed at the time, and as late as 1891 a court declared that "the States may establish a Church or Creed, and maintain them, so far as the Federal Constitution is concerned." Only in the twentieth century have the courts by invoking the Fourteenth Amendment made the guarantee of religious freedom for all citizens a matter for the cognizance of the Federal Courts.

– II –

The laconic brevity and consequent vagueness of the original constitutional provisions make the question of what was meant by them a problem of the historical interpretation of the founders' motives and intentions in declaring them. The First Amendment went into effect November 3, 1791. Meanwhile most of the new states had debated, formulated, and accepted new constitutions, and all had faced and solved in one way or another the problem of church and state. But it was in Virginia that the debates had been most pointed and where the outcome was most clearly and decisively for complete separation. Hence it is to the writings of the Virginians that we naturally turn first for an understanding of what religious freedom meant to those who wrote it into the laws.

Out of the Virginia debates came two classic and definitive statements, Thomas Jefferson's "Bill for Establishing Religious Freedom in Virginia," which went into effect early in 1796, and James Madison's "Memorial and Remonstrance on the Religious Rights of Man" of 1784. The conception of religious freedom that emerges from careful study of these statements may be summarized as follows:

It meant that each individual was to be left free to make up his own mind about religion; he was to have liberty to express his opinions freely, and to seek to persuade others to his view; he was to suffer no deprivations or penalties, civil or otherwise, as a result; and he was not to be forced to contribute to the support of any ecclesiastical institution, even to the one in which he believed. Religion was defined as one's "opinion" (the key word) about "the duty which we owe to our creator, and the manner of discharging it." The right to such opinion was said to be an "unalienable" right, because the opinions of men depend "only on the evidence contemplated in their own minds" and hence "cannot follow the dictates of other men." That is, an unalienable right is of such nature that one cannot relinquish the responsibility for exercising it even if one wants to. "The care

of every man's soul belongs to himself," said Jefferson in his
Notes on Religion. "The magistrate has no power but what the
people gave," and they "have not given him the care of souls
because they could not; they could not, because no man has
right to abandon the care of his salvation to another." Each man
must do his own thinking and believing, as he must do his own
dying.

A church (i.e., an ecclesiastical institution) is, as Jefferson put
it, echoing almost word for word the definition of John Locke,
merely

"a *voluntary* society of men, joining themselves together of their own
accord, in order to the public worshipping of god in such a manner
as they judge acceptable to him and effectual to the salvation of their
souls." It is *voluntary* because no man is *by nature* bound to any
church. The hope of salvàtion is the cause of his entering into it. If
he find anything wrong in it, he should be as free to go out as he was
to come in.

Such a voluntary society may, of course, define and set up its
own standards, and enforce its own criteria for entrance into
membership and for continued fellowship. But "its laws extend
to its own members only."[5] And so far as the civil power is
concerned, a church, as Roger Williams had said in *The Bloudy
Tenent of Persecution,*

(whether true or false) is like unto a Body or College of Physicians in
a City; like unto a Corporation, Society, or Company of East-Indie or
Turkie-merchants, or any other Society or Company in London;
which Companies may hold their Courts, keep their Records, hold
disputations; and in matters concerning their Society, may dissent,
divide, break into Schisms and Factions, sue and implead each other
at the Law, yea, wholly break up and dissolve into pieces and nothing.

without any interference whatsoever.

Finally it meant, as we shall see more clearly below, that the
work of these free churches is the foundation for "order in
government and obedience to the laws." The churches thus make
their necessary contribution to the "public welfare."

– III –

These views are so ingrained in the American mind that it requires some effort to realize that at the time they were considered a very daring innovation—an experiment worth trying but of uncertain outcome. Yet the evidence seems conclusive enough, as two typical quotations from Jefferson will indicate. In his *Notes on the State of Virginia; Written in 1781 . . . [and] . . . 1782*, and first published in Paris in 1785, he noted that

Our sister States of Pennsylvania and New York, . . . have long subsisted without any establishment at all. The experiment was new and doubtful when they made it. It has answered beyond conception. They flourish infinitely. Religion is well supported; of various kinds, indeed, but all good enough; all sufficient to preserve peace and order; . . . Let us too give this experiment fair play . . .

Toward the end of his term as President, Jefferson was sanguine about the outcome of the experiment on a national scale. In a letter of reply to a group of Baptists in Virginia, November 21, 1808, after commending them for consistently standing among "the friends of religious freedom," he said:

We have solved by fair experiment, the great and interesting question whether freedom of religion is compatible with order in government, and obedience to the laws. And we have experienced the quiet as well as the comfort which results from leaving everyone to profess freely and openly those principles of religion which are the inductions of his own reason, and the serious convictions of his own inquiries.[6]

These typical quotations emphasize that leaders like Jefferson considered the practice of religious freedom a great experiment. They also suggest a centrality and stress on the importance of discovering whether this kind of religious freedom was compatible with "order in government and obedience to the laws."

At the time it was not at all obvious that it was, because, as professor W. E. Garrison has pointed out:

For more than fourteen hundred years . . . it was a universal assumption that the stability of the social order and the safety of the state demanded the religious solidarity of all the people in one church. Every responsible thinker, every ecclesiastic, every ruler and statesman who gave the matter any attention, held to this as an axiom. There was no political or social philosophy which did not build upon this assumption. . . . *all,* with no exceptions other than certain disreputable and "subversive" heretics, believed firmly that religious solidarity in the one recognized church was essential to social and political stability.

Granted this, the declaration for religious freedom in the American Constitution was "on the administrative side" one of the "two most profound revolutions which have occurred in the entire history of the church."[7]

– IV –

The question naturally arises as to how this momentous revolution in the thinking and practice of Christendom came to be accepted even as an experiment. In answer it is worth stressing first that the Revolutionary leaders came to see that it was practically unavoidable—that if there was to be a *United* States of America there had to be national religious freedom. The genius of the founding fathers in this matter was not that of the creation of the idea, but rather that of realistic recognition of the "actual condition of things" religious.

Looking back on the period we see that right-wing groups were still most powerful in every area, and not one of them rejected Establishment on principle. But no religious group, or possible combination of groups, was in a position to make a plausible bid for a national Establishment, even had the desire been present. Meanwhile all the religious groups had come to see the possibilities of voluntaryism in the churches through the experience during the great awakenings. At the same time the desire for an Establishment had been weakened and undercut by the general prevalence of rationalistic thinking and pietistic sentiment in the existing churches. The real social and political leaders who gave structure to the new political order were most of them rationalists or Deists, and they renounced Establishment on principle. This was particularly important for the decision against "multiple Establishment," which many found quite acceptable at the time, and for complete separation, which only a few of the less influential sects—notably the Baptists and Quakers—clearly held on principle.

Finally, on the matter of religious freedom, probably all the religious groups were unanimous on one thing: each wanted the complete freedom to propagandize its own view and to work out its own way. It had become obvious to them that the only way that each could get such freedom for itself was to grant it to all the others.[8]

Back of this revolution in practice and hand in hand with it lay the ideological revolution—the tremendously complex and subtle revolution in ways of thinking which was necessary to make the new practice acceptable even as an experiment. Calling attention to one broad characteristic of it will aid our understanding of developments. All the lines of thinking of the eighteenth century converged on the idea of free, uncoerced, individual consent as the only proper basis for all man's organizations, civil and ecclesiastical. This meant that support for enforced uniformity of belief and practice necessarily faded away.

The two dynamic movements of the century which exemplify the transformation in ways of thinking were rationalism and pietism. Rationalism fostered the idea of individual human autonomy guided by the light of Nature and Nature's God, through Reason. "Reason," of course, did not mean merely the process of reasoning, but a basic principle of human nature through which man, the creature, was enabled to read the great revelation of the Creator in His works and to shape his conduct accordingly. The individual was, and could be, moved and guided only by the weight of the evidence contemplated in his own mind—and herein lay his autonomy. Coercion of opinion in the interest of uniformity, Jefferson thought, had served only "to make one half the world fools, and the other half hypocrites."

Pietism also fostered an idea of human autonomy—guidance of

the individual under grace by the Spirit, checked by the objective revelation in Scripture. The individual was and could be moved and guided only by his own personal experience of such grace, and herein lay his autonomy—his independence in Christ. Thus Pietism moved toward *"no creed but the Bible"* and the right of *"private judgment"* under grace, in its interpretation.[9]

Hence the pietist did not have the heart, as the rationalist did not have the head, longer to justify coerced uniformity under Establishment. So during the eighteenth century rationalists and pietists could easily combine forces on the practical and legal issue of religious freedom against the defenders of Establishment who took the traditional view of the matter. Professor Sweet's generalization requires qualification, but it is not too far amiss. It was, he said,

the leadership of such Lockian disciples as Jefferson and Madison, backed by an overwhelming left-wing Protestant public opinion, that was responsible for writing the clauses guaranteeing religious freedom into the new state constitutions and finally into the fundamental law of the land.[10]

It is important to emphasize in passing that for neither the rationalists nor the pietists was acceptance of the principle of free, uncoerced, individual consent an acceptance of guidance through individual whimsey. They did not surrender to the kind of individualism that sets the individual over against the community in an antagonistic relationship, because they envisaged the individual's consent as first to the authorities and laws necessary for stability and order in the community. For both the rationalist and the pietist, the individual became free only as he consented to necessary authority, discipline, and responsibility.

– V –

In this general context we now turn to the important question of the real difference between Establishment and religious freedom—that is, to the essential nature of what Jefferson called the "fair experiment."

Establishment rested upon two basic assumptions: that the existence and well-being of any society depends upon a body of commonly shared religious beliefs—the nature of man, his place in the cosmos, his destiny, and his conduct toward his fellow men—and that the only guarantee that these necessary beliefs will be sufficiently inculcated is to put the coercive power of the state behind the institution responsible for their definition, articulation, and inculcation. At least, it was supposed, there must be enough coercive power to compel attendance upon the teachings, and to suppress or cut off dangerous aberrations.

Thus the whole structure rests upon the common interest in "order in government and obedience to the laws," as Jefferson put it.

Religious freedom did not mean giving up the first assumption, that is, the necessity for the commonly shared basic religious ideas. It meant only the rejection of the second assumption, namely, that the institution(s) responsible for their inculcation must have the coercive power of the state behind it (or them). The essence of the revolution was, then, the rejection of coercion in favor of persuasion.

Looked at in this fashion, religious freedom can be seen to have had some very profound and far-reaching implications that perhaps were not too clearly grasped at the time, and certainly seldom are today.

First, from the viewpoint of the society and the state we may note the following:

There will be a multiplicity of religious groups, or "sects" as the rationalists consistently called them.

Each and every sect will inculcate in its own way the basic religious beliefs that are essential. This is what Jefferson thought had been demonstrated in New York and Pennsylvania. There religion is well supported, he said, "of various kinds, indeed, but all good enough; [because] all sufficient to preserve peace and order."

How much Jefferson's optimistic view was actually based on

observation of the experiment in those states, and how much it was the result of imposing a rationalistic assumption upon the situation, is a moot question. Certainly the rationalists were so imbued with a theory of the essentials of every religion that they were prepared to find what they were looking for in each. Benjamin Franklin reflected these sentiments as an unclouded mirror when he said in his *Autobiography:*

I had been religiously educated as a Presbyterian; and tho' some of the dogmas of that persuasion, such as the *eternal decrees of God, election, reprobation, etc.,* appeared to me unintelligible, others doubtful, and I early absented myself from the public assemblies of the sect, Sunday being my studying day, I never was without some religious principles. I never doubted, for instance, the existence of the Deity; that he made the world, and govern'd it by his Providence; that the most acceptable service of God was the doing of good to men; that our souls are immortal; and that all crime will be punished, and virtue rewarded, either here or hereafter. These I esteem'd the essentials of every religion; and, being to be found in all the religions we had in our country, I respected them all, tho' with different degrees of respect, as I found them more or less mix'd with other articles, which, without any tendency to inspire, promote, or confirm morality, serv'd principally to divide us, and make us unfriendly to one another. This respect to all, with an opinion that the worst had some good effects, induc'd me to avoid all discourse that might tend to lessen the good opinion another might have of his own religion; and as our province increas'd in people, and new places of worship were continually wanted, and generally erected by voluntary contribution, my mite for such purpose, whatever might be the sect, was never refused.[11]

Men whose primary interest was in good citizens, and who could see that even the worst sects "had some good effects" in producing them, were prepared to note that all sects were good enough.

Much more important, however, is the fact that Jefferson's theory implies that the limits even of religious freedom are to be defined by the "public welfare."[12] Apparently the eighteenth-century leaders who fathered the new government with its experiment in religious freedom did not have to wrestle with any outstanding practical consequences of this view, as generations of later justices had to in dealing, for example, with polygamous Mormons or Jehovah's Witnesses whose refusal to salute the flag was widely thought to be inimical to the public welfare. Beginning as the founders did with the assumption that the basic religious beliefs they held were merely the essentials of every religion, they naturally concluded that all religious groups teach and inculcate them under whatever peculiar disguise they may adopt. Hence they could hardly envisage a time when some or even all the religious groups might not teach them at all, or might not teach and inculcate them adequately for the support of the public welfare.

Here, then, is a troublesome lacuna in the theory. But it seems a fair conclusion that (since the public welfare was to set the limits even of religious freedom, and the public welfare is a matter for the state to define) the way was left open for the state, if and when it judged that the religious sects were inadequate or derelict in the matter, to defend itself by setting up the institutions or machinery necessary to guarantee the dissemination and inculcation of the necessary beliefs.

Second, there were also profound implications in this theory for the churches or sects.

The free churches accepted, or had forced upon them *on these* terms, the duty and responsibility to define, articulate, disseminate, and inculcate the basic religious beliefs essential for the existence and well-being of the society—and of doing this without any coercive power over the citizens at all, that is, armed only with persuasive power.

More subtly, they also accepted by implication the typically rationalist view that only what all the churches held and taught in common (the "essentials of every religion") was really relevant for the well-being of the society and the state. Obversely this meant that they accepted the view that whatever any religious group held peculiarly as a tenet of its faith must be irrelevant for the general welfare.

It is hard to escape the conclusion that each religious group accepted, by implication, the responsibility to teach that its peculiar doctrines, which made it distinct from other sects and gave it its only reason for separate existence, were either irrelevant for the general welfare of the nation-community, or at most, possessed only an indirect and instrumental value for it. It is no wonder that a sense of irrelevance has haunted religious leaders in America ever since.

The rationalists were clear on this point, as the quotation from Franklin above makes obvious. Franklin exhibited his consistency when he rejected the minister whose sermons seemed aimed "rather to make us Presbyterians than good citizens"—thus saying in effect that you really cannot do both. All the spectacular success of the free churches in America in effecting numerical growth and geographical expansion, insofar as it has been success in making men peculiarly Roman Catholic, Presbyterian, Methodist, Baptist, Lutheran, or what not (as was most generally the goal), has taken place under this Damoclean sword—the haunting suspicion that somehow relevance to the general welfare decreased in proportion to sectarian success. And hence the prevailing and continuous sense of tension in America between the claims of the religion of the public welfare and denominational religion for supreme allegiance.

In pointing to these implications of religious freedom from the viewpoints of the state and of the "sects," we point to the Trojan horse in the comfortable citadel of denominationalism under such freedom in the United States.

– VI –

Perhaps the most striking power that the churches surrendered under religious freedom was control over public education which traditionally had been considered an essential aspect of the work of an established church if it was to perform its proper function of disseminating and inculcating the necessary foundational religious beliefs. Ideally under religious freedom, as conceived by the rationalists, the free churches might continue to possess such control, since, dividing the population among themselves, each in its own way would inculcate the basic beliefs (the "essentials of every religion") common to all, and necessary for the general welfare.

But for many and complex reasons this proved completely impracticable in the United States. For one thing, the task was too immense to be supported by voluntary churches that claimed as members only 10 to 20 per cent of the total population. And so somewhat by default the state took over what had traditionally been part of the work of the church.[13] If we ask, Why the rise of compulsory free public education? must it not be said that prominent among the reasons was a desire to make possible and to guarantee the dissemination and inculcation among the embryo citizens of the beliefs essential to the existence and well-being of the democratic society?

And who can deny that these beliefs are religious? Certainly this was clearly recognized by early leaders such as Horace Mann, who frankly stood for "nonsectarian" religious teaching in the public schools. But it was soon discovered that there could be no "nonsectarian" religious teaching in America, because religion had been poured into sectarian molds and had hardened in sectarian forms. Thus Horace Mann's brand seemed to many evangelical Protestants to be suspiciously "Unitarian," and at best what passed as "nonsectarian" religious teaching seemed to many Unitarians, Roman Catholics, and others to be evangelical Protestantism. Even the Bible was ruled out, for it could not be read in the public schools except in "sectarian" English translations.

Here are the roots of the dilemma posed by the acceptance of the practice of separation of church and state on the one hand, and the general acceptance of compulsory public education sponsored by the state on the other. Here is the nub of the matter that is all too often completely overlooked. It was very clearly stated by J. L. Diman in the *North American Review* for January, 1876. If it is true, he said,

that the temporal and spiritual authorities occupy two wholly distinct provinces, and that to one of these civil government should be exclusively shut up . . . it would be difficult to make out a logical defense of our present system of public education. If, on the contrary, it be the right and duty of the state to enforce support of public educa- tion . . . [upon all citizens], then our current theory respecting the nature and functions of the state stands in need of considerable re- vision.[14]

Diman's point is based upon the recognition that of necessity the state in its public-education system is and always has been teaching religion. It does so because the well-being of the nation and the state demands this foundation ·of shared beliefs. In other words, the public schools in the United States took over one of the basic responsibilities that traditionally was always assumed by an established church. In this sense the public-school system of the United States *is* its established church. But the situation in America is such that none of the many religious sects can admit without jeopardizing its existence that the religion taught in the schools (or taught by any other sect for that matter) is "true" in the sense that it can legitimately claim supreme al- legiance. This serves to accentuate the dichotomy between the religion of the nation inculcated by the state through the public schools, and the religion of the denominations taught in the free churches.

In this context one can understand why it is that the religion of many Americans is democracy—why their real faith is the "democratic faith"—the religion of the public schools. Such understanding enables one to see religious freedom and separa- tion of church and state in a new light.

One of the most provocative contributions to the discussion of these matters is contained in the final chapter of a book pub- lished in 1952 with the title *What Americans Believe and How They Worship.** The author, Professor J. Paul Williams, pro-

* While my manuscript was being prepared Harper & Row issued a revised and considerably expanded edition of this book. In it Dr. Williams makes the argument of his final chapter even clearer by employing a dis- tinction between *"private, denominational,* and *societal"* forms of religious functioning, and by answering some specific criticisms of his position. However, the basic argument remains the same. Because, with a few minor word changes, all the sentences I have quoted from the 1952 edition in

poses that in order to meet the present crisis "governmental agencies must teach the democratic ideal *as religion*."[15] This is essentially an appeal for a State Church in the United States, and his arguments for it largely parallel those traditionally used to defend Establishments.[16] They are worth examining for they suggest that Americans may now have to take up some of the intellectual business that was laid on the table so long ago. They must face some of the implications of religious freedom that were almost forgotten.

The bulk of Dr. Williams' book is an examination of "the traditional religions" in the United States which leads him to the conclusion that so far as the public welfare is concerned they largely cancel each other out and are irrelevant. In the last chapter entitled "The Role of Religion in Shaping American Destiny" he constructs his thesis.

"A culture", he argues, "is above everything else a faith, a set of shared convictions, a spiritual entity," and its continued health and well-being depends upon the maintenance of this faith in the hearts and minds of the people. Hence "systematic and universal indoctrination is essential in the values on which a society is based, if that society is to have any permanence or stability." This will be recognized as the first assumption underlying an established church.

In the present crisis, he goes on to say, with democracy threatened from all sides "Americans do not even have a clear common conception of what the democratic ideal is," and hence "America runs a grave danger from lack of attention to the spiritual core which is the heart of her national existence. If we are to avoid this danger, democracy must become an object of religious dedication. Americans must come to look on the democratic ideal (not necessarily American practice of it) as the Will of God or, if they please, the law of Nature." This means the articulation, dissemination, and inculcation of beliefs. And in

---

presenting Dr. Williams' position remain in the 1962 edition, I have let my presentation stand. I realize that no such summary can do complete justice to the lucidity and full intent of his argument.

order to achieve this "it will be necessary to mobilize many agencies" among which "the churches and synagogues are obviously first on the list."

But although these religious institutions are already doing quite a bit to bolster democracy, Dr. Williams sees little reason to suppose that they can or will do the job that is necessary on a broad enough scale or fast enough, for "the churches receive but voluntary attention [and that from 'but half the population']; the government may require attention [of 'all the population']." This will be recognized as appeal to the second assumption underlying an established church—the institution responsible for inculcating the basic beliefs must have behind it the coercive power of the state. Naturally Dr. Williams turns to the public-school system. No other agency, he argues, is in as strategic a position to teach democracy and to bring "the majority of our people to a religious devotion to the democratic way of life." But whatever agencies may be enlisted, "we must find ways to awaken in the hearts of multitudes of Americans a devotion to democratic ideals like the devotion given by ardent believers in every age to the traditional religions," even though this means "giving the power of wholesale religious indoctrination into the hands of politicians. . . ."

As for those who object on one ground or another, Dr. Williams' answer is clear and concise. He steps forthrightly into the way left open by the founding fathers. "But at those points where religion is a public matter, those areas which contain the ethical propositions essential to corporate welfare, society will only at its peril allow individuals and sects to indulge their dogmatic whims."

For Dr. Williams, religious freedom means primarily the "freedom to follow conscience in private worship."[17]

It is hard to understand why the publication of these views from such a source apparently attracts little attention. Anson Phelps Stokes' study of *Church and State in the United States* concludes with the suggestion that perhaps concern for religious freedom is being drowned in a sea of religious indifference. That could be part of the answer. Another guess is that knowledge of the history is so eroded that Dr. Williams' position seems utterly foreign and implausible and is not taken seriously.

In the light of what has been said above, I think, it ought to be taken seriously because it has real historical roots in our tradition. What Dr. Williams seems to be saying is that we have tried the "fair experiment" and found that Jefferson was over optimistic in supposing the many sects, armed only with persuasive power, would be effective in inculcating the religious and moral principles necessary for order in government and obedience to the laws. They have failed. Therefore the government in self-defense must step in and do the job, even though this means suppressing some of the "dogmatic whims" of religious individuals and groups. For the well-being of the commonwealth must determine the limits even of religious freedom. Democracy, in a state of siege, must ask that "governmental agencies . . . teach the democratic ideal as religion."

This argument ought to be answered if possible, not ignored.

V

Abraham Lincoln's "Last, Best Hope of Earth": The American Dream of Destiny and Democracy

Our freer, but yet far from freed, land is the asylum, if asylum there be, for the hope of man; and, there, if anywhere, is the second Eden to be planted in which the divine seed is to bruise the head of Evil and restore Man to his rightful communion with God in the Paradise of Good.[1]

Charles and Mary Beard described the first three volumes of their monumental *Rise of American Civilization* as a work which dealt mainly "with the outward aspects of civilization in the United States" expressed in "government, politics, economy, institutions, letters, arts, and sciences." Apparently sensing the inadequacy of such history to explain the primary premise of *a* civilization, they then published a fourth volume in an attempt to "reckon with the intellectual and moral motivation of men and women."[2] In doing so they exemplified the perennial effort to get at the spiritual and ideological bases of the nation—to define the common hopes and fears, ideas and aspirations, that transcend and undergird all the tangible differences between men and fuse them into a coherent whole. This effort is necessary because the vitality of the democracy depends upon the maintenance of diversity, with outward expression in organizations, parties, and factions, until at times there is danger of losing sight of the underlying unity.

Thomas Jefferson, entering into the office of the Presidency after years of bitter controversy had accentuated the differences that obviously divided the new Americans, reminded the people in his first inaugural that

> every difference of opinion is not a difference of principle. We have called by different names brethren of the same principle. We are all republicans—we are [all] federalists.

He could as well have said, we are all Americans, and the principles that we share are greater than the differences that have divided us—the contests in which we engage are as much *within* us as *between* us.

Abraham Lincoln, in a real sense the spiritual center of American history, upon assuming the same high office two generations later when sectional differences were rapidly moving into irrepressible conflict, spoke almost sadly of "our bonds of affection" and "the mystic chords of memory" that "will yet swell the chorus of the Union when again touched, as surely they will be, by the better angels of our nature." In the Second Inaugural he gave a definitely religious content to the "bonds of affection." "Both [North and South, he said] read the same Bible, and pray to the same God; and each invokes His aid against the other." Obviously "the prayers of both could not be answered—[and] that of neither has been answered fully." Why? Because in the movements of human history "the Almighty has his own purposes." This is to say that all the works of finite men stand always under the judgment of the infinite God—and "the will of God prevails." Hence the most that finite men can do in all their striving is to stand "with firmness in the right as God [*now*] gives us to see the right"—the "right" being conformity with the ultimate purposes of the infinite God. But since man is finite he can never be absolutely sure that he rightly senses the will of the infinite God. Finally, then, he must bow in humble acknowledgment that

> if, after endeavoring to do my best in the light which he affords me, I find my efforts fail, I must believe that for some purpose unknown to me, he wills it otherwise.[3]

It is because man is finite that he must be humble in all his relationships with his fellow finite men—that he must approach all the complex problems of human existence finally "with malice toward none; with charity for all"—always with the realization that in the sight of God he may be wrong. No finite man is big enough to cherish malice. Here is the basis for Lincoln's uncanny knack of putting first things first, as when a certain clergyman wrote him expressing the hope that God was on the side of the North. Lincoln replied that this did not worry him, but that he was concerned that the North be on God's side.

It was within this context that Lincoln referred to the preservation of freedom in the Union as "the last, best hope of earth" which Americans might "nobly save or meanly lose."[4] And the genius of the Union—the "new nation, conceived in liberty, and dedicated to the proposition that all men are created equal" —is the principle of "government of the people, by the people, for the people." It is this principle that is "the last, best hope of the earth," and the duty of Americans is to see to it that it "shall not perish from the earth."

Here in Lincoln is found the most profound statement of what Charles and Mary Beard were looking for—the "intellectual and moral motivation" of what Crèvecoeur had called "the American, this new man." One can get at the mind and spirit of a people or nation by ascertaining the breadth and depth of their conception of "where we are and whither we are tending," and their practice can be judged on the basis of their consequent conception of "what to do and how to do it." The first defines their ideal, the second their way—that is, the path to the fulfillment of their ideal.

It is here suggested that for Americans the ideal was defined in terms of "destiny under God," and the way that of what Lincoln called "a constitutional republic or democracy—a government of the people by the same people."[5] America was to fulfill her destiny, under God, by working out in practice and demonstrating for all the world to see, the true possibilities of such government. The ideal and the way were inseparable—that is inherent in the idea of destiny. Hence the practice itself stood always under the judgment of God. Departure from the "way" was not only lamentable, it was insofar rebellion against God and hence always tinged with a sense of profound guilt. This is why, as Santayana put it so well, "to be an American is of itself almost a moral condition, an education, and a career."[6] And here is suggested a way to get hold of the religious roots and heart of America which it is the purpose of this essay to explore.

– I –

A sense of destiny is of course not peculiar to Americans. Such a sense seems to be a necessary ingredient in the self-consciousness of every people; an element common to the mind of every Western nation that helps to define for its people their corporate sense of direction through the vast and misty labyrinth of history. Their sense of destiny is deeply rooted in the formative experiences of a people. But the important thing is the interpretation of the experiences—that subtle combination of insight into, and articulation of, the meaning of the experience that is so deeply persuasive and widely accepted that it becomes a part of the common consciousness and passes into the realm of motivational myths. The experience of the Hebrew people in breaking away from Egypt, crossing the Red Sea, and entering into a land of their own was striking enough to be celebrated in song and story. But the important thing was that this happened to a people who had it in them to translate the experience into "the exodus." That made the difference between merely a successful rebellion of an obscure people, and the myth of a chosen people that through all subsequent history has remained a pillar of fire by night and of cloud by day.

The outstanding peculiarity of the settlement of that part of the North American continent that became the United States was the mixture of peoples of many different traditions. Their most striking experience was that of learning to live together side by side and eventually of launching a new and independent nation. "Here," said Crèvecoeur, "individuals of all nations are melted into a new race of men." Here "from this promiscuous breed" has emerged "the American, this new man" who is "that strange mixture of blood" and traditions "which you will find in no other country."[7]

What then, finally, welded these diverse peoples together and gave them a common consciousness? Obviously it was not the sharing of a common national past, or of a common tradition conveyed in a stream of wisdom literature, of folk tales and myths. In America these people, these immigrants living and working side by side with those from other nations, could not for long continue to think of themselves as peculiarly Englishmen, Germans, Frenchmen, Irishmen, Scotsmen. Gradually the old world consciousness faded into the background as a new world consciousness took shape within them. The emigrant leaving an old world was transformed into the immigrant coming to a new world. In this metamorphosis the old traditions were sometimes forgotten, sometimes strangely mixed, but most commonly they tended merely to cancel each other out in the common confrontation with the new situation.

What these emigrant people really shared was the strangeness, the vastness, the challenges of the new country, and the consciousness of the freedom offered by great space with its untold opportunities. In this situation there emerged the sense that here was opportunity to begin all over again—to be in the new world a new man largely unfettered by tradition, custom, and law. Here, said Crèvecoeur of the transplanted Europeans, "everything has tended to regenerate them."[8] What they shared that bound them together was not a past but the present and a future.

Yet the history of mankind exhibits a massive unbroken continuity which could not be broken even by the emigrants' long step across the ocean. They might forget the past, but the past would condition the way they could think about their present and future. Hence when we say that the various transplanted traditions tended to cancel each other out, we mean the peculiar elements of each—and when Crèvecoeur said that in America "the various Christian sects introduced, wear out,"[9] what he meant was that zealous sectarianism tended to be swallowed up in the larger whole.

During the formative years of English colonization most of the immigrants were Protestants from the Christian nations of Europe. When they came to think about the meaning of the new situation inevitably they thought within the context of this common background. While they shared the sense of new beginnings, they also shared Christian tradition which provided the molds into which their thinking about these new beginnings necessarily ran. What they could think they were doing was determined by what they were at the time—and they were Christians.

Primarily what they shared as Christians was belief in God, the Creator, and His governance of the universe under His providence. Perry Miller has demonstrated this in his two articles on the literature of early Virginia.

The doctrine of providence meant that God governed the universe not only in space but also in time, and as there was an intelligent purpose in each enactment, so all events were connected in a long-range program which men call history.

In this context,

Events were not produced by the blind operations of cause and effect, economic motives, or human contrivances; these were "second causes" through which God worked. The "first cause" was always His will.

Finally, then, the principal human concern in colonization was "neither the rate of interest nor the discovery of gold, but the will of God." Within this climate of opinion every event, great and small, received meaning only as it was related to the purposes of God, and by the same token every event, as Emerson was to note with some nostalgia, was held in its place by the weight of the universe. So it was natural that *Purchas His Pilgrim* should begin the history of Virginia of 1625 with Adam and Eve, in order to "show how God had so managed the past that

English colonization in the present was the fulfillment of His plan."[10]

God did, of course, hold all the nations in the hollow of His hand, and He did use any and all men to effect His ultimate purposes in history. But Christians differed from non-Christians in that they, guided by revelation and under grace, responded and consented consciously and willingly to God's calling. Here is one root of the doctrine of special calling, and the foundation of the idea of a "peculiar people." Cotton Mather but echoed a commonplace when he pointed to the parallel between the exodus of the Hebrews from Egypt and the flight of the Puritans to New England.[11] John Cotton, on the eve of the departure of Winthrop fleet in 1630, preached to the emigrants from II Samuel 7:10:

Moreover I will appoint a place for my people Israel, and I will plant them, that they may dwell in a place of their own, and move no more.

He reminded them that "here is meant some special appointment, because God tells them it by his owne mouth . . . others take the land by his providence, but God's people take the land by promise."[12] And John Rolfe of Virginia was equally sure that the English migration to Virginia was a going forth of "a peculiar people, marked and chosen by the finger of God, to possess it, for undoubtedly he is with us."[13]

In this view the Christian consciously sailed to the new land and planted colonies under a contract or covenant with God.[14] The purposes of God might not be seen clearly or in detail at the time, but it was known that God had a purpose which would be unfolded and thus revealed in the subsequent history, and in His own good time. Such men walked always under the mercy and judgment of God, and knew God through blessings and through adversities. Finally, they thought, men read the purposes of God in the unfolding events of the history they experienced, guided by the Spirit and the light of His word.

Recognition of this conception of providence in the thinking of the time obviates most of the complicated arguments about the primacy of religious, economic, political, or social motives behind the emigration and colonization. To many moderns it comes as a surprise that the contemporaries who wrote about the founding of New England or Virginia were just as aware of economic, social, and political motives, and just as hardheaded about them as the most blatant economic determinists of recent times. But such was the case. God might and did, they thought, use devious methods, luring men through their natural inclinations and even their selfish propensities toward the fulfillment of His ultimate purposes, of which men might not be conscious at all. It is clear, for example, from John Winthrop's account of his reasons for emigrating, that he never thought for a moment that God spoke directly to him, telling him one day to pack up and go to America. Rather God in His infinite wisdom brought about a situation in England no longer tolerable for a gentleman and true Christian, while at the same time He opened in America the opportunity to build the Church of Christ anew together with a Commonwealth suited thereto. Of course He also made it somewhat profitable for commercially minded Christian gentlemen to do so.[15]

This view gave to the everyday events of life under God an experimental and revelatory character. One must constantly in fear and trembling attempt to interpret the "signs of the times" in order correctly to assess the meaning and purposes of God and to act accordingly. The practical everyday life of the individual might in this sense be quite pragmatic, since all that was required of him was to take one step at a time. So, for example, when these colonists experienced reverses and calamities, they were prepared to see them as signs of God's displeasure at their human failure in carrying out the terms of the covenant. The Puritan view of "God's controversy with New England" is well known. But likewise in 1622 the leaders of the Virginia Company were reminded in a pamphlet that their sufferings in and through the colony came because they had failed in their covenant with God.[16] Thus under God there was no "inevitable progress." Success was conditioned upon fulfilling the conditions of the covenant, and men could fail.

Here is the basis for the American sense of destiny under God. The opportunity to begin all over again in the new land was seen as taking place under the infinite wisdom and providence of the Christian God of mercy and of judgment whose will was to be read in the events of the unfolding history itself. Thus the Americans, those new men, came to look upon themselves as a peculiar, a chosen people, set apart by God to serve a peculiar purpose in the history of mankind—a purpose that would be fully revealed in God's good time. This was their destiny which to be known had to be lived out.

– II –

Inherent in this conception of destiny under God, then, was the expectation that the way to its fulfillment would be revealed gradually through the ebb and flow of the daily life of these people. So they were prepared to work it out. And gradually during the complex give and take of the seventeenth and eighteenth centuries emerged the conviction that the way was that of democracy. This conviction was given its classic expression during the last quarter of the eighteenth century, and was then tried in the fires of revolution which burned it deeply into the spirit of the people.

No attempt to present the essence of the democratic way in schematic fashion can be universally satisfying to all, in large part because it was conceived as a way, a path, and not as a static system. But one may speak of certain fundamental beliefs upon which the whole structure of the experiment rests.

First, there was belief in God. "I [or we] believe in God . . ." is the first article of every Christian creed. This means essentially that the believers presuppose in all their thinking that God exists. The God in whom they profess belief is a God of will and purpose, and hence the expression of belief is equivalent to the assertion that there is order and ultimate meaning in the universe which is discoverable at least in part by man. This was one of the central assertions and teachings of Christianity and a basic element in the matrix of all Western civilization.[17]

Second, there was belief in "the people." "The people" is a complex concept, hard to describe and define. "The people" is the very stuff of history—the massive, unbroken stream of human life with its tremendous inertia and momentum—through which the Spirit of God works to the effecting of His infinite purposes. "The people" transcends all individuals and all groups, and even all human conceptions of good and evil. "The people" is the bearer of the wisdom of God for the conduct and guidance of man. As Lincoln summed it up—"the will of God prevails . . . [and] the human instrumentalities, working just as they do, are of the best adaptation to effect his purpose."[18] The voice of the people is the voice of God—in no simple or immediate sense, but rather in the complex sense that Lincoln is reputed to have suggested in the comment that while some of the people can be fooled and hence be wrong all of the time, and all of the people can be fooled and hence be wrong part of the time, nevertheless in the long run it appears that all of the people cannot be fooled and hence be wrong all of the time. This means that the whimsies of the multitude at any point in history need not bespeak the will of the Almighty, but rather that for men there is no higher court of appeal in the long run than the will of "the people" —the stuff of history itself. Ultimately then, "the people shall be judge."[19]

Third, there was the belief that the will of the people which is finally the surest clue to the will of God, can really be known only when all the channels of communication and expression are kept open. The Christian basis for this view is the idea that the Spirit of God cannot be fenced in, channeled through any human contrivances, or its working predicted. "The wind bloweth where it listeth." The eighteenth century gave structure to this dictum in premising the "equality" of all men. This did not mean that all men have equal abilities, talents, or potential possibilities for development, but rather equality in possessing under God and hence by "nature" certain "unalienable" rights as men. An unalienable right is a right the exercise of which the individual cannot give up even if he thinks he wants to. The corollary, or obverse side of an unalienable right is a responsibility.

In either case it is implied that one finds out of what man is capable and hence what man is, by observing what he does under such freedom. The Bill of Rights is the necessary foundation of the democratic way, which is thus seen as a great experiment. Lyman Beecher put his finger on the heart of the Republic when he spoke of the

powerful nation in the full enjoyment of civil and religious liberty, where all the energies of man might find full scope and excitement, on purpose to show the world by one great successful experiment of what man is capable.[20]

The fourth fundamental belief, as Jefferson worded it in his "Act for Establishing Religious Freedom" in Virginia, was

that truth is great and will prevail if left to herself; that she is the proper and sufficient antagonist to error, and has nothing to fear from the conflict unless by human interposition disarmed of her natural weapon, free argument and debate; errors ceasing to be dangerous when it is permitted freely to contradict them.

The dimension of this belief that has tended to fade into limbo is the idea that the truth emerges "from the conflict" itself—that is, that in order for the truth to emerge at all conflict of opinions is essential. This implies a responsibility for each man to contend for the truth as he sees it. Jefferson recognized this implication of his position clearly enough. "Every man," he said, "has a commission to admonish, exhort, convince another of error."[21] It is a complete misunderstanding of the democratic way so conceived to suppose that the happiest state for it is one without conflict. For example, religious freedom was clearly envisaged as the deliberate creation of a situation where every religious opinion and practice, having the right to free expression, would continually contend with all others in order that error might be exposed to view and the truth be recognized. This conception of freedom should be sharply distinguished from the flabby relativistic view that since one opinion is just as good as another, therefore all should be permitted free expression.

It follows that the last thing a true democrat wants is the complete annihilation of the opposition, for this would be to eliminate the possibility of the truth ever emerging. And here is the basis for opposing the view that *laissez faire* is the only option for democracy. For in order to maintain the essential conflict itself, it may at certain junctures be necessary to use the power of the state—the servant of all the people—to encourage, protect, and even to strengthen weak groups—for example, to strengthen agriculture and labor at a time when business threatens to become completely dominant. So Madison contended in the 51st Federalist Paper that

in a free government the security for civil rights must be the same as that for religious rights. It consists in the one case in the multiplicity of interests, and in the other in the multiplicity of sects.

Multiplicity is of the essence of democracy and must be maintained.

– III –

These, then, are fundamental beliefs on which the democracy rests: belief in God, belief in "the people," belief in the voice of the people as the surest clue to the voice of God, belief that truth emerges out of the conflict of opinions. Two comments may be made in enlarging upon some implications of these beliefs.

It is all too commonly supposed even by ardent defenders of it that the democratic way depends upon the essential goodness of the people—that is, that democracy will work only among men of good will. It follows that democracy waits upon all, or a majority, of men to become good. This may be called a "utopian" view since it rests upon the utopian idea of a radical change in human nature. And as men find themselves possessed of less and less belief either in the essential goodness of man, or in the possibility of a radical change in his nature, despair of the democratic way spreads apace.

But as originally conceived our democratic way rested not upon a belief in the essential goodness of man, but upon a realistic view of the essential selfishness, evil, or depravity of all men rooted in the Christian tradition. Lincoln, for example, was clear on this point. "Human nature," he said bluntly, "cannot be changed." And as for human nature, he once remarked that the Bible teaches us that all men are sinners, but he reckoned that we would have found that out merely by looking about us. In brief, the man who by common consent most profoundly articulated the American democratic way had no sentimental illusions about the nature of man—held no utopian view of his essential goodness or of his ultimate perfectibility.

This realistic view of the nature of man is to be seen in connection with the idea of the emergence of the truth from the conflict of opinion itself. The democratic way is the way of open conflict between essentially selfish and biased individuals and groups, each contending for the truth as he sees it in his limited fashion, which may appear to others to be contention for his own selfish interests, under the general aegis of the freedom of each and all so to contend. It is based upon the faith that the maintenance of the give-and-take under such freedom is "the last, best hope of earth." This is a tough faith to hold—but it is the essence of the democratic tradition.

Since both the ideal of destiny under God and the way of democracy were based upon a dynamic or experimental conception of human life under God, the primarily important thing is not where the society and government now are in the process of the great experiment, but the sureness of the people's sense of direction—the firmness of their belief in the essential rightness of the general tendency or movement. So long as there is widespread confidence among the people that the direction and way are basically right, the system is sound and can function even in adversity. And this is essentially a matter of faith—faith in the guidance of God—faith that the democratic way with all its tortuous ambiguities and disappointments is nevertheless the best way yet devised. This is not faith in the present practice of democracy, but belief in the principle that "all men are created equal" and hence that government can and ought to be by the consent of the governed.

If and when such confidence rooted in such faith is undermined, the people lose hope, lose a sense of direction, lose belief in the great experiment itself, and are apt to turn with some hysteria to tangible, technical guarantees of security—to attempts to freeze and preserve what they have. "Where there is no vision the people perish." Hence the *status quo* is enshrined, and attempts made to prevent all deviation, to suppress all dissent, to put a stop to change. One of the most ominous things in the situation today is that increasingly the hope of the people is not based on belief in the great principles and hence on the general rightness of the movement, so much as on belief in a standard of living the primary defense of which is summed up in the phrase, "we never had it so good."

– IV –

In actual practice the democratic way is the way of government by the consent of the governed. This way has realistic and powerful sanctions in the people's right "whenever they shall grow weary of the existing government" to "exercise their constitutional right of amending it, or their revolutionary right to dismember or overthrow it."[22] In order to ensure its successful working it is necessary that such government be always sensitive to changes in the will of the governed, and yet not subject to the sweep and power of their immediate and whimsical desires. It is necessary, therefore, that the will of the governed be expressed and carried out according to established and generally accepted rules that are the result of long historical testing. These rules define the fundamental law under which the free people live, and to which they commonly consent.

Basic here is the majority principle, namely, that so far as the next step is concerned the will of the majority must be supreme.

Hence the elaborate machinery for the correct and peaceful ascertainment of the will of the majority. All minorities must consent to this majority principle if the government by consent is to survive. Hence the government of the free people may, and indeed must, invoke its coercive power against any and all minorities that deny and flout the majority principle—for not to do so is to court anarchy and tyranny.

But if in practice the majority will must prevail step by step, yet the majority may be wrong at any one time, and a majority as well as a minority may be tyrannous.

True it is, that no other rule exists, by which any question which may divide society can be ultimately determined, but the will of the majority; but it is also true, that the majority may trespass on the rights of the minority.[23]

The only safeguard against such trespass is the conviction that under God truth and right are not matters of majority vote. It is for this reason that democracy without faith in God is likely to sink into demagogic mobocracy. Only the belief that majority opinion does not determine truth, places the majority under the obligation and necessity to preserve the right of all minorities to free expression and open propagandization in order that the contention for the truth can go on. Hence the basic right of every minority in the democracy which must be protected is the right to become a majority if it can through free persuasion. This right is protected in the Bill of Rights, which is the keystone in the democratic arch. This is to say that in the democracy the *means* are as much of the essence as the *ends*. Indeed, the democratic faith is essentially a faith in certain means. The democracy cannot be defended with undemocratic means.

Lincoln, in his First Inaugural, stated the majority principle in classic fashion:

A majority held in restraint by constitutional checks and limitations, and always changing easily with deliberate changes of popular opinions and sentiments, is the only true sovereign of a free people. Whoever rejects it does, of necessity, fly to anarchy or to despotism.

Unanimity is impossible; the rule of a minority, as a permanent arrangement, is wholly inadmissible; so that, rejecting the majority principle, anarchy or despotism in some form is all that is left.

This way of government by the consent of the governed, hemmed in as it necessarily is by defined and commonly accepted means, is always subject to abuse for the simple reason that men have never been able to devise a system that would permit freedom to the good while as effectively curtailing the freedom of the evil. Even God, according to Christian tradition, could not or would not devise a universe for men that denied freedom to the devil. Further, government by consent which aims at equal freedom and justice for all, is always ponderous, cumbersome, and slow—or at least it commonly appears so in periods of threat and crisis.

The defenders of such government always and of necessity must labor under the handicap of defending, not a sure thing, but a way of political life conceived as an experiment worth trying in peace and even testing in adversity. The great defenders of the democratic way have not defended it in doctrinaire fashion, but when pressed have said in effect, Where, judging from past human experience, are we to find a better alternative? Thus Jefferson in his First Inaugural,

Sometimes it is said that man cannot be trusted with the government of himself. Can he, then, be trusted with the government of others? Or have we found angels in the forms of kings to govern him? Let history answer this question.

Lincoln echoed the same sentiment in his First Inaugural,

Why should there not be a patient confidence in the ultimate justice of the people? Is there any better or equal hope in the world?

Later he added, making the meaning unmistakably clear, "it is not [a question of] 'Can any of us imagine better?' but 'Can we all do better?' " granted the nature of man and the present historical situation.[24]

Lincoln, even under the tremendous pressures of the Civil

War, never gave a doctrinaire defense of the Union cause, but always presented the contest as part of the great experiment which "embraces more than the fate of these United States." At the beginning he saw that the contest was important because it forced men to ask,

Is there, in all republics, this inherent and fatal weakness? Must a government, of necessity, be too strong for the liberties of its own people, or too weak to maintain its own existence?[25]

And at Gettysburg in November, 1863, he did not celebrate the victory, as one of less rugged faith might well have done, but rather reminded the nation that the war was

testing whether that nation or any nation so conceived and so dedicated can long endure.

We may suppose that he meant what he said—that he did not know with certainty—that he thought the struggle was real and that these "almost chosen" people might indeed "nobly save or meanly lose the last, best hope of earth."

In "secular" language what these most profound defenders of government by the consent of the governed have always maintained is that there are risks involved in any way of life, and men must take chances for the simple reason that they cannot so rig human life as to assure themselves that they are betting on a sure thing. In traditional Christian language this is to say that finite men must live by faith.

– V –

Here, then, are suggested some of the meanings of the American dream of destiny under God and the way of democracy. It is essentially a way of faith—"the assurance of things hoped for, the conviction of things not seen." But the setting suggested above prepares one to understand that while there is in a sense a "democratic faith," yet democracy is not itself the object of religious devotion as some seem to suppose who suggest that the present crisis is such that "governmental agencies must teach the democratic ideal *as religion*."[26] Rather democratic government is merely the most effective and satisfactory instrument that has yet been devised for achieving the high calling of these people to fulfill their destiny under God. Nor does the democratic way rest upon faith in the essential goodness of man or its practice wait upon the successful outcome of a crusade of wholly good men who will throw all the rascals out. For finally the structure as it has evolved in history rests upon faith in the God who is the only object of religious devotion—the Christian God of mercy and of judgment—the God of creation, of providence, and of history. His purposes for the guidance of man are to be read from the unfolding events of history as man experiences it. Lincoln stated it clearly in his reply to the delegation of ministers who came to tell him what the will of God was on emancipation:

I hope it will not be irreverent for me to say that if it is probable that God would reveal his will to others on a point so connected with my duty, it might be supposed he would reveal it directly to me. . . . These are not, however, the days of miracles, and I suppose it will be granted that I am not to expect a direct revelation. I must study the plain physical facts of the case, ascertain what is possible, and learn what appears to be wise and right.[27]

VI

When "Wise Men Hoped": An Examination of the Mind and Spirit of the National Period

During the period between the Revolution and the Civil War certain images of man, society, government, and destiny became so widely prevalent as to be almost universal. A summary presentation of them, with full recognition of the danger of too facile generalization and oversimplification, helps us to understand the great enthusiasm with which people set about putting man's house in order. I am trying to describe a constellation of images which gave shape to a prevailing climate of opinion. Perhaps A. N. Whitehead's phrase "the gospel of individualism" may most appropriately be used as a covering title for this climate. Although they have a certain inner logic and belong together, they were probably never completely spelled out in a formal system. Rather, they were the soil out of which diverse philosophies and theologies grew. In dealing with them we touch upon what Whitehead called the form of the forms of thought of the period.

Whitehead suggested that the peculiar character of this era was due to the fact that "wise men hoped, and that as yet no circumstance had arisen to throw doubt upon the grounds of such hope."[1] Allan Nevins concluded that on the basis of the experience of the Republic down to the 1840s such hope was indeed not unfounded since "all its problems save one (and that terrible indeed) seemed easy of solution." That one problem was slavery, but as yet it was "a cloud no bigger than a man's hand."[2]

The faith of the young Republic seemed to be vindicated. It had separated itself from European control through a successful, albeit conservative, revolution. It had established itself under a Constitution based upon belief in the ability of men to have "good government from reflection and choice" instead of the traditional "accident and force."[3] It had not fallen into the trap of aristocratic and possibly reactionary sentiments set by the Federalists, being led around it by Thomas Jefferson and his Republican party which converted "the main stream of American public opinion to what may be called the sane element in the principles of the French Revolution."[4] It had weathered a second war with England and gained a settlement which a French observer referred to as "the peace that passeth understanding." Nine years later it had issued its second declaration of independence from Europe in President Monroe's famous doctrine. European visitors who earlier had been more inclined to scoff and criticize spitefully (Frances Trollop's *Domestic Manners of the Americans* is a prime example), now came to admire and even to envy and applaud the great experiment.[5] Alexis de Tocqueville saw in it the shape of things to come in Western culture, and give his views classic summary in his *Democracy in America*.

Vindication of the faith of the Republic in the eyes of the world meant in its own eyes confirmation of the rightness of its ideal of "destiny under God" and its way of "democracy." What Lyman Beecher, one of the most perceptive ecclesiastical statesmen of the era, called the great experiment that was "to show the world . . . of what man is capable" if given freedom, seemed already successful. Its light, Beecher added with typical exuberance, shall go up to heaven, and on earth "it will awaken desire, and hope, and effort." The kind of desire and hope it awakened help to define the period's peculiar optimism and belief in man. The effort it stimulated is to be seen in the Revivalism, and in the many humanitarian, moral, and social-reform movements which are so notable a feature of the period. For although the experiment itself seemed to be successful on a grand scale, it was obvious to most leaders that the implications and the practical benefits of democracy must be made to grace all areas of life. And this must be done democratically—that is, voluntarily. Concurrently with the acceptance of religious freedom the principle of voluntaryism came to permeate all areas of life. The reformers, like the revivalists of the period, marched forth armed only with their persuasive powers to organize "free associations" for the accomplishment of their aims. Reform, like salvation and government, could come only through consent.

It is in this broad context that we can see the constellation of images mentioned above. They are six in number.

Central was the image of the free individual. The free individual was the person with full opportunity to develop his every latent possibility or natural power. This concept is to be found within the framework of practically every theology or philosophy of the day. Men might define the nature of man and hence his natural powers and latent potential in quite different ways. And of course the differences between individuals was recognized. But almost all converged on this idea of the free individual. Theodore Parker, who attempted to make a rational system out of New England Transcendentalism, defined the "absolute or natural religion" of free men as "the normal development, use, discipline, and enjoyment of every part of the body, and every faculty of the spirit; the direction of all natural powers to their natural purposes."[6]

Next to be noted is the concept of "perfection." The perfect individual was the fully free individual as defined above—that is, the individual who had developed *his* every potential to the fullest possible extent. This was not to assume that all individuals had the same potentialities. In fact it meant quite the opposite, as we shall note below. Nor was perfection measured against an absolute standard. When the period's greatest revivalist, Charles G. Finney, became professor of theology at Oberlin, he moved with the group there to a view of Christian perfection. Finney defined perfection as complete obedience to the law of

God. That law, he thought, was summarized in the command: "Thou shalt love the Lord thy God with all *thy* heart, and with all *thy* soul, and with all *thy* mind, and with all *thy* strength, and thou shalt love thy neighbor as thyself." From this statement of the command, Finney argued that all that was demanded of the individual was that he love the Lord his God with all his heart, his soul, his mind, his strength—that is, with all the heart, soul, mind, and strength that God had given *him*. On this basis Finney was quite consistent, although he shocked absolutists when he proclaimed that a man, although a "moral pigmy," might in his measure be "as perfect as God is" in literal obedience to the injunction "be ye perfect as your Father in heaven is perfect."[7] Finney was typical of the period in interpreting Christian perfection in the image of the free individual.

The image of perfection was also applied to the understanding of society. A perfect society would be one made up of free individuals. Hence the present aim was movement toward that organization of society which would place fewer and fewer restrictions on the opportunity for all its members to develop all their potentialities. The demand for the removal of such restrictions defined social justice. One can see the drive for this kind of justice behind all the reform movements of the period. It was America's calling, under God, to build a perfect society in this sense, and democracy seemed to be the way thereto.

Movement toward perfection, whether in the individual or in the society, defined the third image to be noted, that of progress. The individual was making progress so long as he was developing his potentialities. In the society, progress was a widening of the possibility for more and more individuals to become "free"— that is, to develop all their latent capacities to the fullest possible extent. During this period progress was evidenced primarily in the general equalitarian tendencies which so impressed Alexis de Tocqueville. The fact that such progress was being made through the democratic way was added vindication of the rightness of the course the Republic was steering. Men predicated their hopes for the future on the continuation of such progress, which would bear "the sovereign individual on his way from complete subordination to the tyranny of the group to that ultimate realization of perfection—untrammeled freedom."[8]

But although evidences of progress were seen in the general leveling tendencies of the time, this did not mean that it was expected that all men would eventually become alike. On the contrary, in a perfect society of free individuals every single person would be unique. This view is perhaps most clearly expressed in Ralph Waldo Emerson's doctrine of representative men. Like all good idealists—and Emerson said Transcendentalism was idealism as it appeared in New England—he began with the intuition (or assumption) that we live in a *Universe*. He adhered to what he called the grand creed—that one mind, one will, pervades everything and is bodied forth in particulars. The Over-Soul is clothed in the flowing robe of events. Individual human beings are such particulars. And each is the representative of one area or aspect of the total Universe, and one only. Hence only as an individual has the opportunity fully to realize his particularity —that is, to become a free individual—can he perform his function in the total scheme of things by truly representing his district of the Universe. It is because every individual is unique in this sense that every heart vibrates with that iron string—"trust thyself." Thus Emerson's Transcendentalism gave the period's image of the free individual cosmic significance. Emerson spoke with some nostalgia of the old Calvinism which in his youth hung like a benediction over New England, holding each man down to *his* place with the weight of the Universe. In his Transcendentalism he pronounced the same benediction over his fellows.

The fourth image in the constellation was that of equality. The period accepted the dictum that "all men are created equal." But they were not presumed to be equal in the sense that all possessed the same capacities, talents, and potentialities, but rather in the sense that they were endowed with the equal right to become free individuals. Thus the period gave its distinctive meaning to the Declaration's phrase, "they are endowed by their Creator with certain unalienable Rights . . . among these are Life, Liberty,

and the pursuit of Happiness." In doing so it gave new life to
the idea of "natural rights" as conceived during the eighteenth
century. As Merle Curti noted, romanticism's "enthusiasm for the
idea of man as man, irrespective of any status acquired by inheritance or education, did blow heat into the Enlightenment's
formula of natural rights."[9]

Men were equal because each had his unique place as a representative man, and his natural right was the right to the opportunity for the full development of his peculiar potentialities. To
Emerson, for example, the equality of all men meant not that
all are alike or have the same interests and capacities but that all
are equally important in the Universe. This he expressed beauti-
fully in his famous "Fable":

> The mountain and the squirrel,
>   Had a quarrel,
> And the former called the latter "Little Prig";
> Bun replied,
> "You are doubtless very big;
> But all sorts of things and weather
> Must be taken in together,
> To make up a year
> And a sphere.
> And I think it no disgrace
> To occupy my place.
> If I'm not so large as you,
> You are not so small as I,
> And not half so spry.
> I'll not deny you make
> A very pretty squirrel track;
> Talents differ; all is well and wisely put;
> If I cannot carry forests on my back,
> Neither can you crack a nut."

In this view the complete individuality was compatible with
the complete equality. In fact, individuality and equality were
inseparable doctrines. The drive for equality was synonymous
with the drive for individuality. It is a grave misinterpretation to

confuse this concept of "individuality" with the post-Civil War concept of "individualism" (or "rugged individualism") which set the individual's interest over against those of the community. Individuality implied that the individual had meaning only insofar as he was part of and, according to his unique gifts, contributed to the community.[10]

Next should be noted the image of voluntaryism. Since consent is of the essence of all co-operative human endeavors, there is hope for progress only insofar as men can be persuaded to want to strive toward perfection for themselves and for their society. Men cannot be coerced into striving to become free individuals. Whitehead traces the lineage of the idea that persuasion rather than coercion is of the essence of Deity back to Plato and the ancient world. In the last half of the eighteenth century it came to practical application, and the nineteenth-century men built theologies upon it. Thomas Jefferson, in defense of his "Act for Establishing Religious Freedom in Virginia" of 1779, argued that

all attempts to influence [the mind] . . . by temporal punishments or burdens, or by civil incapacities . . . are a departure from the plan of the Holy Author of our religion, who being Lord both of body and mind, yet chose not to propagate it by coercions on either, as was in his Almighty power to do. . . .

And Lyman Beecher, in the midst of the theological revolution in New England Calvinism, said that the basic premise of the new theology was that God exercised only persuasive power over men.

Because the period tended to root voluntaryism and the principle of consent in the nature of things, its image of progress should always be interpreted in this light. Consent was a necessary and inviolable aspect of the free individual. Later generations, by mingling traditional Christian views of Providence with conceptions of evolutionary developmentalism, produced a comforting belief in inevitable progress which is sometimes read back into the earlier era. One cannot, however, say unequivocally that progress was inevitable to the mind of the National Period in

America. No doubt a highly optimistic view of the outcome widely prevailed, and perhaps it was expected by most of the reformers that in the long run the perfect society would be achieved. We may take Albert Brisbane's comment in his *The Social Destiny of Man* (1840) as somewhat typical:

Nature . . . has implanted in man an instinct of social progress, which, it is true, will lead him through a series of transformations, to the attainment of his Destiny; but she has also reserved for his intelligence the noble prerogative of hastening this progress, and of anticipating results, which, if left to the gradual movement of society, would require centuries to effect.[11]

But so long as the implications of the image of the free individual were kept in mind, men could not wholly give themselves to the idea of the inevitability of progress. Progress finally depended upon the exertions of free individuals. The struggle was real; every issue was a live issue, and, as Abraham Lincoln was to say, men "may nobly save or meanly lose the last, best hope of earth."

Lastly, in this connection, it should be noted that voluntaryism implied that concerted action of any kind depended upon a contractual relationship between free individuals to accomplish defined objectives. Each free individual must be persuaded and give his conscious consent to the concert of action. Progress toward the perfect society must be furthered by what Lyman Beecher called "voluntary associations of the wise and good." This view motivated and shaped the formation of all the humanitarian movements and reform societies of the day. Indeed, the denominations themselves were little else than great voluntary societies of persuaded and convinced Christians with missionary and educational ends in view.

The sixth and final image in the constellation was that of paternalism. It follows from a strict application of the view of voluntaryism suggested above, that the correction of existing social evils must depend upon persuading those who control and profit from them voluntarily to relinquish their selfish interests in the name of progress. The early reform movements began with the assumption that they could not be coerced. The early temperance movement, for example, depended upon persuading individual drinkers one by one to give up drinking, and persuading individual makers of liquor to stop making it. Early antislavery leaders like John Woolman and Samuel Hopkins depended upon persuading individual slave owners one by one to free their slaves. The colonization movement was postulated upon this premise.

This prevailing faith in persuasion alone, which defines the nature of paternalistic reform, tends to make the National Period appear sentimental to a generation reared in the wisdom of pressure groups, class struggles, and power politics. Such faith in its pure form, however, was never universal in that earlier period. The New England Puritans of the seventeenth century had held and applied what even our generation might consider a more realistic view of the relationship between persuasive and coercive power. Their descendants in the first half of the nineteenth century, of whom Lyman Beecher may be taken as a representative, recognized that

in a free government, moral suasion and coercion must be united. If children be not religiously educated, and accustomed in early life to subordination, the laws will fail in the unequal contest of subduing tigers to their yoke. But if the influence of education and habit be not confirmed and guarded by the supervening influence of law, this salutary restraint will be swept away by the overpowering force of human depravity. To retrieve therefore our declension, it is indispensable, not only that new fidelity pervade the family, the school, and the church of God, but that the laws against immorality be restored to their ancient vigor.[12]

Perhaps more important for the future was the fact that the prevailing conception of the nature of democratic government itself tempted even the most sentimental of reformers to reach for the state's coercive power without necessarily realizing the implications of what he was doing. The representative government was conceived as the servant of the people. In practice "the people" meant the majority. Lincoln stated the majority principle with classic clarity in his First Inaugural: "A majority held in restraint by constitutional checks and limitations, and always changing easily with deliberate changes of popular opinions and sentiments, is the only true sovereign of a free people." In this context as soon as the leaders of a reform movement gained, or thought they could gain, a majority vote for their particular measures, they were tempted to grasp the coercive power of the government to impose their reform upon all. Sooner or later practically every one of the great reform societies faced this issue. The temperance movement split in 1836 over the question of whether it should continue dependence upon persuasion alone or should work henceforth for legislative regulation or prohibition.[13] Leaders of the antislavery movement divided on this point from the beginning. For the same reasons some less worthy movements, such as the anti-Masonic and the anti-Catholic, were injected into politics in some areas.[14] Some voluntary societies indeed were launched with the idea of "selling" a particular movement to the government which would then give its financial support and use its coercive power if necessary. An outstanding example is the Colonization Society formed in 1816.[15] And Arthur Bestor has convincingly argued that most, if not all, of the communitarian societies formed during the period were conceived as "patent-office models of the good society."[16]

The point I wish to emphasize here is that while this reach for the coercive power of the government by the reformers suggests a lack of clarity in their grasp of the principles of voluntaryism and paternalism, yet the inconsistency was not as great as may at first appear. For in the American scene the government itself could rather easily be regarded as a great voluntary reform society with power to regulate the conditions for membership in it.

In passing it should be noted that there are evidences during this period of a loss of faith in persuasion alone—that is, in paternalistic reform. Orestes A. Brownson and Theodore Parker, for example, were apparently persuaded by the national elections of 1840 and 1844 that the people might be duped into voting against their own best interests. They began to adumbrate a theory that vested interests would not relinquish power and prerogatives until and unless compelled to do so by superior power. Parker, in his final analysis of the American situation, held that "the organized trading power" which seeks gain with small regard to justice and is "amenable only to the almighty dollar" was really dominant. But, he argued, because of the nature of the democracy "the organized political power," which is commonly subservient to the trading power, may eventually be used by the people to control that power. In such control he increasingly put his faith.[17] Here is one bit of evidence for the emergence in the United States of radical theories of social reform, rejecting paternalism from the top down in favor of reform brought about through mass movements from below. But in the National Period such views were a minority report.

The constellation of images or doctrines we have discussed fairly well defines the mind and spirit—"the intellectual and moral motivation of men and women"—which lay back of the particular movements and general thrust of the National Period.

Perhaps one more ought to be added—"the principle of automatic harmony"—the assumption that there could be no ultimate contradiction between the personal interests of free individuals and the perfect society. Paul Tillich makes much of this as the "one presupposition . . . always present, sometimes avowed, sometimes tacit" at the time.[18] But I think there is a real danger of distortion if too much emphasis is placed on this principle in interpreting the mind of the National Period. It can, for example, induce one to read back into that Period's conception of "individuality" the post-Civil War conception of "individualism." In a sense of course the assumption of such harmony is implicit in the images of the free individual and the perfect society. But the free individual was always defined in the context of a society made up of other free individuals—and ultimately in a Universe —which curbed his personal individualism by reference to the basic right of all others to become free. Indeed, infringement of this unalienable right defined injustice. This gave tremendous impetus to the attack on social evils of all kinds. But the later individualism came to mean in practice that no matter what an individual did in following his own even selfish desires or whims it would ultimately be seen as in harmony with the best interests of the whole society. This naturally cleared the way, and provided justification, for the unrestrained and ruthless exploitation of natural and human resources on the part of the new tycoons who were largely uncurbed by the older sense of justice based on the images of the free individual and his unalienable right to equality.

In this essay I have attempted to deal with what Charles and Mary Beard called "the interior aspects" of the period between the Revolution and the Civil War, by sketching a constellation of images that seem to have been almost universally present: the free individual, the perfection of the individual and of society, progress, equality, voluntaryism, and paternalism. It should be stressed that these images constituted a constellation that must be seen as a whole, for any one cannot be understood apart from all the others. When grasped as a unit they give content to the mind of that amazing period, so unlike our own, when "wise men hoped." They help us to understand what goals promoted the tremendous exertions for the betterment of the lot of men.

The period is a bit incredible to us for we see it through the dark veil of intervening experiences. The reform movements, insofar as they were crusades for universal social justice, fell so short of their goal as largely to be excursions into frustration—a seedbed for cynicism. This left its mark on the American spirit. Practically all the crusading energies of the period were drawn into the antislavery movement and thence sucked into the whirlpools of Civil War which eventuated in "the tragic era" and what has been called "the moral collapse of government and business."

Early in the 1890s one of America's most acute foreign observers, James Bryce, said bluntly in summing up: ". . . the government and institutions, as well as the industrial civilization of America, are far removed from that ideal commonwealth which

European philosophers imagined, and Americans expected to create."[19] And yet, so abundant were the natural resources, and so great the human energies generated during the National Period, that several years were to elapse before a significant number of Americans began to raise serious questions about the direction they had taken. Now, after two world wars separated by the greatest depression, and in the shadow of a mushroom-shaped cloud, our "wise men" seem to project only gloom. Perhaps if they would look back at the National Period, as Nathaniel Hawthorne looked back on his brief experience at Brook Farm, they might conclude with him that foolish and sentimental as they now seem, those wonderful people "had struck upon what ought to be a truth" about man, a truth which he hoped posterity would dig up and profit by.

VII

Denominationalism: The Shape of Protestantism in America

The Christianity which developed in the United States [after 1800] was unique. It displayed features which marked it as distinct from previous Christianity in any other land.[1]

Professor Latourette's generalization applies primarily to the institutional forms rather than to the theology of Christianity in the United States. The basis of the institutional uniqueness has been the free church idea. The phrase, free churches, is used in various ways—sometimes to designate those churches of congregational polity, sometimes those peculiarly distinguished by their liberal views. But properly the phrase designates those churches under the system of separation of church and state. Here the qualifying word "free" is used in the sense of independent and autonomous and in the context of long tradition refers to those churches that are independent of the state and autonomous in relation to it.

The denomination is the organizational form which the free churches have accepted and assumed. It evolved in the United States during the complex and peculiar period between the Revolution and the Civil War.

The denomination, unlike the traditional forms of the church, is not primarily confessional, and it is certainly not territorial. Rather it is purposive. And unlike any previous church in Christendom, it has no official connection with a civil power whatsoever. A church as church has no legal existence in the United States. It is represented legally by a civil corporation in whose name the property is held and the necessary business transacted. Neither is the denomination a sect in a traditional sense and certainly not in the most common sense of a dissenting body in relationship to an established church. It is, rather, a voluntary association of like-hearted and like-minded individuals, who are united on the basis of common beliefs for the purpose of accomplishing tangible and defined objectives. One of the primary objectives is the propagation of its point of view, which it in some sense holds to be true. Hence to try to divide the many religious bodies in the United States under the categories of "church" and "sect" is usually more confusing than helpful, especially since by long custom "church" is commonly used in a way that implies approbation, and "sect" in a way that implies derogation.

Keeping these considerations in mind, I have for the sake of variety followed the practice common in America when discussing the Protestant bodies, of using the words "church," "sect," and "denomination" interchangeably. Our terms clarified, let us examine some of the elements that were woven into the denominational structure during the formative years and which subsequently have conditioned the thought, life, and work of American Protestantism down to the present.

– I –

In Christendom from the fourth century to the end of the eighteenth, Christianity was organized in an established church or churches. The one Church reached its peak in expression and power during the twelfth and thirteenth centuries. At that time it actually possessed and wielded tremendous tangible, overt power in the affairs of men, and more subtly, tremendous and formative cultural power in the souls of men. The heart of this Church was creedal or confessional belief in supernatural power mediated to men through the sacraments. It claimed inclusiveness and universality as the one true Church of Christ on earth, but by the same token it was necessarily exclusive. Outside the Church and its sacraments there was no salvation, although this had to be asserted with humility because ultimately only God knew His own with certainty.

The Reformation broke up this tangible unity of the one Church in Christendom. It claimed to be not a revolt from the church *but* merely an attempt to reform the church from within, a position inherently validated by the true principles of the Church itself. These had become so inextricably mingled with the organizational forms and practices that honest re-formation meant revolt from the existing institution. This revolt coincided with the emergent self-consciousness of the modern nations, behind which was the complex of economic, social, and political movements that ushered in and shaped modern Western civilization.

Inevitably the spiritual reformation and consequent institutional fragmentation of the Church developed affinities with the rising national consciousness. Thus the effort to reform the Church found diverse expressions in the nations—Lutheranism within the realms of the German princes and the Scandinavian countries, Anglicanism in England, Reformed in Geneva and Scotland, and so on.

The conflict culminated in the Thirty Years' War that devastated Europe. The Westphalian settlements of 1648 marked a grudging recognition of the necessity to live-and-let-live within the several territorial areas. The basis for the churches that thus emerged was both confessional and territorial. And each of these churches in its own territory and in its own way continued to make the claims traditionally made by the one true Church. Each as a Church assumed the traditional responsibilities, and each clung to the long-established principle of religious uniformity enforced by the civil power within a commonwealth. These were the churches of the right wing.

Meanwhile in the turmoil of re-formation, certain heretical individuals and movements had emerged that, appealing to the commonly accepted authority of Scripture, began to claim freedom of religious belief and expression as a right. These were the sects of the left wing. They were voluntary groups without status or social responsibility or power. From the viewpoint of the official churches they were schismatic as well as heretical and hence thought to be subversive of all order whether civil or ecclesiastical. And so almost universally strenuous repressive measures were invoked against them.

– II –

Representatives of practically all the religious groups of Europe, both right and left wing, were transplanted to that part of America that was to become the United States. There they learned in a relatively short time to live together in peace under the genial aegis of the Dutch and English combination of patriotic-religious fervor, toleration, cynicism, simple desire for profits, efficacious muddling through, and "salutary neglect" that made up the colonial policy of these nations. The eventual result was that by 1787, after independence was won, the new nation had to honor the practice of religious freedom if it were to exist as a nation.

It was of course recognized that this was a departure from the prevailing Christian tradition of almost fourteen hundred years. But by this time many both within and without the religious groups were in a mood to agree with Thomas Jefferson:

As to tradition, if we are Protestants we reject all tradition, and rely on the scripture alone, for that is the essence and common principle of all the protestant churches.[2]

Even so, the transplanted offshoots of Europe's state churches —the right-wing groups—retained their position of prestige and lominance in the new land throughout the colonial period. At the close of the Revolution the four largest and most powerful religious groups were the Congregationalists, the Anglicans, the Baptists, and the Presbyterians. Of these four, the Baptists held nowhere near the position of power and respect accorded the other three. There followed in size the Quakers, the Lutherans, the German, and the Dutch Reformed. The Methodist body, still in swaddling clothes in the Anglican manger, was twelfth in size.[3]

To be sure the dominant, powerful, and respected right-wing churches had experienced considerable internal change during the vicissitudes of the colonial period, especially during the upheavals growing out of the great revivals. But there was as yet little indication that the church patterns of America would be markedly different from those of Europe. Ezra Stiles' prediction in 1783 that no doubt the future of Christianity in America would lie about equally with Congregationalists, Presbyterians, and Episcopalians, seemed eminently plausible.

The radical change in the relative size of the religious bodies in America took place during the brief period between 1787 and 1850. By the middle of the nineteenth century, the Roman Catholic Church, which at the close of the Revolution was tenth in point of size and everywhere except in Pennsylvania laboring under some civil restrictions, was the largest. Second in size were the Methodists, followed by the Baptists, Presbyterians, Congregationalists, and Lutherans. Seventh in size were the Disciples—an upstart group less than twenty years old. The Protestant Episcopal Church had fallen to eighth place, while, perhaps most amazing of all, Joseph Smith's Mormons were ninth.[4]

Since this configuration of relative size has persisted in the United States for more than a century—with a few notable exceptions such as the Congregationalists' drop from fifth to ninth place—we may speak of these years as the "formative" period for the American denominations.[5]

– III –

Our concern is with the mind and spirit of these "free" churches—their genius which was woven from many diverse strands during this formative period, and how this genius continued to define the direction, life, and work of American denominations.

Religious freedom and the frontier provided the broad ideological and geographical setting in which these developments took place. The first meant the removal of traditional civil and ecclesiastical restrictions on the expressions of the religious convictions and even the whimsies of men. The frontier provided the necessary space and opportunities in which such expressions could thrive. Together, this combination of freedom and opportunity created what Whitehead called the "Epic Epoch of American life,"⁶ the period of "Freedom's Ferment" as Alice Felt Tyler most aptly dubbed it.

I base my interpretation of this "epic epoch" on the conviction that what individuals and groups do when given freedom depends upon what they are when such freedom is offered. Hence, an understanding of the development of what we note as characteristic traits of the denominations hinges in large part upon a study of the characteristic attitudes and practices that came to be accepted during the colonial period. In keeping with this suggestion I shall take up in somewhat schematic fashion several important elements, ideas, or practices that went into the making of the denominations, and which together gave and still gives them their distinctive character.

A

The first to be noted is the "sectarian" tendency of each American denomination to seek to justify its peculiar interpretations and practices as more closely conforming to those of the early church as pictured in the New Testament than the views and policies of its rivals. This tendency is closely related to a kind of historylessness exhibited, as Professor Latourette has pointed out, in the marked tendency of American Protestantism during the nineteenth century "to ignore the developments which had taken place in Christianity in the Old World after the first century."⁷

This antihistorical bias itself has long historical roots. Roman Catholicism developed the idea of the Bible as the Word of God within the context of the church which through apostolic succession from Peter was the bearer of the tradition. The purity and authority of the church in speaking out of the tradition was in turn guarded by the sacraments of baptism and ordination. Thus the church, as the continuing, tangible historical reality, always stood as interpreter of the Word to the individual, and in this sense spoke out of the tradition with authority equal to that of the Bible.

The Reformers, in revolt against the church as it then existed, appealed over the practices of the church to the Word as found in the Bible. But the Reformation which took shape in the right-wing Lutheran, Anglican, and Reformed versions, held the doctrine of the Word together with doctrines of the church and ministry in such fashion as to guard against individual "enthusiasm" and to preserve the sense of the unbroken historical continuity of Christianity.

The left-wing sects, in their fight for existence against almost universal opposition, sought a source of unquestioned authority that would undercut all the tradition-based claims of both Roman Catholics and right-wing Protestants over them. They found it in the Bible, which as the commonly recognized Word of God they proposed to place directly in the hands of the Spirit-guided individual Christian as his only necessary guide to faith and practice. The common thrust of these groups was toward *"no creed but the Bible"* and the right of "private judgment," under grace, in its interpretation.[8] In practice this meant an appeal over all churches and historical traditions to the authority of the beliefs and practices of primitive Christianity as pictured in the New Testament.

In America, although the churches of the right wing were everywhere dominant during the colonial period, the situation in the long run played into the hands of the left-wing view. For there, under the necessity of living side by side with those from other lands and different backgrounds, the transplanted national and religious traditions tended to cancel out each other's angularities. Crèvecoeur clearly delineated this tendency, and attributed it to the fact that

zeal in Europe is confined; here it evaporates in the great distance it has to travel; there it is a grain of powder inclosed, here it burns in the open air, and consumes without effect.[9]

Nevertheless as Christians, whether Lutheran, Anglican, Congregational, Presbyterian, Baptist, Quaker, or what not, all shared the Bible—the center and symbol of a common Christian beginning and heritage, and for all the highest authority. Hence each, in defense of its peculiar way against the others, was increasingly pressed to fall back on this one commonly recognized authority and to argue that its denominational teaching most closely conformed to the Biblical patterns. Unlike their European parents, the transplanted right-wing churches of America never possessed or were soon shorn of effective coercive power to suppress dissent and enforce uniformity. Their leaders were almost forced to enter the argument—if at all—pretty much on the terms originally set by the left-wing groups.

Meanwhile the common sense of opportunity to begin all over again in the new land, which was so characteristic a feature of the mind of the early planters, also worked to erase the sense of continuity with the historic church and to accentuate the appeal to the teachings of Jesus and the practices of primitive Christianity. Even to nominal or cultural Christians of the seventeenth century, this opportunity was bound to be interpreted as an occasion ordained by God to begin again at the point where mankind had first gone astray—at Eden, the paradise of man before the fall. Here is deeply rooted the commonly observed and usually irritating assumption of innocence on the part of many Americans.[10]

But to ardent churchmen and Biblicists the fresh start in the New World was seen as a providential chance to begin over again at a selected point in history where it was thought the Christian Church had gone astray. John Cotton was not unusual in speaking of the churches formed by the Puritans in New England as exceptionally close to what would be set up "if the Lord Jesus were here himself in person."[11]

Both the pietistic and rationalistic movements of the eighteenth century, independently, worked to the same general end. The personal religious experience emphasized by the pietists was assumed to be a duplication of the experience of New Testament Christians. And rationalistic reformers, in their battle against existing ecclesiastical institutions, soon learned to appeal to the pure moral teachings of Jesus whom they saw as the first great Deist. The teachings of Jesus formed the norm by which the churches could be judged and found wanton. In essence the views of pietists and rationalists were so close together on this point that both could agree with the Unitarian Joseph Priestley that the story of the Christian Church was largely a sordid history of the "corruptions" of pure Christianity through the inventions and contrivances of clever men. Both reached the same conclusion that the forms, practices, and traditions of the historic church were neither binding nor pertinent to their day.

In summary, the constellation of ideas prevailing during the Revolutionary epoch in which the denominations began to take shape were: the idea of pure and normative beginnings to which return was possible; the idea that the intervening history was largely that of aberrations and corruptions which was better ignored; and the idea of building anew in the American wilderness on the true and ancient foundations. It is notable that the most successful of the definitely Christian indigenous denominations in America, the Disciples of Christ, grew out of the idea of a "new reformation" to be based, not on new insights, but on a "restoration" of the practices of the New Testament church—on which platform, it was thought, all the diverse groups of modern Christendom could unite as they shed the accumulated corruptions of the Church through the centuries. Typically American, this beginning over again was not conceived as a new beginning, but as a picking up of the lost threads of primitive Christianity.[12]

In practice the assumption of the normative character of the moral teachings of Jesus or of the New Testament religious experience and ecclesiastical forms, which undercut appeal to all intervening traditions, actually limited the restrictions placed on the ardent men and women who were engaged in building new churches in the new land. The content of the rationalists' interpretation of the pure religion and morals of Jesus turned out to be surprisingly like current Deistic views. The pietist just as easily found his emphasis on religious experience indigenous to the New Testament. And each found his version of "the church" to be identical with the Church of the Bible. Hence those in both camps were free to move with the tides of history, pragmatically, experimentally—incorporating as much of the traditional and the new in their structures as to each seemed valid and desirable. Here is part of the explanation of the often puzzling combination of Biblical authoritarianism with experimental and pragmatic activism in American religious life.[13]

Men of some historical learning and consciousness, like the doughty John W. Nevin of the German Reformed Church's Mercersburg Seminary, protested that the "sectarian" appeal to

private judgment and the Bible involves, of necessity, a protest against the authority of all previous history, except so far as it may seem to agree with what is thus found to be true; in which case, of course, the only real measure of truth is taken to be, not this authority of history at all, but the mind, simply, of the particular sect itself. . . . A genuine sect will not suffer itself to be embarrassed for a moment, either at its start or afterwards, by the consideration that it has no proper root in past history. Its ambition is rather to appear in this respect autochthonic, aboriginal, self sprung from the Bible, or through the Bible from the skies.[14]

By 1849 when this was published, it was a passing voice crying in the lush wilderness of the American free-church system whose promoters had no mind to be bound by the past and little thought that wisdom might be found, even by American churchmen, between the first and the nineteenth centuries. In spite of an almost universal appeal to the authority of the Bible, and a tendency to literalistic interpretation of it, the architects of the American denominations appear to have been surprisingly unbound by a sense of tradition. It must be added that their freedom in this respect was largely the appearance or feeling of freedom possible only to those ignorant of their history. Hence in a sense the very freedom which they felt and acted upon, a freedom without historical perspective, served many times to bind them to the obvious tendencies of the moment. In all innocence they built into the life of the denominations what time and tide happened to bring to their shores. And each tended to sanctify all the various elements of doctrine and practice that it adopted, under the supposition that it but followed a blueprint revealed in the Word of God.

B

The second element to be noted is the voluntary principle. Voluntaryism is the necessary corollary of religious freedom. Resting on the principle of free, uncoerced consent, the several religious groups became voluntary associations, equal before, but independent of the civil power and of each other.[15] What the churches actually gave up with religious freedom was coercive power. The revolution in Christian thinking which they accepted was dependence upon persuasion alone.

The religious groups were somewhat prepared to accept such dependence by their experiences during the great colonial revivals that swept the country from the 1720s to the Revolution. The revivals in every area led to conflict between their supporters and the defenders of the forms and practices of right-wing Protestantism, and in every case the revivalists triumphed, insofar as the acceptance of their methods was concerned. The revivals had demonstrated the possibilities of persuasion. Subsequently, they taught confidence in it. Once this battle was won in the churches, the principle of voluntaryism became a leaven in the mind and practices of the religious groups, conditioning their development.

Conceiving the church as a voluntary association tends to push tangible, practical considerations to the fore by placing primary emphasis on the free, uncoerced consent of the individual. A recent history of Congregationalism, published by that denomination's press, declares that "a Congregational church is a group of Christians associated together for a definite purpose, not because of peculiarities of belief," and the members of local churches "are not asked to renounce their previous denominational teachings but are asked to join in a simple covenant pledging co-operation and fellowship."[16]

The center of a denomination, as of any other voluntary association, is a tangible, defined objective to which consent can be given. During the actual struggles for religious freedom, the common objective was recognition of the right to worship God in public as each saw fit, free from traditional civil restraints or disabilities. Once this was achieved, each group was free to define its own peculiar objectives.

In relation to the voluntary principle Christianity itself tends to be conceived primarily as an activity, a movement, which the group is engaged in promoting. If the group *has* a confessional basis, its attitude toward it is likely to become promotional and propagandistic, as in the case of Missouri Synod Lutheranism. Anything that seems to stand in the way of the effectiveness of such promotion is likely to be considered divisive, a threat to internal unity and group effectiveness. In this context, theology as an attempt to define and clarify intellectual .positions inspires discussion, differences of opinion, even controversy, and hence is considered divisive. The strong tendency to dampen serious discussion of theological issues in most groups comes from just this attitude which strengthens the general anti-intellectual bias inherent in much of revivalistic pietism. This in turn helps to account for the surprising lack of interdenominational theological discussion, or even consciousness of theological distinctiveness among the many groups. "Fundamentalism" in America was a movement that tried, among other things, to recall these denominations to theological and confessional self-consciousness. It was defeated in the major denominations, not so much by theological discussion and debate as by effective political manipulations of denominational leaders to sterilize this new "divisive" element.

Voluntaryism further means that a powerful selective factor is at work in the choice of denominational leaders, since such leaders finally gain and hold support and power in the group through persuasion and popular appeal to the constituency. This means that whatever else top denominational leaders *may be*, they *must be* denominational politicians. Tocqueville was surprised to find that everywhere in America "you meet with a politician where you expected to find a priest."[17] Similar factors are of course at work in the American Republic at large. All the factors that Lord Bryce pointed out as militating against the great man's chances of becoming President of the United States operate in the same fashion in the selection of a President of the American Baptist Convention.

Voluntaryism also means that each group has a kind of massive and stubborn stability, inertia, and momentum of its own, deeply rooted in, and broadly based upon, the voluntary consent of the individuals composing it. Here is the real basis for the tremendous vitality of these denominations. The inherent inertia is likely to become evident especially in periods of internal stress or of external threat—as some proponents of mergers have learned to their consternation.

In Chapter IV I have noted how the acceptance of religious freedom and consequent voluntaryism on the rationalists' terms implied that tenets peculiar to a group were unimportant for the general welfare—something which helps to explain why so many religious leaders in America are constantly haunted by a sense of being irrelevant in decision-making centers.

C

The third element to be noted is the place of the mission enterprise in the life of the denominations.

Since the free churches of America are voluntaryistic and purposive, the defined objectives of a group are peculiarly definitive and formative.

It is a commonplace that pietism became dominant in the American churches at the beginning of the nineteenth century. Pietism as a movement in the churches stressed personal religious experience and commitment expressed in Christian works of evangelization and charity. Hence a concomitant of pietism wherever it appeared—in German Lutheranism, in English Methodism, in American colonial revivals—was always a renewed interest in missions. The tendency of pietism as of voluntaryism is to place the central emphasis on the objectives of the group which makes the missionary program of a denomination, both home and foreign, definitive for it.

Missions, of course, are an aspect of the broad work of evangelization—the winning of converts through persuasion. But since conversion always takes place in the context of a group, evangelization necessarily has two aspects: the conversion of the individual to God and the individual's commitment to the particular group which defines for him the nature of the Christian life. The two aspects are separable, and the second may come to outweigh the first, placing the denomination under pressures to accept as members all who will co-operate in furthering the work of the local church or denomination which we saw in the quoted passage on the Congregationalist's conception of their church. For this reason the originally very exclusive sectarian denominations in America have tended to move in the direction of loosely inclusive membership where agreement upon the church's purposes overshadows the conversion itself.

The fact that the denomination is a voluntary association has had an effect also upon the conduct of the over-all evangelistic mission program. Since success depends upon persuasion, various aspects of the program, like home and foreign missions, necessarily compete for attention and funds within the denomination. Similarly, the several areas of the foreign field compete, with the result noted by H. W. Schneider, that

in the twentieth century, as well as in the nineteenth, the most popular mission fields were still those areas in which "heathenism" was most spectacular—India, China, and "darkest Africa."[18]

Just as voluntaryism and sense of mission form the center of a denomination's self-conscious life, so they provide the basis for the interdenominational or superdenominational consciousness and co-operation which has been such an outstanding aspect of the American religious life. This is seen in the host of inter- or superdenominational societies—the American Board of Commissioners for Foreign Missions, The American Home Mission Society, the Bible Society, the Tract Society, the American Sunday School Union, the Temperance Society, the Colonization and Anti-Slavery Societies, the Y.M.C.A., and the Federal and National Councils. Very typical is the description of the Interchurch World Movement launched in 1919 as a

cooperative effort of the missionary, educational, and other benevolent agencies of the evangelical churches of the United States and of Canada to survey unitedly their present common tasks and simultaneously and together to secure the necessary resources of men and money and power required for these tasks.[19]

The goal of these movements is the same as that within individual denominations, namely, to present the achievement of certain defined objectives in such a way as to enlist the support of individuals. It should be noted that most of these societies were not formed by the co-operative activity of denominations as such, but rather by individuals from various denominations in voluntary associations. In this sense they have been superdenominations, many times in recognized competition with the denomination, a competition well reflected in the Old School Presbyterian attitude toward the A.H.M.S. and the Baptist attitude toward some of the work of the Bible Society.

There have been, of course, outstanding examples of genuine co-operation among denominations as such. The Congregational-Presbyterian Plan of Union of 1801 and the later Accommodation Plan and more recently the Federal and National Councils are examples. But the basic form is the same, in this case co-operation for the accomplishment of tasks too large for one group to do alone.

Here is the basis for the persistent American view that an ecumenical movement must begin with working together rather than with agreement on fundamental theological propositions; on "life and work" rather than on "faith and order." American churchmen tend to be committed to this emphasis because of the nature of their long and successful experience in interdenominational co-operation.

Since the missionary enterprise plays a central and definitive role in the American denomination's self-conscious conception of itself, even slight changes in the conception of the mission works subtle changes in the character of the denomination itself. An understanding of the changing motifs of missions in America contributes greatly to an understanding of many denominational developments.

During the formative period of 1783 to 1850, the most prevalent conception of the missionary enterprise in all the evangelical denominations was that of individualistic winning of converts one by one to the cause of Christ. To be sure, it was assumed by most that, as Rufus Anderson, secretary of the A.B.C.F.M., put it in 1845, "that point being gained, and the principle of obedience implanted, and a highly spiritual religion introduced, social renovation will be sure to follow." And he went on specifically to reject as a direct objective of missions the "reorganizing by various direct means, of the structure of that social system of which the converts form a part."[20]

Similarly, as Wade C. Barclay's second volume of his *History of Methodist Missions* makes clear, the Methodists commonly accepted Wesley's injunctions to his preachers which was written into the first discipline—"You have nothing to do but to save Souls." Bishop McKendree in 1816 had anticipated Rufus Anderson's general position in his answer to the question, What may we reasonably believe to be "God's design in raising up the Preachers called Methodists"? which was "to reform the continent by spreading scriptural holiness over these lands."[21] One cannot say, therefore, that these leaders gave no thought to "social renovation"—but rather that believing as they did that it would automatically follow upon the dissemination of "scriptural holiness," they took a great deal for granted. Time has not borne out their optimism.

This general conception of the mission enterprise largely defined the objectives of all the evangelical denominations during the first three quarters of the nineteenth century. In a real sense, each became a great missionary organization devoted to pressing the claims of the Gospel wherever there was an opportunity. By the same token, every member was a missionary, either actively as a consecrated worker in the field or through his enlistment in and support of the common enterprise. Thus the General Assembly declared in 1847 that

The Presbyterian Church [U.S.A.] is a missionary society, the object of which is to aid in the conversion of the world, and every member of this church is a member of the said society and bound to do all in his power for the accomplishment of this object.

It was this that shaped and gave direction to each budding denomination.

But during the last quarter of the nineteenth century and the opening years of the twentieth, real belief in the all-sufficiency of this kind of missions declined, at least among those of the top leadership in most of the large denominations. During this period enlightened theological professors hand in hand with "Princes of the Pulpit,"[22] responding to the impact of scientific thinking in the garb of evolution and to the deplorable economic and social conditions in the burgeoning industrial society, shaped the "new theology" and the "social gospel." Inevitably as their views came to prevail the conception of the work of the church underwent changes, and missions were metamorphosed from the simple task of winning converts to which, it was assumed, all else would be added, to the complex task of participating actively in social betterment and reconstruction. Foreign missions, from being simple outposts of Christian evangelization, became outposts of the latest technological, medical, agricultural, and educational knowledge and practice being developed in the United States. This view of missions received most frank expressions in the "layman's inquiry" published in 1932 as *Re-Thinking Missions.* "We believe," the inquiry states,

that the time has come to set the educational and other philanthropic aspects of mission work free from organized responsibility to the work of conscious and direct evangelism. We must . . . be willing to give largely without any preaching, to cooperate whole-heartedly with non-Christian agencies for social improvement. . . .[23]

This of course was conceived as "Christian" work—but by what standards? Why should the devoted young medical missionary in Africa, China, or India be closely examined regarding his views of the Trinity of the Virgin Birth, or on any other "merely" theological views for that matter? Meanwhile as Professor Winthrop Hudson has made clear,[24] in the United States itself Christianity was so amalgamated and identified with the American way of life that it was difficult for denominational leaders to distinguish what was peculiarly "Christian" in the work from the general culture. In this situation Christian missions were easily metamorphosed into attempts at intercultural penetration.[25] "The Christian," said the laymen's inquiry,

will therefore regard himself as a co-worker with the forces within each such religious system which are making for righteousness.[26]

In the long run the results were somewhat embarrassing since while the younger churches throve in every mission land, yet in general it was easy for the mission lands to accept the technology while in reaction rejecting the Christianity which had been assumed to be inseparable from it. In brief, the revolt of the "colonial" missionary countries of the East, armed with the latest "Christian" know-how of the West, somewhat undercut belief in this kind of missions, which meant the undercutting of the denominations' conception of their life and work at home.

Here is one root of much of the present confusion and distress in the American denominations. No longer really believing either in the sole efficacy of a simple Christian evangelization or in the salutary effects of cultural interpenetration under Christian auspices, their purposive core and sense of direction is destroyed and they are set adrift.[27] Perhaps one hopeful element in the picture is that this, among other things, is pressing even American churchmen to re-examine the meaning of the Church not only as "life and work" but also as "faith and order."

The same principle applies to such outstanding interdenominational movements within the country as the Y.M.C.A. and the Federal Council. The "Y," a product of the revivalism of the second quarter of the nineteenth century,[28] had as its original objective the evangelization of uprooted men in the traditional fashion. Beginning with this primary purpose it added libraries, reading rooms, inexpensive hotels, and recreational and other facilities as a means thereto. But as belief in simple evangelization declined the facilities themselves tended to take the leading role in the program, until today the primary appeal of the "Y" is likely to be as a community welfare organization which is somewhat embarrassed by its earlier evangelistic emphasis.

The Federal Council, originating in 1908, was described by one of its historians as a marriage of American church unity or co-operative movements with the concern for social service.[29] Thus it reflected the changed conception of the primary work of the church at the time of its origin, as Walter Rauschenbusch clearly stated.[30] It was conceived by such leaders as Graham Taylor as a co-operative movement among the churches in the interests of social justice, and C. Howard Hopkins referred to it as "the climax of official recognition of social Christianity. . . ."[31] Its first outstanding pronouncement was its "Social Creed of the Churches" adopted in the meeting in Chicago in 1912.[32]

On the one hand, then, the Council can be seen as an expression of the basic genius of the American religious organizations—voluntary association in the interests of effective evangelization. But on the other hand it reflects the changed conception of "evangelization" from the traditional winning of individual souls to Christ coupled with charitable amelioration of distress to the winning of people to concern for social justice based if necessary upon radical social reconstruction.

D

To historylessness, voluntaryism, and the mission enterprise, we must add a fourth element, revivalism, to our list of shaping influences in American denominational Protestantism.

In the English colonies, as uniformity enforced by the civil power broke down and dependence upon persuasion and popular appeal for recruitment increased, revivalism soon emerged as the accepted technique of the voluntary churches. Not without protest, of course, for the traditionalists of the old-line churches correctly sensed that the revivalists "stressed evangelism more than creed."[33] Thy tried like King Canute—and about as effectively—to exercise a measure of control over the incoming tide.

Early revival leaders in the colonies like the Tennents among the Presbyterians and Jonathan Edwards of the Congregationalists, who were long accustomed to sober but effective periods of spiritual refreshing in their parishes, apparently stumbled upon the practice, as witness Edwards' narrative of "surprising" conversions. But they, and especially their followers of lesser stature and more tenuous roots in the churchly tradition, became enthusiastic imitators of the glamorous free-wheeling Anglican revivalist, George Whitefield, whose career, like the Sorcerer's great broom (in the hands of less skillful manipulators), was multiplied in innumerable splinters.

But if the colonial situation worked for the acceptance of revivalism, the situation under religious freedom in the new nation tended to make it imperative. As Professor Garrison has succinctly put it,

With 90% of the population outside the churches, the task of organized religion could not be limited to encouraging "Christian nurture" . . . in Christian families, or to ministering to old members as they moved to new places farther west. It had to be directed toward that 90%. What they needed first was not nurture or edification, but radical conversion, . . . [and since they] followed no chiefs . . . they had to be brought in one by one.

"It is small wonder," he correctly continues, "that the revivalists put on all the heat they could and with some notable exceptions, appealed to the emotions more than to the intelligence."[34] There is the heart of the matter. Revivalism in one form or another became the accepted technique of practically all the voluntary churches, the instrument for accomplishing the denominations' objective of evangelism and missions.

As a commonly accepted practice, revivalism exerted a strong influence upon the patterns of thought and organization of the Protestant denominations. The "revival system" came to be much more than a recruiting technique. Some colonial churchmen correctly sensed this, and many of their predictions about the long-range effects of revivalism on the churches were fulfilled in the years following independence. What they saw was that revivalism tended to undercut the traditional churchly standards of doctrine and practice.

There are several reasons why this is so. In the first place, revivalism tends to produce an oversimplification of all problems, both because the effective revivalist must appeal to the common people in terms they can understand and because he must reduce all the complex of issues to a simple choice between two clear and contrasting alternatives. Said one convert of "Priest [John] Ingersoll," as the father of the famous agnostic was called, "he made salvation seem so plain, so easy, I wanted to take it to my heart without delay."[35] How simple it could be made is indicated by "Billy" Sunday's proclamation:

You are going to live forever in heaven, or you are going to live forever in hell. There's no other place—just the two. It is for you to decide. It's up to you, and you must decide now.[36]

In the second place, the revivalist gravitates almost inevitably toward the idea that "whosoever will may come." This pull, coupled with the necessarily concomitant stress on personal religious experience in "conversion," tends to make man's initiative primary. Revivalism thus tends to lean theologically in an Arminian or even Pelagian direction with the implicit suggestion that man saves himself through choice. As John W. Nevin complained in *The Anxious Bench,* published in 1843, under revivalism it is the sinner who "gets religion," not religion that gets the sinner.

In the hands of New England revivalists in the line of Timothy Dwight, Lyman Beecher, and Nathaniel W. Taylor, Calvinism was "modified" almost beyond recognition by the emphasis placed on their interpretation of "free-will." The foundation of their theological system, said Beecher, was that even God exerts only persuasive power over men.[37] This emphasis in turn bolsters the notion that converted men create the church—an idea paralleled in the political realm by the notion that the people create the government. In such a politico-religious vein Charles G. Finney declared that "the devil has no right to rule this world" and the people ought "to give themselves to God, and vote in the Lord Jesus Christ, as governor of the universe."[38]

In the third place, revivalists are strongly tempted to stress tangible results and to justify whatever means will produce them. Even Edwards defended the preaching of terrifying "hell-fire" sermons with the comment that he thought it not amiss to try to frighten men out of hell. And Finney and his friends justified their "new measures" largely on the ground that they got results. Lyman Beecher and his alter ego, Nathaniel W. Taylor, almost made "preachableness" in revivals normative for doctrines, and Daniel Day Williams has pointed out that for some of their revivalistic heirs in New England "the ultimate standard for judging every doctrine and every practice of Christianity was thus first, Will it help or hinder the salvation of men?"[39] This pragmatic emphasis on results reached a peak in the eminently persuasive albeit muddled thinking of Dwight L. Moody who reputedly said he was an Arminian up to the cross but Calvinist beyond—and who declared forthrightly that "it makes no difference how you get a man to God, provided you get him there."[40] This emphasis culminated in the spectacular career of "Billy" Sunday and his professional imitators with their elaborate techniques for assessing *their* contribution to the Kingdom of Heaven and the Church of Christ on earth by counting the number of *their* converts.

In the fourth place, revivalism as voluntaryism tended to bring a particular type of leader to the fore—men close to the people who could speak their language and rouse their emotions. During this formative period educated, cultured, and dignified religious leaders like Timothy Dwight, John Witherspoon, and William White were replaced in their denominations by demagogic preachers and revivalists—men like Peter Cartwright, C. G. Finney, Henry Ward Beecher, and Joseph Smith.

This tendency should be seen in the context of the general leveling or equalitarian trend of the times. The parallel development in the political sphere is striking. With the passing of the older revolutionary leaders, the removal of restrictions on popular suffrage, the removal of the barriers between the people and the government, and the shift from Federalism and Jeffersonianism to Jacksonian democracy, the "orator" able to appeal in Congress to his peers declined in importance and the popular leaders of the masses increased in influence.[41] Lord Bryce in commenting on the Presidency contrasts the "intellectual pigmies" who followed Jackson with the men of education, administrative experience, largeness of view, and dignity of character who had preceded.

As revivalism came to pervade the denominations with its implication that life in a church was a struggle across dull plateaus between peaks of spiritual refreshing, not only was "Christian nurture" in the churches slighted, it was given a reverse twist. Bushnell pointed this out in his complaint that far from encouraging the child to grow up in the church as a Christian never knowing himself to be otherwise, the revival system encouraged him to grow up in flagrant sin in order that by contrast he would better know himself as a Christian through the crisis experience of conversion. The revivalists' emphasis that Christ came to save sinners had the effect of encouraging the church to nurture sinners in order that it might save them.

Not only did revivalism tend to neglect the Christian nurture of children in the church, it tended also adversely to effect the minister's function as the shepherd of his flock. For inevitably the sober local pastor increasingly was judged by his ability to create the proper build-up and setting for the periodic revival campaigns in his church. And naturally ardent members of the congregation were quick to compare him unfavorably with the more colorful albeit less responsible roving evangelists. Many a church prayed the prayer, "Lord, send us a man like Finney!" And the stock answer to decline and apathy in a local church was to import a forceful revivalist to "revive us again!" just as the stock answer to troubles in the country was likely to be the importation of a morally impeccable plumed knight in shining armor to lead a great crusade for spiritual renovation and to throw the rascals out.

It is perhaps anticlimactical to suggest here that revivalism tended to foster an anti-intellectual bias in American Protestant-ism. The oversimplification of issues, the primary emphasis on a personal religious experience, and the standard of success as numerical results minimized the traditional role of the church and its ministers in intellectual leadership.

Revivalism with these tendencies was a central element in the structure of the Protestantism that gained religious freedom. In subsequent years, it was an important factor in shaping the exercise of that freedom. There were those in the formative years who, from the viewpoint of classical Protestantism, regarded the sweep of the revival system with alarm. They voiced a strong and cogent protest. Most notable perhaps was John W. Nevin whose *The Anxious Bench* was an attack on the whole "new measure" revival system. He contrasted it with the "system of the Cate-chism." Similarly, Horace Bushnell, a Connecticut Congregation-alist, voiced a milder protest in his work on Christian Nurture published in 1847. But by and large revivalism made a clean sweep in practically all the denominations. Lyman Beecher noted with some amazement that even Emerson's "corpse cold" Unitarians in Boston attempted to hold revivals, but he was inclined to agree with Theodore Parker that they lacked the essential piety and warmth for the work and hence succeeded only in making themselves a bit ridiculous. Among the denominations, the Presby-terians made the most consistent and determined stand against the more radical effects of the system. In turn they suffered fragmen-tation, ridicule, and abuse for their defense of traditional standards of doctrine and polity.[42] Even Lutheranism, its confessional-ism undercut by rationalism and pietism, was swept by revivalism as the replies to Nevin's work indicate. Despite the efforts of confessionally minded men from within, Lutheranism was probably saved from becoming just another typical American denomination by the great influx of new Lutheran immigrants.

Surveying the scene as a whole, the historian of Presbyterianism in America was not far wrong when he said that "the Great Awakening . . . terminated the Puritan and inaugurated the Pietist or Methodist age of American church history."[43]

E

The fifth element to be noted is the churches' general flight from "reason" in reaction to the Enlightenment during the Revolutionary Epoch, and the concomitant triumph of pietism.[44]

Once religious freedom was accomplished and a popular interpretation of the French Revolution in America brought the theological issue of "reason" *versus* revelation to the fore, pietism rapidly aligned itself with classical right-wing scholastic orthodoxy in opposition to rationalists and all their works—now included under the blanket term "infidelity." By and large, except perhaps for Unitarianism, the bulk of American Protestantism turned against the ethos of the Enlightenment and thereafter found itself either indifferent to, or in active opposition to, the general spirit and intellectual currents of modern Western civilization. Thereafter the bulk of American Protestantism was molded primarily by pietistic revivalism and scholastic orthodoxy. The former made personal subjective religious experience basic, while scholastic orthodoxy defined the professed content of theology.

Pietism as a movement has been peculiarly amorphous in character and intellectually naive. The early leaders, intent on cultivating individual Christian piety in the churches—whether Spener and Francke in German Lutheranism, or the Wesleys in English Anglicanism—never conceived their work except as a movement within the saving forms of a church in the interest of revitalizing its Christian life. Only so does Wesley's use of the text, "Is thine heart right, as my heart is with thy heart? . . . If it be, give me thine hand,"[45] make sense. And if the context of a church is absent this can and has led to strange bedfellows for Christians. For pietism, cut off from the forms of a traditional church and by itself made the guiding genius of a denomination, has successively lent itself to whatever live movement seemed to give structure to current problems and their solutions.

Thus, as suggested, it lent itself to the battle for religious freedom as structured by the Rationalists in the eighteenth century. During the Revolutionary Epoch when the issue seemed to be "reason" *versus* revelation, it as easily lent its warm heart to hardheaded scholastic orthodoxy. However, this alignment was largely based on the theological issue. But at the same time pietists tended to endorse the "moral and social ideals and attitudes" of the emerging modern age. Here is the real basis for that strangely divided or schizophrenic character of American Protestantism that has baffled so many historians and observers. The two Randalls, John Herman Senior and Junior, stated the situation clearly in their *Religion and the Modern World* of 1929:

> Western society confronted the disruptive forces of science and the machine age with a religious life strangely divided. On the side of moral and social ideas and attitudes, of the whole way of living which it approved and consecrated, Christianity had already come to terms with the forces of the modern age. . . .
>
> On the side of beliefs, however, Christianity in the early 19th century had not come to terms with the intellectual currents of Western society. It found itself, in fact, involved in a profound intellectual reaction against just such an attempt at modernism. . . .
>
> Thus it was that Christianity entered the 19th century with its values belonging to the early modern period, to the age of commerce and individualism, and its beliefs thoroughly medieval and pre-scientific.[46]

This schizophrenia has affected every area of the American denominational life and work. It helps to explain why during the course of the nineteenth century the denominations so easily came to sanctify the ideals and spirit of the rising industrial, acquisitive, bourgeois society at the same time that they jettisoned the scientific underpinnings of the modern age.

When at the close of the Revolutionary era evangelical Protestantism parted company with the intellectual currents of the modern world, an ever-widening chasm grew between "religion" and "intelligence." Americans since 1800 have in effect been given the hard choice between being intelligent according to the prevailing standards in their intellectual centers or being religious according to the standards prevalent in the denominations. This is really no secret. One of the most commonly accepted generalizations is that during the nineteenth century the churches lost most of the intellectuals. As early as 1836 Orestes A. Brownson noted that "everybody knows, that our religion and our philosophy are at war. We are religious only at the expense of our logic [or knowledge]."[47] A more orthodox brother expressed approximately the same sentiment in more euphemistic fashion:

There is an impression somewhat general . . . that a vigorous and highly cultivated intellect is not consistent with distinguished holiness: and that those who would live in the clearest sunshine of communion with God must withdraw from the bleak atmosphere of human science.

Or, as he put it more bluntly at the end of the same article,

It is an impression, somewhat general, that an intellectual clergyman is deficient in piety, and that an eminently pious minister is deficient in intellect.[48]

His article, contrary to its purpose, leaves one with the feeling that the impression was not unfounded.

F

The sixth and final formative element to be noted is the competition among the denominations. In good rationalistic theory, which was basic, competition among the several religious sects was of the essence of the free church idea under the system of separation of church and state. It was, indeed, the true guarantee of the preservation of "religious rights" as James Madison suggested in the 51st Federalist Paper.

The free churches were not reluctant to accept this view since "in the existence of any Christian sect" the

> presumption is of course implied, if not asserted . . . that it is holding the absolute right and truth, or at least more nearly that than other sects; and the inference, to a religious mind, is that the right and true must, in the long run, prevail.[49]

If theoretical considerations made competition among the religious sects acceptable, the practical situation made it inevitable. The free churches were confronted with a rapid-growing and westward-moving population, approximately 90 per cent of which was unchurched. This virgin territory for evangelization promoted revivalism which offered a way of reaching individuals in groups. At the same time, it intensified the rivalry among the free, absolutistic groups competing in the vast market of souls. This competition generated tremendous energies, heroic sacrifices, great devotion to the cause, and a kind of stubborn, plodding work under great handicaps that transformed the religious complexion of the nation. But it cannot be denied that, as L. W. Bacon said of a specific situation during the colonial period, many times "the fear that the work of the gospel might not be done seemed a less effective incitement to activity than the fear that it might be done by others."[50]

This of course was competition between Christian groups sharing a common Christian tradition and heritage, and indeed really in agreement upon much more than they disagreed on. It was not competition between those of rival faiths, but competition between those holding divergent forms of the same faith—and probably not the less bitter for being a family quarrel. This fact meant that ever-changing patterns of antagonism and competition were developed, and, by the same token, ever-changing patterns of alignments and co-operation.

Robert Baird in his *Religion in America*, first published in 1844 at the time when the competition was most keen, divided all the denominations into the "Evangelical" and the "Unevangelical." The former when viewed in relation to the great doctrines which are universally conceded by Protestants to be fundamental and necessary to salvation . . . all form but one body, recognising Christ as their common head.[51]

The latter "either renounce, or fail faithfully to exhibit the fundamental and saving truths of the Gospel."

Roman Catholics belong to the latter classification, for although "as a Church [they] hold those doctrines on which true believers in all ages have placed their hopes for eternal life" yet they "have been so buried amid the rubbish of multiplied human traditions and inventions, as to remain hid from the great mass of the people."[52] According to Baird, then, Roman Catholics stood in a special category. The great unbridgeable division was between those who "recognize Christ as their head" and those who did not. Notable among the latter were Unitarians, but Universalists, Swedenborgians, Jews, Deists, Atheists, and Socialists were also included. This commonly accepted schematic categorization set the patterns of competition and co-operation among and between the groups.

A Roman Catholic threat could unite all the other groups—even the Evangelical and Unevangelical—in a common front of opposition, especially when as in the West attention was directed to the supposed social and political threat of the Catholic Church to "free institutions."[53] On the other hand, evangelicals might upon occasion borrow a weapon or accept aid and comfort from Roman Catholics in opposition to Unevangelicals. Evangelicals would of course unite against Unitarians and Universalists. Conservative Unitarians might in the stress of conflict with "the latest form of infidelity" seek substantial aid from the stanchest of the orthodox, as when Andrews Norton of Harvard had the Princeton Presbyterian attacks on Transcendentalism reprinted in Boston.[54] Baptists and Methodists, although antagonists on the frontier, might easily combine against Presbyterians and Episcopalians. But finally each sect stood by itself against all others, a law unto itself in defense of its peculiar tenets which it implicitly held as absolute.

The general effect of such competition was an accentuation of

minor as well as substantial differences—the subjects of baptism
and its proper mode, ecclesiastical polity, the way of conducting
missionary work, pre- and postmillennialism, "Vater unser"
versus "unser Vater" in the Lord's Prayer[55]—and a submergence
of the consciousness of a common Christian tradition. Such competition helped sometimes to make sheer stubborn perpetuation
of peculiarities a chief objective of a group long after real understanding of them had faded into limbo. And lastly, this vitiating
competition many times produced a somewhat less than charitable attitude toward other Christian groups and even the kind of
sardonic jealousy reflected in the reputed remark of the Baptist
revivalist who in commenting on his meetings said, "We won only
two last night, but thank God the Methodists across the street
did not win any!" In the long run these more questionable results of the competition have been most obvious and most generally lamented.

Nevertheless it must be recognized that such competition and
conflict is inherent in the system of free churches, and as Talcott
Parsons observed, it would exist "even if there were no prejudice
at all, . . . a fact of which some religious liberals do not seem to be
adequately aware." In contemporary terms, this is "a struggle
for power among [the] religious denominations,"[56] as each tries
to extend itself. So long as the total membership of the denominations was but a fraction of the national population, this aspect of
the competition was largely obscured. But as the percentage of
church membership rises higher in relation to total population, it
becomes increasingly clear that each may be seeking to extend
itself at the expense of others, as, for example, when Southern
Baptists "invade" Northern (now American) Baptist territory,
and Roman Catholics "invade" traditionally Protestant rural areas.

Meanwhile, however, other factors have tended to a general
erosion of interest in the historical distinctions and definable theological differences between the religious sects. Increasingly the
competition among them seems to stem from such non-theological
concerns as nationality or racial background, social status, and
convenient accessibility of a local church. Finally what appears

to be emerging as of primary distinctive importance in the pluralistic culture is the general traditional ethos of the large families, Protestant, Roman Catholic, and Jewish.[57] If this trend continues, the competition inherent in the system of church and state separation, which served to divide the religious groups in the first place, may work eventually to their greater unity.

How a group uses its freedom, I submitted earlier, depends largely upon its character when such freedom is offered. In our context, religious freedom and the challenge of the frontier's unchurched shaped certain colonial religious patterns into the structure we recognize as American denominationalism. We have seen how competition, made keen in an environment of freedom, has promoted revivalism as a technique, voluntaryism as a cohesive base, and historylessness as a cast of mind. Withal has come an anti-intellectual bias and a sense of purposive enterprise which is peculiarly reflective of the nineteenth-century American society in which the Protestant denominations throve.

VIII

American Protestantism Since the Civil War.

I. From Denominationalism to Americanism

By the decade 1850 to 1860 denominationalism was generally accepted in the United States and was assumed to be the proper organizational form of Christianity under religious freedom and the separation of church and state. Meanwhile the most widely prevalent outlook in the denominations was that of evangelical and revivalistic Protestantism. It is the argument of this and the following essay that during the second half of the nineteenth century there occurred an ideological amalgamation of this Protestantism with "Americanism," and that we are still living with some of the results.

It is a commonplace that toward the end of the nineteenth century Protestantism largely dominated the American culture, setting the prevailing mores and the moral standards by which personal and public, individual and group, conduct was judged. If a culture is the tangible form of a religion, in the United States that religion was Protestantism. As H. Paul Douglas put it, "despite multiplying sectarian differences, Protestantism's prevalence tended to create a Protestant cultural type. . . . It was a triumph of religion still on the communal level."[1] Down to the present a rebel in America has to rebel against these standards in order to acquire the name.

To leaders in the free churches, inasmuch as their measure of Christian humility permitted, such dominance was a source of pride and a basis for self-approbation because it demonstrated

their success in meeting the terms implied in the original acceptance of the fact of separation of church and state. With religious
freedom, the churches had given up coercive power and had
assumed the responsibility collectively to define and inculcate in
the population the basic beliefs necessary for the being and the
well-being of the democratic society,[2] while armed only with
persuasive power. Their dominance seemed to demonstrate that
they could do this effectively. Then with the Civil War the North
became dominant, and "to Protestants of the Northern States,
the years of the Civil War furnished the supreme vindication" of
their way.[3] The free churches seemed to have been tried and
found adequate, and it is little wonder that in spite of theological
differences and multiplying sectarian divisions, "in its most
characteristic pronouncements, American Protestantism substan-
tially approved the church-state status quo."[4]

What was not so obvious at the time was that the United
States, in effect, had two religions, or at least two different forms
of the same religion, and that the prevailing Protestant ideology
represented a syncretistic mingling of the two. The first was the
religion of the denominations, which was commonly articulated
in the terms of scholastic Protestant orthodoxy and almost universally practiced in terms of the experimental religion of
pietistic revivalism.

The second was the religion of the democratic society and
nation. This was rooted in the rationalism of the Enlightenment
(to go no farther back) and was articulated in terms of the destiny
of America, under God, to be fulfilled by perfecting the democratic way of life for the example and betterment of all mankind.
This was a calling taken as seriously as ever a Christian saint had
taken his peculiar vocation. Said one of its high priests in 1826:
"We stand the latest, and, if we fail, probably the last experiment
of self-government by the people."[5]

This religion was almost universally practiced in terms of the
burgeoning middle-class society and its "free-enterprise" system,
the most persuasive argument for which was the plain fact that
it worked to the economic and general material betterment of
men. Andrew Carnegie, in summarizing his version of its benefi-

cent effects, could say that such "is the true Gospel concerning Wealth, obedience to which is destined some day to solve the problem of the Rich and the Poor, and to bring 'Peace on earth, among men Good-Will.' "[6]

The high degree of amalgamation of these two faiths took place during the decades following the Civil War. But developments in the first half of the century had prepared the way for the mingling of such diverse ideological elements. The widespread triumph of revivalism in the denominations tended to erode their theological defenses and critical acumen. The reaction in the free churches against the "infidelity" of the eighteenth century threw them back upon scholastic orthodoxy for their intellectual substance, while at the same time practical necessity induced them to accept the emerging civilization which was guided by the spirit and ideas of the Enlightenment. Meanwhile the pietistic emphasis on personal religious experience was twisted into a version of Pascal's "the heart has its reasons, which reason does not know," which provided an excuse for giving up the wrestle with the intellectual problems posed by the modern age. This was not confined to the uneducated revivalists on the geographical frontier and the ignoramuses on the fringes of social and intellectual respectability. Horace Bushnell's distinguished theological career began when, during a revival in Yale College in 1831, he finally burst out:

O men! what shall I do with these arrant doubts I have been nursing for years? When the preacher touches the Trinity and when logic shatters it all to pieces, I am all at the four winds. But I am glad I have a heart as well as a head. My heart wants the Father; my heart wants the Son; my heart wants the Holy Ghost—and one just as much as the other. My heart says the Bible has a Trinity for me, and I mean to hold by my heart. I am glad a man can do it when there is no other mooring.[7]

Thereafter, aided and instructed somewhat by Samuel Taylor Coleridge, he spun out over a long period of years his own reflections on the Christianity of the heart that was secure from the "speculations of the philosophers and literati"—indeed, even from "the manner of the theologians"[8]—all of whom were thought to have an exaggerated regard for logical intellectual structures. A significant end result of this attitude was Lyman Abbott's glorying in the fact that at Plymouth Church "we do not ask what men believe,"[9] a sentence in which "care" might be substituted for "ask."

It is unnecessary to dwell upon the point that such a view made religion almost impervious to the "acids of modernity" which were already eating away the faith of many; gave theology a security largely untroubled by the problem of its relationship to the emerging scientific world view; and placed the question of the Christian's role as a businessman and citizen in the democratic society beyond the ken of practical theology. Meanwhile "a smug preoccupation with the salvation and perfection of the individual"[10] largely pervaded the revivalistic denominations, tending to focus their attention on the personal vices and morals of individuals, until such personal habits as smoking, drinking, dancing, and Sunday observance became the outstanding criteria of Christian character. From the midst of this period came Daniel Dorchester's exultation that "under Protestantism, religion became purely a personal thing, passing out from under the exclusive control of the sacraments, the arbitrary sway of assumed prerogatives, into irrepressible conflicts with individual lusts and worldly influences."[11]

Francis Wayland, Jr., an outstanding Baptist minister and leader, had foreseen something like this outcome as early as 1842 and was very unhappy about it. Looking around, he noted that

one man asserts that his religion has nothing to do with the regulation of his passions, another that it has nothing to do with his business, and another that it has nothing to do with his politics. Thus while the man professes a religion which obliges him to serve God in everything, he declares that whenever obedience would interfere with his cherished vices, he will not serve God at all.

Wayland was grieved to observe that "the pulpit has failed to meet such sentiments at the very threshold, with its stern and uncompromising rebuke." The root of the difficulty in the

churches, he thought—sensing the emphasis of pietistic revivalism—is that "men are told how they must feel, but they are not
told how they must act, and the result, in many cases ensues, that
a man's belief has but a transient and uncertain effect upon his
practice."[12]

But since men, if not given instruction and guidance in such
matters as citizenship and conduct in business by ministers and
theologians in their churches, will nevertheless be instructed and
guided by some prevailing code, the effectual abdication of the
Protestant churches meant that the ideas and ideals of the
emerging acquisitive society were generally accepted without
criticism.

Hence the dichotomy, noted and stated so well by the two
Randalls, between the professed religious beliefs of the denominations and the "moral and social ideals and attitudes, . . . the whole
way of living" which they "approved and consecrated." On the
side of the latter, they readily came "to terms with the forces of
the modern age," but "on the side of beliefs" not only did they
"not come to terms with the intellectual currents of Western
society" but they were "involved in a profound intellectual reaction against just such an attempt at modernism" as was implied
therein.[13] A not unexpected result was that when in 1897 George
A. Gordon surveyed the scene with critical eye he concluded
that the theological problem of the day was the almost complete
"absence of a theology giving intellectual form and justification
to the better sentiment of the time." For example, he added,
"among almost all our effective preachers the sympathies are
modern; but in the greater number the theology is either ancient
or nonexistent. In either case, the mass of prevailing emotion and
practical activity has no corresponding body of ideas in league
with it." The theological "scheme entertained is usually some
decrepit modification of the Calvinistic kind . . . while the purposes, sentiments, and practical outlooks are all of this new and
greater day."[14] "We need," he concluded, "a temple for the intelligence."

However, as the nineteenth century had moved into the balmy

days of the Victorian age, the democratic society with its "free-enterprise" system proved obviously beneficial in terms that could be measured in incomes and material goods. As this happened, activistic American Protestants lost their sense of estrangement from the society, began to argue that it was profoundly Christian, and to explain and vindicate it in a jargon strangely compounded out of the language of traditional Christian theology, the prevalent common-sense philosophy, and *laissez-faire* economics. The way to such compounding was oiled by popularized versions of the teaching of such men as Bushnell and his disciples that the form of expression in words was relatively unimportant. This tended to sanctify ambiguity in theology.

In the context of this general interpretation of developments, it is not too difficult to understand why an aura of religious consecration came to surround the acceptance and promulgation of the syncretistic point of view. Especially important in this regard was the matter of religious freedom—how it was originally conceived and by whom. In the first place, it was the rationalists who made sense out of it theoretically and, on the basis of their theory, worked out the legal and political forms for the separation of church and state. In the second place, the churches accepted religious freedom and separation in practice, although there was little obvious theoretical justification for it in the classical Protestant theology which they professed. They accepted it in practice as a good thing, but on the rationalists' theoretical terms. The prevalence of pietistic and, later, romantic sentiments enabled such theoretical ambiguity to go largely unquestioned. Nevertheless, the rationalists' theory had far-reaching and devastating implications so far as the free churches were concerned. Most important was the implication that only what the religious "sects" held and taught in common (the rationalists' "essentials of every religion") was relevant to the public welfare of the new commonwealth. For the obverse side of this was that what each group held peculiar to itself, and hence what gave it its only reason for separate existence, was irrelevant to the general welfare for the whole commonwealth. No wonder that a sense of irrelevance has always haunted

the most sectarian religious leaders in America. Further, the competition between the religious groups inherent in the system of
religious freedom has always augmented the sectarian emphases
while at the same time such emphases on peculiarities undercut
the sense of relevance to the life of the whole commonwealth.

This dilemma has troubled some religious leaders in America
from the beginning. It is revealed, for example, in the typical
insistence in 1848 of Professor Bela Bates Edwards that "perfect
religious liberty does not imply that the government of the
country is not a Christian government." But the most he could
assert positively was that there is a "real, though indirect, connection between the State and Christianity."[15] But what is the
nature of this indirect connection? Tocqueville saw it more
clearly than most. While supposing that there was some "direct
influence of religion upon politics in the United States," he concluded that its indirect influence was still more considerable, and
added in explanation,

The sects which exist in the United States are innumerable. They all
differ in respect to the worship which is due from man to his Creator;
but they all agree in respect to the duties which are due from man to
man. Each sect adores the Deity in its own peculiar manner; but all
the sects preach the same moral law in the name of God.

He also saw that the situation involved spiritual and mental
compartmentalization, and what he said of Roman Catholics
might also be applied to Protestants. Their priests in America, he
thought,

have divided the intellectual world into two parts: in the one they
place the doctrines of revealed religion, which command their assent;
in the other they leave those truths, which they believe to have been
freely left open to the researches of political inquiry. Thus the Catholics of the United States are at the same time the most faithful believers and the most zealous citizens.[16]

The same kind of compartmentalization was exhibited by John
Leland, the Baptist elder and perennial democrat, who on the
matter of religious freedom spoke, on the one hand, "as a re-

ligionist" and, on the other hand, "as a statesman," coming to separate conclusions in each that would be hard to reconcile theoretically.[17]

In brief, Christianity was made relevant to the public welfare at the expense of cherishing unresolved theoretical difficulties. And so long as these remain unsolved, discussions of the sects' relation to the general welfare are likely to remain ambiguous. For example, the common fervency of the insistence upon the dogma of "real, but indirect connection," which, I take it, has usually meant what Tocqueville noted, that the religious denominations in common inculcate the same basic moral standards which are the foundation of the Republic. This it is that makes their work relevant to the general welfare of the democracy. And this amounts to tacit acceptance of the rationalists' view of the matter.

Meanwhile the whole grand dream of American destiny, under God, instrumented through the democratic way while its tangled roots drew nourishment from many different soils in past centuries, was nevertheless profoundly religious in origins and conception. Hence the democratic faith had always a positive and apparently independently legitimate place in the religious affections of the people. This the free churches, in order to make themselves relevant, have always been under pressures to accept on faith and to sanctify.

Grant all this, plus the prevalence of a fuzzy and amorphous intellectual structure in the religious groups, and the way is left open for the uncritical adoption of whatever standards do actually prevail in the society. Hence, as noted, the American denominations have successively lent themselves to the sanctification of current existing expressions of the American way of life.

John Herman Randall, Jr., by taking a more theoretical route as befits a philosopher, arrives at the similar conclusion that "Protestantism left the way open for the assimilation of any pattern of values that might seem good in the light of men's actual social experience . . . [and] has thus tended to become largely an emotional force in support of the reigning secular social ideals."

However, it is not quite fair to conclude, as he does, that Protestantism has offered "*no* opposition to any ideal deeply felt" and "no independent guidance and wisdom,"[18] although the denominations have always exhibited a surprising lack of ability to launch a cogent criticism of their culture. During the period we are discussing such criticism was almost nonexistent. "The most significant feature of the New Theology" of the period, as W. S. Hudson makes clear, "was its lack of normative content," which made it "compatible with every conceivable social attitude."[19] It is not to be wondered at that businessmen, who during the great depression looked to their churches for guidance, complained that they received back only the echoes of their own voices.

But whatever historical explanations are accepted as most plausible, there remains the general agreement that at the time Protestantism in America achieved its greatest dominance of the culture, it had also achived an almost complete ideological and emotional identification with the burgeoning bourgeois society and its free-enterprise system. This gives point to Henry May's thesis that "in 1876 Protestantism presented a massive, almost unbroken front in its defense of the social status quo."[20]

Furthermore, Protestants, in effect, looked at the new world they had created, were proud of its creator, and, like Jehovah before them, pronounced it very good. A widespread complacency, a smug self-satisfaction with things as they were (or as they were supposed to be), settled upon them as soot settles on Chicago. This complacency, while a bit incredible to the mid-twentieth century, is not too difficult to understand historically. To do so, it is necessary to keep in mind the almost universal prevalence of a providential view of history—which itself is no mean evidence for the cultural dominance of the denominations. Late in 1864 Horace Bushnell proclaimed:

We associate God and religion with all that we are fighting for. . . . Our cause, we love to think, is especially God's and so we are connecting all most sacred impressions with our government itself, weaving in a woof of holy feeling among all the fibres of our constitutional polity and government. . . . The whole shaping of the fabric is

Providential. God, God is in it, everywhere . . . every drum-beat is a hymn, the cannon thunder God, the electric silence, darting victory along the wires, is the inaudible greeting of God's favoring work and purpose.[21]

Granted this sentiment, it was natural that the outcome of the Civil War should suggest to those of the North that "the sword of victory had been wielded by the arm of Providence." At the same time many in the South tended humbly to submit "to the inscrutable ways of the same Power."[22] So the young South Carolinian interviewed by John Trowbridge had concluded, "I think it was in the decrees of God Almighty that slavery was to be abolished in this way, and I don't murmur."[23]

However, the ways of Providence were not to all as inscrutable as to Abraham Lincoln, who, after plumbing the awful depths of the war's events, spoke of the altogether righteous judgment on both North and South of the Almighty who has His own purposes in history—purposes which might not fully coincide with the desires of either side. Lincoln concluded in humility that it behooved finite men to proceed "with malice toward none, with charity for all."

There was little of such humility in the heart and hardly a hint of such somber mystery tingeing the thought of the Rev. Henry Ward Beecher—that magnificent weathervane of respectable opinion. When in May, 1863, he addressed the anniversary meeting of the American Home Missionary Society in Chicago, he exulted, "see how wonderfully . . . God, in his good providence, is preparing us for the work." For "while the South is draining itself dry of its resources . . . the Northern States are growing rich by war." "And what does it mean but this—that God is storing us with that wealth by which we are to be prepared to meet the exigencies which war shall bring upon us?"

And what exigencies are to be brought upon us? Beecher expressed no doubts:

We are to have the charge of this continent. The South has been proved, and has been found wanting. She is not worthy to bear rule.

She has lost the scepter in our national government; she is to lose the scepter in the States themselves; and this continent is to be from this time forth governed by Northern men, with Northern ideas, and with a Northern gospel.

The reasons were clear to Beecher: "this continent is to be cared for by the North simply because the North has been true to the cause of Christ in . . . a sufficient measure to secure her own safety; . . . and the nation is to be given to us because we have the bosom by which to nourish it."[24]

Instructed by such religious leaders, it is not to be wondered at if the final victory was widely interpreted as a vindication of the righteousness of the cause of the victors. And this in turn easily merged with a vindication of what the victorious North was rapidly becoming—an industrialized civilization under business control. For, to quote a college textbook, "the Northern victory meant that certain forces and interests, long held in check by the combination of the agricultural South and West, could now have free and full play. . . . Finance and industrial capitalism could move forward to completion without effective opposition."[25]

From here it was but another short step to the enshrinement of the political instrument which, in the hands of Providence, had guided the Union to victory over slavery and disunion. By 1865 a writer in the Methodist *New York Christian Advocate* had already proclaimed that "we find the political parties of the day so made out, that it may . . . be determined on which side an orderly and intelligent Protestant will be found, and on which the profane, the dissolute and the Romanist."[26] The Republican party, said Henry Wilson, contained "more of moral and intellectual worth than was ever embodied in any political organization in any land. . . . [It was] created by no man . . . [but] brought into being by Almighty God himself." This, of course, meant enshrinement of what the party became soon after Lincoln's death, when "it allied itself with the forces of corporate industry, which represented a greater investment of capital and, consequently, a greater concentration of power in politics and economic life than the slaveholders had ever dreamed of possessing."[27]

But if Americans were idealistic, they were also pragmatic. If it appears that they too simply saw the smiles of beneficent Providence in the trinity of Northernism, business, and the Republican party, it must also be remembered that the system appeared to work—to produce tangible fruits in the great and obvious material prosperity that o'erspread the land like a flood and promised, eventually at least, to saturate all levels of society. Thousands of inventions, garnered up and universally applied by free and daring enterprisers, revolutionized transportation, communication, agriculture, and industry, while the prevailing system seemingly distributed the benefits more widely and equitably than any had before it.[28] It was these tangible results that provided the most convincing argument for "the American way of life" and tended to dampen all critical, as well as carping, voices in whatever realm as "un-American." Further, as time passed, a rather definite and complete ideological structure—constituting an explanation and defense—was compounded out of conservative *laissez-faire* economic theory, the common-sense philosophy of the schools, and the orthodox theology of the churches.

The foundation of the whole structure was the idea of progress. It was belief in progress that made tolerable the very rapid changes to which people were being subjected, as well as some of the less desirable aspects of what was happening. The idea of progress was compounded of the Christian doctrine of Providence and the scientific idea of evolution and was summed up in the slick phrase popularized by John Fiske and Lyman Abbott: "Evolution is God's way of doing things." So, for example, it could be proclaimed as late as 1928 that "the fact of human progress is seen to be part of the inevitable evolutionary process; and religious faith seeks in the cosmos which produced us and which carries us along the evidence of the activities of God."[29]

To those standing on such a teleological escalator, change held no terrors. Undesirable features of the passing scene might be endured with patience bred of the knowledge that they would inevitably be transcended, since, as Henry Ward Beecher assured a Yale audience, "man is made to start and not to stop; to go on,

and on, and up, and onward . . . and ending in the glorious liberty
of the sons of God."[30] Meanwhile, as John Bascom had said,
"death is of little moment, if it plays into a higher life. The insects
that feed the bird meet their destination. The savages that are
trodden out of a stronger race are in the line of progress." And
"we—we as interpreters—are not to bring higher and impossible
motives and feelings into a lower field."[31]

That such sentiments were not restricted to well-placed leaders
is suggested by the lyrics of popular gospel songs that common
people sang in their churches:

> He leadeth me; O blessed thought!
> O words with heavenly comfort fraught!
> Whate'er I do, where'er I be,
> Still 'tis God's hand that leadeth me.

And when bleak failure seemed to encompass them and canker-
ous despair threatened to eat away their souls, they sang,

> We wonder why the test
> When we try to do our best.
> But we'll understand it better by and by.

The understanding on all levels was aided by the articulation
of a constellation of basic doctrines which gave plausibility to the
idea of progress by explaining its practical workings in human
society. One of the most complete statements of these doctrines
was achieved by Andrew Carnegie in his article called "Wealth,"
which appeared in the June, 1889, issue of the *North American
Review*. It was described by the editor as one of the finest articles
he had ever published.

Carnegie eschewed airy speculation and proposed to speak of
"the foundations upon which society is based" and of the laws
upon which "civilization itself depends"—the laws which "are the
highest results of human experience" and "the soil in which
society so far has produced the best fruit." He added as an ana-
thema, "Objections to the foundations upon which society is
based are not in order."

First was the familiar law of the sacredness of property or the right of every individual to have and to hold and be protected by the government in the possession of whatever property he could get.

Second were the twin laws of competition and the accumulation of wealth. The competition is for property, and these laws explain the way in which property gets distributed in a society. All men enter into the competition. But men differ in inherent aptitudes or talents in relationship to it. Some men are gifted with a talent of organization and management which invariably secures for them "enormous rewards, no matter where or under what laws or conditions." Ergo, "it is a law, as certain as any of the others named, that men possessed of this peculiar talent for affairs, under the free play of economic forces, must, of necessity, soon be in receipt of more revenue than can be judiciously expended upon themselves." In brief, "it is inevitable that their income must exceed their expenditures, and that they must accumulate wealth." The wealthy man Carnegie regarded as the victim of circumstances over which he had no control.

Carnegie was realist enough to recognize that society pays a great price for the law of competition which indeed "may be sometimes hard for the individual." Nevertheless, since this law has produced "our wonderful material development, . . . it is best for the race, because it insures the survival of the fittest in every department." This suggests a rather clear and universal, not to say comforting, criterion for judging who are the "fittest" in every area of the society.[32]

The Rt. Rev. William Lawrence of Massachusetts propounded his ecclesiastical version of the agnostic's sentiments in an article published in January, 1901.[33] Sensing "a certain distrust on the part of our people as to the effect of material prosperity on their morality," he suggested that it would be well to "revise our inferences from history, experience, and the Bible" and shed that "subtle hypocrisy which has beset the Christian through the ages, bemoaning the deceitfulness of riches and, at the same time, working with all his might to earn a competence, and a fortune if he can." Having rid himself of such false inferences and hypocrisy, man may now recognize two great guiding principles for his life. The first is that it is "his divine mission" to "conquer Nature, open up her resources, and harness them to his service." The second is that "in the long run, it is only to the man of morality that wealth comes" for "Godliness is in league with riches." This being the case, the good Bishop added, "we return with an easier mind and clearer conscience to the problem of our twenty-five billion dollars in a decade," confident that "material prosperity is in the long run favorable to morality."

Third was the law or rule of stewardship, which followed upon the views of the sacredness of property and the laws of competition and accumulation. In brief, the use and disposition of the property, as well as its mere possession, are sacred to the man who accumulates it. God gave it to him by endowing him with certain talents, and he is responsible for it *to God* alone, and certainly not to the lesser fit in the community.

"We start," said Carnegie, "with a condition of affairs under which the best interests of the race are promoted, but which inevitably gives wealth to the few." And "thus far . . . the situation can be surveyed and pronounced good." Therefore, the "only question with which we have to deal," he continued, is "What is the proper mode of administering wealth after the laws upon which civilization is founded have thrown it into the hands of the few?" There were, he thought, but three possibilities. The few might leave it to their families, they might bequeath it for public purposes, or they might administer it during their lives. He rules out the first two as irresponsible, even coming to the radical conclusion that the state might well confiscate through inheritance taxes at least half of fortunes so left.

The true duty of "the man of Wealth" is to live modestly and unostentatiously, "provide moderately for the legitimate wants of those dependent upon him," and, beyond that,

to consider all surplus revenues which come to him simply as trust funds, which he is . . . strictly bound as a matter of duty to administer in the manner which, in his judgment, is best calculated to produce the most beneficial results for the community . . . thus becoming the mere agent and trustee for his poorer brethren, bringing to their service his superior wisdom, experience, and ability to administer, doing for them better than they would or could do for themselves.

The main rule to be followed is to help those who will help themselves and to eschew the indiscriminate charity which presents "one of the most serious obstacles to the improvement of our race," by encouraging "the slothful, the drunken, the unworthy." To this we shall return in the next essay.

Here it is necessary to note only that such stewardship was taken seriously by many wealthy men of the day and produced in them an honest and consecrated devotion to their sacred duties which only the sneering souls of the mean in mind could belittle. In 1856 John P. Crozer was awed to note that "wealth flows in from all sources." This, he added, made him feel "as often before, in making up my yearly accounts, oppressed with the responsibility of my stewardship. I am, indeed, perplexed how I shall use, as I ought to, the great and increasing stores of wealth which God has bestowed upon me." "I love to make money almost as well as a miser," he wrote a year later, and added, "I love to give it away for charitable purposes." But he realized, as he searched his soul, "I . . . must set a guard over myself, lest the good designed be lost in the luxury of giving." For

excuses are so easily framed, and the heart of man so deceitful, that one can easily reason himself into the belief that, all things considered, he has done pretty well. I find such a process of reasoning in my own mind; but calm reflection tells me that I have not done well. I am a very unprofitable servant to so good a Master; and as he has made me the steward of a large estate, it becomes me "to lend it to the Lord" freely of my substance.

Still troubled, he prayed with real humility, "O my lord, if it is thy righteous pleasure, direct me clearly and decisively to some path of duty and of usefulness, apart from the absorbing influence of wealth and worldly mindedness."[34]

Later, of course, when such devoted stewards were harassed

by the rise of the unfit and strikes rocked their companies, this paternalistic conception of stewardship would show another face, as when George F. Baer, president of the Philadelphia and Reading Railway, wrote in 1902 to an inquirer:

> I beg of you not to be discouraged. The rights and interests of the laboring man will be protected and cared for—not by the labor agitators, but by the Christian men to whom God in His infinite wisdom has given the control of the property interests of the country, and upon the successful management of which so much depends.[35]

Meanwhile, as intimated previously, Protestantism—at least in the respectable churches—effused a benign sanctity over all. The older people's churches were rapidly becoming middle class, at least in mentality and leadership. As A. M. Schlesinger, Sr., says, even the Baptists "abandoned their contempt for wealth," as God gave gold in abundance to some of their more worthy members.[36] In 1866 a writer in the *Christian Advocate* was pleased to note that "by virtue of the habits which religion inculcates and cherishes, our Church members have as a body risen in the social scale, and thus become socially removed from the great body out of which most of them originally gathered." And he added with a hint of smugness, "this tendency of things is natural and universal, and in its results unavoidable; perhaps we might add, also, not undesirable."[37]

At the same time, American scholars, many of them ministers turned professors, worked out, as Henry May says, "a school of political economy which might well be labeled clerical *laissez faire*." The ideological amalgamation of which we have spoken is best and most clearly illustrated here. Said the Rev. John McVicker of Columbia: "That science and religion eventually teach the same lesson, is a necessary consequence of the unity of truth, but it is seldom that this union is so satisfactorily displayed as in the researches of Political Economy."[38]

Americans, in spite of the long century of relative peace and stability in the world following 1814 and their almost complete freedom from embroilment in European affairs, were never complete isolationists in spirit. From this they were saved by the strong sense of destiny under God which pervaded their thinking from the beginning. By 1825 Francis Wayland, Jr., had already proclaimed sentiments that should have raised eyebrows in Europe: "What nation will be second in the new order of things, is yet to be decided; but the providence of God has already announced, that, if true to ourselves, we shall be inevitably first."[39]

The keynote of the American idea of destiny was struck by John Winthrop in his address "Written on Boarde the Arrabella" in 1630. He said: as

for the worke wee haue in hand, it is by a mutuall consent through a speciall overruleing providence, and a more than an ordinary approbation of the Churches of Christ to seeke out a place of Cohabitation and Consorteshipp vnder a due forme of Government both ciull and ecclesiasticall.

If we are faithful to our covenant with him, Winthrop continued,

wee shall finde that the god of Israell is among vs . . . when hee shall make vs a prayse and glory, that men shall say of succeeding plantacions: the Lord make it like that of New England: for wee must Consider that wee shall be as a Citty vpon a Hill, the eies of all people are vpon vs.[40]

Thenceforth throughout American history this strong sense of particular calling, of destiny under God, has remained a constant part of the ideological structure of the nation. In the Discourse quoted above, Francis Wayland, Jr., echoed Winthrop when he wrote, "Our power resides in the force of our example. It is by exhibiting to other nations the practical excellence of a government of law, that they will learn its nature and advantages, and will in due time achieve their own emancipation."[41] Already, he thought, "our country has given to the world the first ocular demonstration, not only of the practicability, but also of the unrivalled superiority of a popular form of government."[42]

William R. Williams in 1846 more obviously wove the strands of evangelical Christianity into those of American destiny. "Our

Heavenly Father has made us a national epistle to other lands," he wrote.

> See that you read a full and impressive comment to all lands, of the power of Christian principle, and of the expansive and self-sustaining energies of the gospel, when left unfettered by national endowments, and secular alliances. The evangelical character of our land is to tell upon the plans and destinies of other nations.[43]

Clothed in various languages in various times and places, the theme of American destiny has remained the same, although God, like Alice's Cheshire Cat, has sometimes threatened gradually to disappear altogether or, at most, to remain only as a disembodied and sentimental smile.

It was the idea of destiny which added "the inducements of philanthropy to those of patriotism" in the American mind and broadened the idea of progress and its laws to include all of humanity. America's destiny came to be seen as her call to spread the amazing benefits of the American democratic faith and its free-enterprise system throughout the world, gradually transforming the world into its own image.

The idea of destiny tempered Bishop Lawrence's belief that "Godliness is in league with riches." The call for today, he argued, is for

> the uplift of character . . . and every means of culture; . . . and, above all, the deepening of the religious faith of the people; the rekindling of the spirit, that, clothed with her material forces, the great personality of this nation may fulfill her divine destiny.[44]

When Lawrence wrote this in 1901 the United States, fresh from its venture in imperialistic war, was already beginning to be impressed by the meaning and possibilities of her physical power. The idea had been hatched that the power as well as the wealth was given by divine appointment to be used.

Josiah Strong, erstwhile Congregational pastor in Cheyenne, Wyoming, and at the time secretary of that denomination's Home Missionary Society, sounded the Christian version of this view in his very popular book *Our Country* published in 1885.[45]

Strong argued that the Anglo-Saxon race—and in the United States all immigrants soon become Anglo-Saxon—is the bearer of two closely related ideas, Civil Liberty and "pure *spiritual* Christianity." Ergo, "the Anglo-Saxon . . . is divinely commissioned to be, in a peculiar sense, his brother's keeper." And when we add to this the equally obvious fact of his "rapidly increasing strength in modern times . . . does it not look as if God were not only preparing in our Anglo-Saxon civilization the die with which to stamp the peoples of the earth, but as if we were also massing behind that die the mighty power with which to press it?"

Citing the Americans as "the noblest; for we are 'The heirs of all the ages in the foremost files of time,'" he explained that God, with infinite wisdom and skill, was training them "for an hour sure to come"—the hour of the "final competition of races." He had no qualms about the outcome: "Can anyone doubt that the result of this competition of races will be the 'survival of the fittest'?" Standing firmly on the evolutionary escalator, he proclaimed the present knowledge that the "inferior tribes were only precursors of a superior race, voices in the wilderness crying; 'Prepare ye the way of the Lord!'"

So this influential Congregational leader admired God's "two hands"—with one of which He was "preparing in our civilization the die with which to stamp the nations" while with the other He was "preparing mankind to receive our impress."

With such well-nigh infallible religious guides abroad in the land, it is small wonder that a mere junior Senator, Albert J. Beveridge, of Indiana, was prepared to defend annexation of the Philippines on January 9, 1900, with the words:

We will not renounce our part in the mission of the race, trustee, under God, of the civilization of the world. . . . He has made us . . . the master organizers of the world to establish system where chaos reigns. . . . He has made us adepts in government that we may administer government among savage and senile peoples. . . . And of all our race, He has marked the American people as His chosen Nation to finally lead in the regeneration of the world. This is the divine mission of America, and it holds for us all the profit, all the glory, all the happiness possible to man. We are trustees of the world's progress, guardians of its righteous peace. The judgment of the Master is upon us: "Ye have been faithful over a few things; I will make you ruler over many things."[46]

Finally, "exhibiting a nugget of gold, he cried: 'I picked this up on the ground in one of these islands. There are thousands of others lying about.' "

A Christian note of profounder depth was struck, however, by Senator George F. Hoar, who rose merely to say: "The Devil taketh him up into an extremely high mountain and showeth him all the kingdoms of the world and the glory of them and saith unto him, 'All these things will be thine if thou wilt fall down and worship me.' "[47]

We have noted then that the bulk of American Protestantism achieved during this period a working ideological harmony with the modes of the modern industrialized civilization, the free-enterprise system, and the burgeoning imperialism. Professor W. S. Hudson, treating the more purely theological aspects of this development in a most discerning book on *The Great Tradition of the American Churches*, makes good his claim that "the New Theology was essentially a culture religion."[48] The doctrines of the "gospel of wealth" in the context of the idea of destiny under God gave a satisfactory explanation of the facts of human life as experienced in the United States. It should never be forgotten that at this time the observational order coincided in high degree with the conceptual order and that such coincidence defines social stability.

This it was that created an atmosphere in which those actually in control—the only people that really mattered—could live at ease in the vast expanding new Zion. This was Edith Wharton's "age of innocence," Henry S. Canby's "age of confidence"; and its flower was a host of middle-class "fathers" of the type pictured by Clarence Day. Perhaps its outstanding characteristic was complacency, based on the feeling that God was in His heaven and all was right with the world. Surveying the period in retrospect, we may agree with Whitehead that "the prosperous middle classes, who ruled the nineteenth century, placed an excessive value upon placidity of existence." With Whitehead, we can affirm that this is hardly a sufficient basis for an enduring culture.[49]

Looking backward today from a world which promises to be very different from that Utopia which Edward Bellamy anticipated in 1888, it seems obvious enough that the outward harmony was achieved by overlooking certain incongruous elements in the situation that had troubled only such gloomy and lonesome prophets as Nathaniel Hawthorne, Herman Melville, Walt Whitman, and Henry Adams. The world that seemed so fine and stable to Carnegie and Bishop Lawrence, to Crozer and Henry Ward Beecher, to Josiah Strong and Russell Conwell—to all the "fathers" of Day's type—was about to explode. The period of cultural triumph of the denominations merged—not with a whimper, but with a bang—into the period of upheaval and crisis.

IX

American Protestantism Since the Civil War.

II. From Americanism to Christianity

In the preceding essay we described the metamorphosis of Protestantism in the United States in its ideological amalgamation with "Americanism." This was still a period of fervent devotion, but the object of devotion had been subtly changed under the appearance of enlargement to include a particular system of social, political, and economic life. "In ages of fervent devotion," Tocqueville noted, "men sometimes abandon their religion, but they only shake it off to adopt another. Their faith changes the objects to which it is directed, but it suffers no decline."[1] This was the kind of change we have described. There was no outward appearance of decline in religious activities or denominational prosperity. Indeed contemporary statistical studies suggested a period of organizational vitality and exceptional growth, during which the denominations were rapidly bringing the unchurched into their folds. For this reason the rightness of the general outlook seemed to pass the pragmatic test—the system worked, as serious and able students like Daniel Dorchester took pains to point out.[2]

Meanwhile the ideological amalgamation of Protestant denominationalism and Americanism went on. The situation was ironic. While Protestant leaders were very much aware of the evils resulting from a formal connection between church and state they were, to say the least, less conscious of the equally grave perils in religious endorsement of a particular way of life. Consequently under the system of official separation of church and state the denominations eventually found themselves as completely identified with nationalism and their country's political and economic systems as had ever been known in Christendom.

A crisis in the life of these denominations naturally resulted when spectacular upheavals suggesting possible breakdown prompted many leaders to question the adequacy of the existing social and economic systems, while at the same time the relevancy of the churches' theology was challenged as never before.

The simple thesis of A. M. Schlesinger, Sr., guides the following discussion of developments, namely: that during the last quarter of the nineteenth century organized religion in America met two great challenges—"the one to its system of thought, the other to its social program."[3]

The challenge to the system of thought was spearheaded by the persuasive sway of evolutionary thinking, appearing first in the work of Darwin and Spencer and soon pervading all areas of intellectual life. The challenge to the social program of the denominations came first in the form of unbearable conditions in the expanding industrial cities and then in a series of spectacular upheavals that shook the social structure to its foundations.

It is important to note that these two challenges, which threatened to shatter both the ideological and the practical worlds of the denominations, were concurrent. In this perspective the wonder is not that there was a great deal of confusion, inanity, and hysteria but that as much sanity and order prevailed in them as actually did. Indeed, one of the most thorough students of the era concluded that "during this period of recurrent depression, doubt and struggle the Protestant churches still maintained, to a greater extent than is usually realized, their historic position of intellectual and moral leadership."[4]

– I –

The social program of the denominations was firmly rooted in the long Christian tradition of charity: the amelioration of distress, feeding the hungry, clothing the naked, visiting the sick and

imprisoned, and giving the cup of cold water for Jesus' sake
and not the titillation of human pride. The ideal in this respect was
" 'the man of feeling' . . . the feeling of the renewed heart, enlarged as is the range of human wretchedness, purified by the
indwelling Spirit of God, and ennobled by the model on which
it is formed," as two Scottish ministers wrote of the Rev. Ezra
Stiles Ely in 1829.[5]

But the exercise of Christian charity came to be hemmed in by
current modes of thinking. In the first place, it was to be exercised
wisely, which meant with a realistic regard for what Horace
Bushnell called the laws of trade. Among these were the im-
mutable "laws of current price" which he thought automatically
set the price of farm products and determined "the wages of hand
labor."[6] In 1868 the Rev. John Bascom of Williams College invoked these laws against proposed eight-hour-day legislation.
He argued that any attempt to interfere with their working in
the interests of abstract justice or the amelioration of distress was
to attempt "a substitution of civil for natural law" and to
demonstrate "the impossibility of affecting favorably or shifting
the conditions of society except in connection with the forces
that give rise to them."[7]

Recognizing this, Bushnell continued that "the merchant . . .
should do his trade by the strict law principles of trade, and never
let his operations be mixed up with charities." Hence his two
ideal merchants

were never known to veer by a hair from integrity in any transaction
of business, but they would have veered a hundred times a day, falling
into a muddle where all distinctions of principle are lost, if they had
not done their trade as trade, under the law of trade, and reserved
their charities—all their sympathies, allowances, mitigations, merciful
accommodations—for a separate chapter of life.[8]

Andrew Carnegie, in his famous article on "Wealth," intimated
clearly enough that to pay higher wages than the market demanded in an effort to distribute wealth more equitably was just
such a mistaken mixing of trade and charity and violated the

rich man's responsibility to administer his wealth "for the community far better than it could or would have done for itself."[9]

In this view he was backed by the natural theology of Professor Bascom, who held that while ultimately selfishness will be "steadily softened into a just and generous regard of the good of others," meanwhile the only "basis of simple justice, of pure economic right, and . . . the only one on which the claims of all parties can find firm, constant, and conclusive adjustment" is that of "sharp competition, of a stern and unscrupulous use of the advantages which the market affords." Therefore, for example, "if a workman wishes higher wages than the employer is willing to pay, he has but one test of the validity of his claim . . . and that is his ability to secure elsewhere the sum demanded." This, he explained, "is commercial law, commercial justice, a practical and final decision of all questions, beyond which there is the opportunity for no claim, as there is for no coercion."[10]

Under these rubrics Carnegie castigated the writer of philosophic books who confessed that he had given a quarter to a man who approached him on the street. This, thought Carnegie, was a flagrant example of indiscriminate charity and was probably "one of the most selfish and very worst actions" of this man's generally worthy life.[11] The Rev. Charles Wood was even more dogmatic than Carnegie. He was convinced that "begging on the streets, and from door to door, is a *habit*, acquired after an experience of its success. . . . In nine cases out of ten there is no necessity, no pressure of want at all." Rather, "it is prompted by a low, indolent spirit, which seeks to gratify its selfish lusts, at the expense of the virtuous and good." Furthermore, he added, revealing a widespread prejudice, "four-fifths, if not nine-tenths, of all our street beggars and paupers are of one nationality and of one form of religion." Therefore, he argued, "street begging should be made an offence in the eyes of the law, and should be strictly visited by a suitable penalty."[12]

In the second place, the exercise of charity was limited and conditioned by the prevalent view that most poverty was the direct result of vice and sin. Carnegie was convinced that "in alms-giving more injury is probably done by rewarding vice than by relieving virtue," and his true reformer was "as careful and as anxious not to aid the unworthy as he is to aid the worthy."[13]

These views also had clerical approval in high places. Henry Ward Beecher thought that while there may be reasons of poverty which do not involve wrong, nevertheless, "looking comprehensively through city and town and village and country, the general truth will stand, that no man in this land suffers from poverty unless it be more than his fault—unless it be his *sin*." Happily, he added, "there is enough and to spare thrice over; and if men have not enough, it is owing to the want of provident care, and foresight, and industry, and frugality, and wise saving. This is the general truth."[14] In 1873 the reviewer of Charles Loring Brace's *The Dangerous Classes of New York* . . . in the *Presbyterian Quarterly and Princeton Review*, commented that "in this city . . . as a general rule, poverty comes from vice, rather than vice from poverty."[15] The Rev. Charles Wood, writing in the same *Quarterly* a year later, was positive that "pauperism and vagrancy are *crimes*, and should be *prevented* or *punished*." And, he added, "it is even doubtful whether the indirect *injury* done by our voluntary, benevolent associations, and 'missions for the relief of the poor' . . . does not overbalance the good which they accomplish." For, he continued, perhaps with a tinge of professional jealousy, "the only institutions, or organized societies" which can insure the punishment or prevention of vagrancy and pauperism are the "divine institutions" of "the family, the *church* and the state." "All other institutions should be associated with and subordinated to these." Only "good homes, pure churches, and well administered laws, will either prevent or punish the crimes of our lowest classes."[16]

John Bascom was made of even sterner stuff. "The staple with which Providence has to deal in the races of men," he pontificated, "is ignorance and indolence interstratified with sin—stupidity made heavy, solid, opaque, and gritty with a wicked will" until the unpliant and stubborn mass can only be broken and ground and reformed by the strongest and harshest of machinery. Unpitying poverty, absolute and severe want, must be allowed to force action, to sharpen instincts, to strengthen the will. War and pestilence must winnow the feeble races, lest they swarm in vile, unprofitable life.

Hence "God's method," with which Bascom seemed to be completely familiar, is the "melancholy work of scouraging on the backs of the blind and perverse," and wisdom recognizes that "the loitering, unambitious poor still reserve for themselves the lash of necessity, are checked in increase . . . by hardship and disease, and left under the severe hand of physical law," which treats them "according to the dulness and sin that is in them." Therefore he who would be philanthropic must choose either to rob intelligence and industry of their reward, or to cast off the unworthy, leaving them "to the fruits of their folly, till the bitterness of sin shall aid in working its cure, and help to create [in them] an appetite for something better." Meanwhile he concluded it is foolish to try to "undo by a trick of management and new relations the work of sin, and unbind its heavy burdens."[17]

Christian charity came to be incased in this hard shell of sanctified realism that sought to protect it from foolishness. Nevertheless the sheer existence of conditions in the growing industrial cities[18] increasingly constituted a challenge to human decency as well as to Christian conscience, which made its impact. Walter Rauschenbusch, who in 1886 went to the Second German Baptist Church on West Forty-fifth Street in New York apparently to save individual souls, found himself confronted with "the endless procession of men 'out of work, out of clothes, out of shoes, and out of hope,' that wore down the threshold and wore away the hearts of the sensitive young pastor and his wife." No doubt this experience put him in a receptive mood to be awakened "to the world of social problems" by Henry George,[19] who was reminding the clergy that kindness, generosity, and other amiable virtues were no longer sufficient—that "what is needed is justice."[20]

Meanwhile, because the denominations were rapidly becoming

middle class in outlook and constituency, their social program was also challenged by the loss of working people. "We make the statement without fear of contradiction, and therefore without apology," said Charles Wood in 1874, "that the poor are not provided for, nor are they wanted as a part of the congregations which worship in the majority of our city churches." This indifference on the part of the churches, he added, when "taken in connection with that of the poor themselves to their own spiritual instruction, only shows the pitiable condition in which they are placed."[21] Even Henry Ward Beecher, although less obviously perturbed by it, recognized in 1874 that in "the average churches in New York and Brooklyn, from Murray Hill downward . . . it will be found that the aristocratic and prosperous elements have possession of them, and if the great under-class, the poor and needy, go to them at all, they go sparsely, and not as to a home." And, he added with surprising candor, "our churches are largely for the mutual insurance of prosperous families, and not for the upbuilding of the great underclass of humanity."[22]

Out of these factors created by the rise of great industrial cities came the many movements of charity and philanthropy and definite attempts to appeal to workers which are delineated so well by Aaron I. Abell in his study of *The Urban Impact on American Protestantism, 1865-1900*.[23] City rescue missions, homes of various kinds, the Salvation Army, the Volunteers of America, institutional churches, and a host of other instruments for meeting the situation were devised and grew apace. And these, in turn, had their effect. The efforts expended through them were somewhat successful in alleviating distress but were more important in holding significant numbers of the workers. These urban workers exerted an influence in the churches, since "the wage-earning masses expected religion to establish ultimately a more equitable economic and industrial order."[24]

Nevertheless, as Henry May notes, "until they were shocked by a series of violent social conflicts, most Protestant spokesmen continued to insist that all was well." Until then, "greed at the top could be ignored or accepted as a tool of progress," while "misery at the bottom could be waved aside as inevitable or, at most, treated by a program of guarded and labeled philanthropy."[25]

The upheavals which challenged the magnificently complacent outlook of the period came out of the discontent smoldering in agriculture and labor. Speaking broadly, the woes of the farmer were attributable to the rapid industrialization of the country, with the attendant ascendance of a business mentality and the lure of businesslike practices. This is the situation which a textbook writer discusses in the aptly titled chapter "Capitalism Captures the Farmer." After picturing the farmers' plight, he concludes that "in the placid language of economics this was marginal living; in the realistic language of life it meant futility and desperation."[26] Hamlin Garland, spokesman for the revolt of the sons of "the middle border," used such realistic language in dedicating his *Main Travelled Roads*, published in 1891, to "my father and mother whose half century of pilgrimage on the main travelled road has brought them only pain and weariness." Out of the pain and weariness, the futility and desperation, came the sporadic movements of revolt—the Grange movement (Patrons of Husbandry) of 1867 and following; Greenbackism in the middle of the seventies; the Farmers' Alliance movement following 1880; the merging of these movements in Populism (the Peoples' party) in 1891; and their final culmination in merger with the Bryan Democrats for the great free-silver campaign of 1896.

But Protestant spokesmen, as revealed in the religious press, actually gave these manifestations of farmer unrest relatively little attention. No doubt this was because their attention was centered upon the more spectacular uprisings of labor. The Bureau of Labor reported 23,798 strikes in the nineteen years from 1881 to 1900, involving 6,610,000 workers and 132,442 plants. Four of the strikes were particularly explosive. First were the railroad strikes in 1877—called by the author of *Raintree County* "another Sumpter"—which spread out over the Pennsylvania, the Baltimore and Ohio, and New York Central. Pitched battles involving workers, police, militia, and federal troops were fought in many cities; property damage was immense, and sober men had visions of mobocracy and revolution. Second was the Haymarket affair in Chicago. In a clash between pickets and police at the McCormick Harvester Plant early in May, 1886, six pickets were killed and several wounded. At a protest meeting held the following day in Haymarket Square a bomb was thrown which killed eight policemen and injured twenty-seven persons. The trial, which resulted in seven "anarchists" being condemned to death (four were hanged, one committed suicide, two had sentences commuted to life imprisonment), revealed widespread alarm. Following the Haymarket affair came the strike of the Carnegie Steel Plant in Homestead, Pennsylvania, in 1892. There, during a battle between three hundred Pinkerton "detectives" and the workers, ten were killed and sixty wounded. This strike was stopped only when eight thousand state militia were called out. Fourth was the great strike at the Pullman Palace Car Company in 1894 when President Cleveland—over the protests of Governor Altgeld of Illinois—sent two thousand federal troops to "guard the mails," and the injunction was effectively used against the unions. Henry May holds that of all the strikes this one most alarmed the middle-class public.[27]

Meanwhile 1893 was a bleak and dangerous year. The depression which gripped the country was perhaps the greatest challenge the political and economic institutions of the United States faced between the Civil War and the great depression from 1929 to 1937.[28] Starvation, suffering, and hopelessness stalked the thousands of unemployed and frightened the comfortable. Revolution seemed imminent to many when bands of workers—"General" Jacob S. Coxey's "army" is the most famous—marched upon Washington seeking recognition and relief.[29]

Religious leaders were prepared, after a fashion, to meet such unprecedented upheavals. Regarding strikes, John Bascom had argued that while they represent the simple assertion of a right and therefore could not be condemned on moral grounds, yet they were rarely necessary because "the causes which justify a rise of wages will usually, by the inevitable laws of trade, quietly secure the result." Therefore, in those cases where "the clamor becomes loud and the measures violent," this fact alone is almost sufficient to mark "the absence . . . in the relation of the parties, of those grounds which render the claim just."[30] And in the midst of the troubles of 1893, Andrew Preston Peabody, who taught ethics and religion at Harvard, dismissed labor organizations with the remark: "That they are tolerated in what pretends to be a free country, or by any government less barbarous than that of Dahomey or Ashantee, is to me an unsolvable mystery."[31]

We are not surprised to note that men of such preparation reacted first with amazement and fear and cried out for the suppression of the "mobs." Not untypical were the comments of the *Christian Union* in 1877: "There are times when mercy is a mistake, and this is one of them." The *Independent* burst out hysterically:

If the club of the policeman, knocking out the brains of the rioter, will answer, then well and good; but if it does not promptly meet the exigency, then bullets and bayonets, canister and grape—with no sham or pretense, in order to frighten men, but with fearful and destructive reality—constitute the one remedy and the one duty of the hour. . . . Napoleon was right when he said that the way to deal with a mob was to exterminate it.

As late as 1892 a writer in the *Christian Advocate* thought that the duty of every patriot was to "hope for the best, and say only those words which will tend to the maintenance of law." Meanwhile "if he has any abstract theories for bettering the human race, this is no time to ventilate them."[32]

But by that time many religious leaders were already deeply troubled. "In the darkest hours of the Civil War," said a writer in the *Christian Advocate* in 1886, "we never felt more sober than today."[33] Even John Bascom had noted in 1868 that in the contest between capital and labor "employers, frequently few in number, can easily come to a tacit understanding without attracting public attention, and steadily resist the natural forces which are tending to press up the price of labor," while "the workmen, on the contrary . . . feel keenly the immediate necessity of continuing labor on the best terms they can make."[34] Noting that any sudden inflation of prices finds laborers the losers, he argued that since the Civil War the condition of workmen had become worse while manufacturing profits rose.

The first reaction of the editors of the *Congregationalist* to the Homestead strike was to compare the owner's hiring Pinkerton men to shoot the strikers with "lynchers . . . taking the law into their own hands" because impatient with the regular processes of justice. "Some legal requirement and provision for arbitration" seem to be absolutely necessary, they argued, because these enterprises "employing many thousands of men and affecting widely the interests of the people . . . are not merely private property." Therefore the skilled workmen at Homestead "cannot rightly be dispossessed of their positions by mere arbitrary conditions imposed by their employers," any more than a big corporation can rightfully be "blocked in carrying on its business by the arbitrary demands of labor organizations."[35]

In the September issue of 1892 the editors of the *Andover Review*, commenting on Homestead, held that while law and order must be given immediate and absolute precedence, nevertheless "the maintenance of order in congested labor districts is not the settlement of the labor question." The question of the day, they continued, is that of the "personal rights in equity in the plant which the men had contributed so much to build up by their skill and character." For, contrary to Carnegie's "benevolent millionairism," the growth and "reputation of the Carnegie works . . . are due, not simply to the energy and business sagacity of the owners, not simply the enterprise in the managers, not simply to improved machinery, but equally to the coöperation of the skilled workmen employed." And while it may be legal, it just isn't equitable "whenever a question of work or wage arises, for the management to say, if you don't like the place you can quit."

The editors concluded that "there can be no further progress in the adjustment of labor and capital, and no permanent safety for the wage system, as the method of industrialism, until these rights in equity are in some way acknowledged." And unless they are, "the wage system will certainly and justly lose its place as the accredited method of industrial business, and something will be devised which will express in larger degree than wages the interest of labor in the means and agencies of production." Finally, the editors muttered, in what sounds like a threat, if management continues to insist simply upon legal rights in the wage system against rights in equity, "the appeal will be taken to politics, and the appeal of industrialism to politics is the first and a long step toward State Socialism."[36] Here then were emerging cogent criticisms of the existing American way of life based on a rejection of some of the most sacred doctrines of the gospel of wealth.

So far as the Protestant denominations were concerned, the significance of the great social upheavals was that they forced in many minds consideration of the question of the adequacy of charity as then understood and interpreted. Could it guide the social program of the free churches or suggest ways to meet the vast new problems of the industrialized civilization? "Do I mean to say that Christian philanthropy is a failure?" asked Charles Worcester Clark in an article published posthumously in 1893.[37] "Certainly not; only that the time has come earnestly to consider whether its field ought not to be extended so as to cover the cause of the evils it is already doing so much to alleviate." "Charity," he explained, "whether public or private, mainly deals with results, to mitigate effects; public action must be applied to the industrial system itself, in order to prevent a continuation of their causes." In brief, "our philanthropy must concern itself not only with private helpfulness, but with public reform and economic reorganization." This, he thought, will be objected to as wholly unprecedented by those who "do not even try to solve the social problem, save in the same old way," but "I merely contend that, in view of the industrial revolution wrought by science and invention during the past century, the burden of proof rests on those who maintain that the old ways are sufficient under the new conditions, no less than on those who demand a change."

In this general context we are better able to understand the great gulf between the views of John Bascom and Henry Ward Beecher and those of Francis Greenwood Peabody, who in 1900 in a book called *Jesus Christ and the Social Question* argued that "the social question of the present age is not a question of mitigating the evils of the existing order, but a question whether the existing order itself shall last. It is not so much a problem of social amelioration which occupies the modern mind, as a problem of social transformation and reconstruction." The demands, he continued, are "not patronage, but justice; not the general distribution of superfluous wealth, but the righteous restitution of wealth to those who have created it."[38] This indicates a mood widely prevalent at the turn of the century. It was an outlook in sharp contrast to that prevailing during the seventies and eighties. It marks the emergence of the social-gospel movement in the denominations.

– II –

Meanwhile, referring back to Schlesinger's thesis, the denominations' system of thought was also being challenged and shaken as never before in America, even during the heyday of infidelity. For concurrent with the social upheavals which attended the "economic revolution" and "industrial metamorphosis"[39] came the full impact of Darwinian evolutionary thinking, which appeared to strike at the very root of Christianity and all religion. Because it was posited upon the induction that "all life developed from pre-existing life,"[40] evolutionism seemed to remove the creating Deity and His providence from the origin and direction of the world and to erase the created boundary between man and the other animals, placing all upon a continuum. This appeared to do away with the object of Christian devotion and to destroy the foundations of Christian ethics.[41]

It was this evolutionism which "germinated ideas wherever it penetrated, and it penetrated everywhere."[42] The so-called "new history," was based upon the application of evolutionary theories to the understanding of the past. The "higher criticism" of the

Bible was largely the application of the new history to the sacred volume.[43]

Evolutionary thinking was certainly nothing new in Western civilization, and its sudden sway in America is not accounted for simply by the convincing empirical documentation of Darwin and the pursuasive universality of Spencer's systematization. It was a period of great changes in the structures of the culture, but it is "the rate rather than the fact of change [which] endows the forty years after 1860 with epochal attributes."[44] It was evolutionary theories, sanctified by the traditional Christian doctrine of Providence, which spawned the general idea of "progress" and made the rapid change tolerable and even exhilarating.

Evolutionary theories were an aspect of the world view of modern science and at the time gave structure to its cosmology. Their tremendous appeal forced theology at last to try to come to terms intellectually with the world view of modern science. Since the end of the eighteenth century the bulk of the Protestant denominations had embraced classical orthodoxy sentimentalized by pietism and divorced from the mind and spirit of modern civilization. Evolutionism forced the denominations to take up again the intellectual business laid on the table at the opening of the nineteenth century and largely ignored during the intervening busy years of institutional proliferation and growth. The issue between science and theology could no longer be ignored. The pathetic nature of the denominations' position is suggested by the fact that when in 1926, in Dayton, Tennessee, "twelve unlettered hill-men were constituted a jury to decide the most momentous issue of modern thought," Tom Stewart, the public prosecutor, could ask in all seriousness, "Who says we can't bar science that deprives us of all hope of the future life to come?"[45] There indeed is the place for tears.

Struck by what appeared to be mutiny in the social and economic areas at the very time when ideological winds were sweeping them from their old theological anchorages, the denominations seemed in danger of floundering. Derisive gods might have found grounds for sardonic laughter in the situation.

The social outlook of the denominations was seen to be inadequate during this period because it was too modern—too completely geared to the prevailing outlook—while their theology
was largely irrelevant because it was too anachronistic—too out
of touch with contemporary currents of thought.

The two challenges, to return to Schlesinger's terms, went
hand in hand.[46] The growing industrial system created the great
cities, which became the centers for the development and easy
dissemination of new knowledge and havens for the new religious, social, and economic heretics. Meanwhile some of the
denominationally supported educational institutions, including
church-related seminaries, were reaping a harvest from the
acquistive, exploitative, middle-class social structure in the form
of large gifts from Carnegie's peculiarly endowed individuals
who, willy-nilly, accumulated wealth. Such gifts, by making
these schools financially independent of their denominations,
had the effect of freeing their administrators and professors from
direct denominational control. This, of course, was not entirely
unappreciated. One suspects a bit of existential involvement when
Harvard's Professor Peabody says his "intercourse with rich men
has been such as to make me thank God for them, and deprecate
with my whole soul the leveling doctrines" now being advocated.
On the next page he notes the number of professorships such
men had endowed.[47]

Just when many young men were imbibing relatively advanced
theological notions in the German universities and returning to
teaching positions in the theological schools of America, several of
these schools were given the wherewithal to free their professors
from church control. In several instances when denominations
attempted to discipline wayward professors, their schools, in
effect, simply declared their independence. This development
permitted the cultivation of modernistic or liberal approaches to
the several theological disciplines by men who were not necessarily responsibly related to the churches at all. Such professors
were always in danger of becoming preciously exotic, and even
contemptuous of the denominations' level of enlightenment. This

helps to explain why the controversy between science and theology in America was not settled when and because a handful of such professors in the seminaries accepted evolutionism, any more than it was settled when and because several outstanding, but practically independent, ministers, like Henry Ward Beecher and his worthy successor, Lyman Abbott, decided in sweet reasonableness that it was "God's way of doing things."

When religious leaders in the denominations were forced at last to consider the complex theoretical and practical issues between science and theology, they reacted according to their individual light, which in turn (to mix the metaphor) depended upon the theological stream or tradition they were standing in at the time. For our purposes one can distinguish three broad strands in American Protestant thought during this period.[48] The first was traditional orthodoxy or Biblical authoritarianism, which provided what Hopkins aptly calls the "frozen foundation of complacency" characteristic of "conventional, institutionalized, orthodox Protestantism."[49] It was frankly supernaturalistic in outlook, and it maintained a solid core of doctrine, even if the doctrinal outlines might be fuzzy, except in such uncorruptedly stanch men as Charles Hodge, professor of theology at Princeton from 1822 to 1878. Hodge possessed an uncanny ability to reduce the profound complexities of the Christian walk in the modern world to a kind of rough-hewn, orthodox simplicity.

In general the men in this tradition met the challenge to their way of thinking with pietistic indifference, with strong dogmatic denials, or with open contempt, as when a writer in the *Princeton Review* declared that "we can even afford to acknowledge our incompetence to meet them in argument, or to answer their objections; and yet our faith remains unshaken and rational."[50] They tended to meet the challenges to the churches' social program first with surprise and anger and then with increased efforts through charity. By and large they were slow and reluctant to criticize the existing social order and inclined to be critical of those who did.

The second strand was that of romantic liberalism—or "progressive religion"[51]—which was rooted in philosophic idealism and appealed in one way or another to intuition. The romantic movement in America during the early nineteenth century spawned transcendentalism among New England Unitarians. The descendants of transcendentalism in America, however, have by and large been outside the regular denominations. To be sure, Unitarianism later digested Emerson and even Parker—under pressures from the ill-fated Free Religious Association organized in 1867.[52] But the real religious descendants in America of the transcendentalist movement would seem to be the host of "cults" bred of the new-thought movement, an outlook that has recently been slipping into the Protestant churches through the back door[53] and may result in revolutionary changes.

Meanwhile romanticism swept through the fold of Connecticut's Congregational orthodoxy and, as Perry Miller has noted, with Horace Bushnell this "Calvinism itself was, as it were, transcendentalized."[54] Granted this, perhaps the most significant thing Bushnell did, so far as the future of American Protestantism was concerned, was to maintain his position within Congregationalism, which gradually managed to digest this form of romanticized orthodoxy. In the long view, Emerson and Bushnell represent aspects of the same religious movement in America, but, thanks to Bushnell, it took root in the denominations and flowered as "liberalism."

For Bushnell the central problem of his early life was that of the relationship between the dogmatic formulations of his inherited orthodoxy and the world of science. Thus torn, as he put it, between his head and his heart, he chose to follow his heart; and finally his solution "came to him at last, after all his thought and study, not as something reasoned out, but as an inspiration,—a revelation from the mind of God himself." He had experienced the direct, intuitive perception of "the Gospel"— of "God in Christ."[55] For him this was the Christian experience and, as such, was as real and unassailable as were all other direct perceptions.

This it was that provided succeeding generations of romantic liberals in American Protestantism a basis for Christian faith that could not be harmed by all the "acids of modernity." Men of this sentiment during the nineteenth century moved in one of two possible directions in meeting the challenge of science to theology: they might "abstract religion from the realm of scientific verification"—and hence of criticism—or they might "claim for the data of religious experience the same scientific status as the data of the physical sciences and to build thereon an empirical science of theology."[56] The doctrine of immanence became central—God was seen as revealing himself in all of history. Religion was defined as "the gradually developed experiences of men who had some perception of the Infinite in nature and in human life."[57]

Men in this tradition faced evolutionism with an equanimity of soul that bordered on the blasé, as witness Lyman Abbott's *Theology of an Evolutionist,* published in 1897. Beginning with a romantic teleology, they produced a facile harmonization of science with Christiantiy over which one's mind may glide unruffled by any angularities of meaning. Their minds were unshackled from tradition (we are "to look for our experience of God in our own times and in our own souls," said Abbott).[58] They believed in developmental progress. Rooted in Bushnell's thinking, they retained a sense of the importance of nurture in a community and hence were sensitive to the ill effects of adverse environments. When men in this tradition faced the challenge to the churches' social program they tended to become social critics and even prophets. Commonly it is these men, of whom Washington Gladden is an outstanding example, who come to mind when we think of the social gospel.

The third strand in American Protestantism when the conflict between science and theology became irrepressible is that of scientific modernism—the way of building a religion "out of the materials furnished by the several sciences."[59] Perhaps this position was most pithily put by Shailer Mathews in his *The Faith of Modernism.*[60] Modernism, he said, "is the use of the methods of modern science to find, state and use the permanent and central values of inherited orthodoxy in meeting the needs of a modern world." Of course, at this time "science" included the burgeoning disciplines of scientific psychology, sociology, anthropology, and history.

While romantic liberalism seems to have been characteristic of ministers in the churches, scientific modernism was the forte of professors in the schools. Men in this stream adopted evolutionism as a scientific hypothesis, on the basis of which they became socio-historians, developed the psychology and sociology of religion, or expounded a "scientific" philosophy of religion that threatened sometimes to crowd Christian theology out of the seminaries. When they faced the social crisis, they tended to maintain a proper scientific objectivity and, under the compelling impulsion "to reach beliefs and their application in the same way that chemists or historians reach and apply their conclusions,"[61] they tended also to abandon normative pretensions for descriptive analysis. One of their characteristic social products was the kind of settlement houses which were founded as middle-class outposts in the urban slums, where students might become acquainted at first hand with the life of the lower classes and study conditions among the denizens of these modern jungles,[62] perhaps even salvaging some wrecked lives.

Each of these strands—Biblical authoritarianism, romantic liberalism and scientific modernism—had origins far back in the history of America and, indeed, of Christendom. On the generally amorphous topography of the American religious mind they did not run as discrete streams. They crossed and recrossed in complex ways in different individuals and groups. Elements of each were mingled in ever-changing kaleidoscopic patterns by highly individualistic and unconsciously syncretistic thinkers. Nevertheless the strands are definable—these traditions existed in the American Protestant churches, and no doubt parties would eventually have grown up around them in the denominations in any case. But the impact of evolutionism accentuated their differences by giving them a common center of interest—or of opposition—and led to controversies that intensified the prevailing ideological turmoil. However that may be, it is clear that when both the denominations' way of thinking and social program were challenged, there was a great deal of confusion in Protestant theology in America. Schlesinger's "organized religion" was by no means a massive unity either organizationally or ideologically.

In 1881 Daniel Dorchester, noting the several signs of religious progress, was enthusiastic because now "theology is less scholastic and repulsive, has less of pagan adulteration, has been lubricated and broadened, and is better for its siftings."[63] But from the standpoint of the mid-twentieth century the lubrication appears less salutary, and we are more inclined to agree with H. S. Commager that "during the nineteenth century and well into the twentieth, [organized] religion prospered while theology went slowly bankrupt."[64]

– III –

If we look into this extremely complex situation for one central thread upon which to string our interpretation, I think we find it in the unfolding change of attitude toward *laissez-faire* individualism rooted in the doctrine of automatic harmony.[65] What was changing was a whole climate of opinion. In its issue of September 8, 1892, *The Congregationalist* struck the keynote of the changing time: "Modern economy has . . . made the mistake of assuming that free competition would guarantee just exchanges and hence realize industrial justice." But "the trust in free competition has failed to realize the Christian idea of fair exchange."[66] Even more pointed was the statement of Charles Worcester Clark: "In the early part of this century . . . the conditions essential for the justification of the *laissez-faire* theory of political economy were present: freedom to move from place to place, and from industry to industry, wherever the best chance offered." But "that fair field for individual merit to prove itself and win its due reward has been our pride so long that it is hard to believe it gone. But it is gone."[67] And some clergymen, at least, were canny enough to take the attitude expressed by

Washington Gladden: "If 'the old order changeth giving place to new,' we may as well have our eyes open to what is going on and make our peace with the order on the best possible terms."[68]

If it be asked what was the cause of the extremely rapid change that was taking place, the reply must be that the important thing was modern science—science as an outlook or way of thinking—and the consequent technological developments.[69] It was science in these two senses that transformed the outward face of human living more in two generations than had been the case in all the previous centuries. It was this that Woodrow Wilson had in mind when he reminded the members of the G. A. R. in 1915 that the nation in which they then lived was not the nation for whose union they had fought. And Henry Adams had already muttered, "My country in 1900 is something totally different from my own country in 1860."

On the technological side, the symbol of the science which created this new world was the machine, which may stand broadly for the instruments created by man for the control and use of physical nature. In this, man was tremendously successful —so successful, indeed, that modern man's fears have moved from "nature's" epidemic diseases, earthquakes, winds, floods, and fires to the "machine" which seems to have taken on a life of its own, becoming the monster of Frankenstein. Henry Adams pictured the predicament of modern man as that of the creator of the dynamo who has inadvertently grasped the two poles and can therefore neither let go nor control his own actions.[70] The flower and focus of the "machine" was the modern city, the product of technological industrialism. The problems created by the machine were accentuated and seen in relief in the urban centers.

When the Frankenstein possibilities of the "machine" became apparent, the most common way of stating the basic problem of the age was to say that it was the need of control. Looking back from the vantage point of 1909, Washington Gladden recalled how, as early as 1860, "the amount of titanic energy which was even then finding vent in the life of . . . greater New York" impressed upon him "a vivid sense of the impersonality and brutality of the whole movement, of the lack of coördinating intelligence," and placed him in a position where he

could not help wondering whether in liberating the force which gathers men into cities, and equipping it with steam and electricity, a power had not been created which was stronger than the intelligence which seeks to control it; whether such aggregations of humanity, with wills no better socialized than those of the average nineteenth-century American, are not by their own action self-destructive.[71]

In September, 1892, the editors of the *Congregationalist* approved Professor H. C. Adams' statement of the question: "The monopoly problem of today is really this—shall organized industry, with its positive benefits and great possibilities, be directed for personal or for public ends?" And "shall this tremendous industrial power be in the arbitrary control of individuals, or be exercised under conditions of responsibility?"[72]

This way of looking at things became widespread during the last quarter of the nineteenth century and, broadly speaking, gave shape and meaning to the social question, defining for many the nature of the crisis. An English writer, surveying in 1901 "a century's progress in religious life," summed it up very well: "The first half of the [nineteenth] century was individualistic; the second half has tended to become collectivistic. Freedom was the earlier ideal, brotherhood is the later." For "the policy of *laissez-faire* is thought to have broken down, and the State is repeatedly called upon to take over and control the interests of the community."[73]

– IV –

The social-gospel movement must be seen within the context of the widespread feeling that planned social and economic controls in the interests of justice were becoming necessary, and that this would be contingent upon a revolution in thinking and attitudes as well as in practice. There would have to be a change in thinking and attitudes because the mind that had so successfully created and used the "machine" was individualistic, and constitutionally opposed to planning and controls in social and economic matters. Further, these attitudes had accumulated powerful pragmatic and religious sanctions.

Recognition that there was a social program became almost universal. A. I. Abell makes the point that so large did it loom over the denominations' life that, for the time at least, doctrinal, creedal, and polity questions both within and between denominations tended to be subordinated. Even the Episcopalians, he notes, toned down or dropped their differences to make the keynote of their General Convention in 1880 " 'not the restatement of dogma, but the urgency of Christian work.' "[74]

All, of course, did not accept the view of the nature of the "social question" noted above. *The social-gospel movement was the response in the denominations of those who did.* This seems to be the one common characteristic useful in defining it, for the social-gospel movement cannot be defined theologically or institutionally. It was never incorporated in any independent new organizations; it did not result in any new denominations. The theologies associated with the movement were many and as diverse as the diverse and individualistic religious pattern in America could provide. Indeed, down at least to the 1930s, theology in relation to the movement was in a real sense fortuitous and instrumental. It was in reality a movement in the denominations looking for theological roots.

Walter Rauschenbusch recognized this clearly and began his *Theology for the Social Gospel,* published in 1917, with the statement that "we have a social gospel. We need a systematic theology large enough to match it and vital enough to back it." Therefore he devoted the first three chapters to the attempt "to show that a readjustment and expansion of theology so that it will furnish an adequate intellectual basis for the social gospel, is necessary, feasible, desirable and legitimate."

To be sure, the general situation we have described tended to give the movement a kind of theological complexion. The leaders found that the prevailing individualistic outlook of pietistic revivalism and the "gospel of wealth" rooted in traditional orthodoxy was not a congenial atmosphere for their views. Hence they were almost forced into the paths of the reconstructive movements in theology. The social gospel became the church party platform of all theological progressives, liberals, or modernists—of all those movements that represented attempts to come to terms with the ideas and spirit of modern civilization while maintaining continuity with the Christian tradition. There was never, however, the one-to-one relationship suggested by G. G. Atkins when he described the social gospel and liberal theology as being as interlocking as were the "old Gospel" and economic conservatism.[75] Nevertheless the attraction of liberals to the social gospel placed leadership of the movement in the hands of informed people—those in the churches who were most in touch with current intellectual life. This in turn gave the movement an eggheadish complexion which was to prove a fertile seedbed for opposition in the denominations.

Once the concern for social reconstruction in the interests of equity and justice became widespread among individuals, all views were bound to be aired. The nature of the denominations as voluntary associations meant that any man who could gain a pulpit and the backing of a local congregation, a denominational post, or even a professorship had a secure platform from which to speak and propagandize. And they all did.

Further, every concern or idea, in order to survive in a denomination, had to be incarnated in a movement. The drive of such movements eventually and inexorably led to attempts to capture the denominational organization itself. Finally, since the missionary enterprise was central in each denomination, it was recognized that those who could define its nature would control the denomination's life. Hence the movement generated the drive to shift the conception of the evangelistic work of the churches from individualistic revivalism to social reconstruction —and its success in this respect should not be underestimated.[76] "It is true the work of the Church has been markedly individualistic," a speaker patiently explained to the congregation at Plymouth Church, Brooklyn, New York, in 1897, but now changed conditions have served "to make it alive to its social obligations and duties." This, he thought, was "the difference between *remedial* Christianity and *preventive* Christianity. That is to say, the social work of the Church in the past . . . has been to remedy the effects of evil which have been left to work themselves out and multiply themselves in fresh evil effects." However, "to-day the Church has aroused itself to this: it is our business to strike deeper, to get at the roots of these evils and remove them,—and then we shall be under no necessity to remedy their effects."[77]

The second important factor was the theological confusion and turmoil that prevailed—or, perhaps better, "the absence of theology in the supreme sense of that word," as George A. Gordon suggested in 1897,[78] at the time when the "acids of modernity" were eating away at traditional religious beliefs. People thus set afloat spiritually could still cling to belief in "Christian" work which was relevant to immediate situations. There was assurance and comfort to be found in the thought that perhaps the Christian could not go too far astray when feeding the hungry, clothing the naked, visiting the sick and imprisoned, and giving the cup of cold water for Christ's sake. Perhaps it was never formulated in just this fashion, but one profound appeal of the social-gospel movement was that it made possible for many idealistic Americans continued belief in Christianity if only "for the work's sake." No doubt what many nominally Christian people really came to believe in was the work of social betterment and renovation.

In order to understand the sweep and scope of the movement in the denominations, it is helpful to see it through the eyes of one of its most active leaders in the years just before World War I. Writing the Foreword for his book *Christianizing the Social Order* in October, 1912, Walter Rauschenbusch gave as one reason for such a work that "outsiders misjudge the part which the churches are taking in the impending social transformation because they are ignorant of the quiet revolution that is going on in the spirit and aims of the American churches." Indeed "few, probably, even of those who are taking an active part in their social awakening, realize fully the far-reaching importance of this great historic movement." There was taking place, he thought, "a great change" in "the life of this nation," which he compared to an individual's experience of conversation and interpreted as "the stirring of God in the souls of men." Among "the people in the churches, who have long been consciously religious, the new thing is the social application of their religious life." For "the old current of their religion is pouring into a broader channel of social purpose, and running with swift flow toward the achievement of public justice and love." Indeed this is increasingly felt to be "the great business of religion."

Rauschenbusch was elated at the change that had taken place. He could, as he said, look back to the time before 1900, which "pioneers of Christian social thought in America" recalled "as a time of lonesomeness [when] we were few and we shouted in a wilderness." But since 1900, he thought, "the able ministers who were not already physically or mentally old by 1900, and who were not rendered impervious by doctrinal rubber-coating of some kind, have been permeated by the social interest almost in a body," until today "perhaps the most convincing proof of the spread of the social interest in the ministry is the fact that the old men and the timid men are falling in line."

But what pleased him most of all was that "the social interest in the Church has now run beyond the stage of the solitary pioneer. It has been admitted within the organizations of the Church." Indeed, as C. Howard Hopkins puts it, social Christianity had become "official." For between 1901, when the General Convention of the Protestant Episcopal Church and the National Council of Congregational Churches "took preliminary action leading toward official social-service programs," and 1912, when Rauschenbusch was writing, all the great denominations took official action through the creation of boards, committees, councils, and so on—of social action.[79] Outstanding was the Methodist Federation for Social Service, organized in Washington, D.C., in December, 1907, as "an effort to apply the sane and fervid spirit of Methodism to the social needs of our time."

The "climax of the official recognition of social Christianity was attained in the organization of the Federal Council of the Churches of Christ in America in 1908." In 1912 it adopted its famous "social creed," patterned after the Methodist "creed" of 1908. Hopkins concludes that social Christianity reached its popular peak with the Men and Religion Forward Movement of 1911 to 1912—the very time when Rauschenbusch was writing. This movement Hopkins describes as "the most comprehensive evangelistic effort ever undertaken in the United States," and, he adds, it was "virtually converted . . . into a social gospel campaign."[80] Rauschenbusch had concluded in 1912 that "the movement has probably done more than any other single agency to lodge the social gospel in the common mind of the Church."[81]

It is indicated that the social-gospel movement was one of great proportions in the denominations on the eve of World War I. A revolution in outlook was taking place in the churches, which is epitomized in the comment of an English writer: "A hundred years ago the dominant idea in religion was the salvation of the individual soul; to-day it is the redemption of society." "Formerly," he added, "it was said that attendance at the weekly prayer meeting was the test of the vitality of a church; now we look for the gauge in its social activities." However, "there is no need for these to supersede the prayer meeting," although "it is now the case that the Church best reveals the energy of its spiritual life by the self-sacrificing devotion of its social work."[82]

Keeping in mind that central to the social-gospel movement was reaction against the individualism of pietistic revivalism, the identification of Protestant Christianity with economic *laissez faire* and the exploitation of natural and human resources characteristic of industrial capitalism, we can understand why the movement tended to swing to the opposite extremes of substituting social concern for individual Christian experience; of identifying the gospel with current schemes for reconstructing society; of judging the work of the church on the basis of its effectiveness in furthering social reform; of substituting sociology for theology. How far this tendency ran it would be impossible to measure. That it existed is beyond question. It suggests the emergence of a syncretistic outlook in opposition to that of the gospel of wealth. Probably in the early 1930s the liberal Protestant clergyman in America was apt to be as blindly a Democrat or Socialist as his predecessor around 1885 had been a Republican.

– V –

It is against this background that fundamentalism is to be seen. Most simply, the fundamentalist movement was the organized reaction in the denominations to the real and supposed tendencies of the social-gospel movement. It was as broad, complex, and amorphous as what it opposed. This suggests a political rather than a theological definition. The common use of "fundamentalist" to designate any and all theological conservatism is confusing, especially since so many clever liberals used it as a derogatory term for all those to the right of their own enlightened position. I would like to restrict "fundamentalist" to point to those movements, within denominations or interdenominational, organized for the purpose of combating "liberalism" by capturing and controlling ecclesiastical machinery.

The rise of self-conscious liberal or modernist movements—meaning thereby all the attempts to reconcile Christian thinking and practice with the ethos of the modern world—indicates that for many people the traditional formulations of Christian faith had largely lost their meaning. Many accepted the modernistic formulations. Others were unable to recognize the "old-time religion" in new garb and clung desperately to the familiar forms even at the expense of rejecting the modern world.

On the one hand, then, fundamentalism was a genuinely conservative movement in the denominations. The intention behind it was to preserve the true Christian religion, and to conserve continuity with the heritage. Its sound positive sentiment was the conviction that the Christian Church ought to be rooted in recognizable Christian experience, and belief explained and defended systematically in a theology. On the other hand, however, fundamentalism was a truly reactionary movement of resistance to change. The church member who felt he was being swept against his will into strange new currents and who instinctively grasped at anything that gave promise of not being carried away in the general flood, was a ripe candidate for a fundamentalist movement.

In a sense the fundamentalist was more theological-minded than his liberal opponent. But so desperate was he to defend and preserve his parochial version of Christian belief that he tended to suspect thinking itself and dogmatically to assert on the basis of supposed traditional authority what he conceived to be the essentials of the faith. The "fundamentals"[83] that were asserted were not theological at all, but pretheological dogmas and, by the same token, they were to be posttheological. They were the firmly planted posts of the stockade into which Christian thought was to be drawn for defense. Whatever thinking was permitted was limited to placing stronger posts in this stockade.

Obviously this outlook was incompatible with the mind and temper of the modern world. And because evolutionism was the cornerstone of contemporary scientific thinking it was natural that evolution became the theological shibboleth of fundamentalism. As E. E. Aubrey put it, the fundamentalist attacks on the Darwinian theory are not merely superstitious recalcitrance. "They are based on sound suspicions that to yield an inch is to expose the citadel of their system to destruction." For "it is not merely the origin of man which is involved but the scientific approach as such; and the evolutionary point of view spells destruction of dogmatic finality."[84] The fundamentalist was quite aware of what he was fighting for. But his theological weapons were so obsolete that the movement soon lost whatever appearance of intellectual leadership and constituency it may have had. The tragedy is that in real imagination and intelligence, religious conservatism was so utterly bankrupt at the time. All its checks drawn on pietistic revivalism and literalistic Biblicism bounced. For this reason the fundamentalist movement became (as all conservative movements lacking imagination and intelligent leadership become) merely a political power-group movement in the denominations. One prototype of all American fundamentalists is the Congregational minister in Connecticut, who a century before told Lyman Beecher and Nathaniel W. Taylor—the current liberals—"I may not be able to think and argue as well as you can, but I know what the people in the churches—the constituency—will stand." He did. And he created a great deal of trouble.

Fundamentalism is, I suppose, as old as Christianity. But the historians of what we call the fundamentalist movement in America commonly trace its origins to Bible, prophecy, and premillennialism conferences in the 1870s. The crystallization of such a definable power movement in the denominations, as we have noted, may conveniently be dated with the publication of the twelve small volumes of *The Fundamentals* between 1910 and 1915.[85] It is significant that this is precisely the period of the height of the social-gospel movement. Publication of these volumes was financed by two laymen, and by the time that the twelfth volume had appeared it was claimed that some three million copies had been distributed to religious leaders all over the world—about one million outside the United States.

In 1919 the World Christian Fundamentals Association was formed because "it was no longer deemed sufficient to carry on a general propaganda through conservative interdenominational agencies, but the denominational machinery must now be captured for the same end."[86]

It is unnecessary to rehearse the movement in each of the denominations. Essentially, the aims were the same in each; the strategies and techniques varied according to the general cultural level of the group and the form of church polity. In each denomination the fundamentalists attempted to gain control of theological education, the missionary enterprises of the group, and the denominational machinery and to affirm and impose doctrinal standards that would successfully exclude those who did not accept the "fundamentals." The fundamentalists did not actually win in any major denomination. But they were defeated more by the clever maneuvering of astute denominational leaders than by direct discussion of controverted theological issues. If during the course of the controversies the fundamentalists tended to become primarily antiliberals, the liberals tended to become primarily antifundamentalists. For about fifty years after the upheavals beginning around 1875 the liberals and modernists had all the advantages of moving with the currents of the times. Accepting evolutionism as the basic postulate of their thinking, the liberals of the 1920s and early 1930s, whose outlook had been formed before World War I, tended to assume their movement was the best because the latest, and to refer to all their critics as "fundamentalists." The outstanding modernist, Shailer Mathews, reputedly wrote them off as his "contemporary ancestors."

The positive practical thrust of the liberal-modernist movement was toward social reconstruction on the basis of principles thought to be implicit in the social teachings of Jesus. But while they thus presumed to judge existing social institutions, they did not commonly bring themselves under the same critical judgment. They tended to make God their omnipotent ally who guaranteed the successful culmination of their plans. In 1925 Shailer Mathews told the Stockholm Conference that our recognition of "the divine presence as furthering and assuring the permanent success of a sacrificial social-mindedness is the modern equivalent of the apostolic preaching of the Kingdom of God."[87] If the theology of the fundamentalists was archaic and anachronistic, that of the liberals was secularized and innocuous.

On the positive side, the fundamentalists insisted that if Christianity was to survive, it must maintain an identity in keeping with its historical character; while the liberals insisted that if Christianity was to survive it must come to terms with the main currents of modern thought and the social revolutions of the twentieth century. Insofar, both were essentially right. Both were wrong when they failed to recognize the validity and necessity of the other's point.

– VI –

This essay builds upon Professor Schlesinger's thesis that during the last quarter of the nineteenth century both the way of thinking and the social program of organized religion in the United States were challenged. I have tried to delineate the nature of the challenges, and the very complex nature of the reactions to them. In doing so I have tried to make clear how all the diverse movements and ways of thinking emerge naturally out of the peculiar character of the American Protestantism that was challenged. This approach, it is hoped, will help us to realize that all had legitimate historical roots in the American experience. Each was limited and partial primarily because each failed to grasp the totality of that experience and latched onto a part of it only.

My story concludes around 1930. Since then there has been a general stirring in the denominations, characterized by attempts to evaluate critically both the life and work and the faith and order of the free churches in America. Although appearing in different garbs in different denominations and groups, so that one cannot speak of a precisely definable general movement, the stirrings seem to exemplify a common spirit. Certainly among its characteristics are a heightened theological consciousness, a willingness to re-examine the traditional content of the Christian faith of Protestants, a critical attitude toward the liberalism and modernism of the immediate past, and positive attempts to revitalize the life of the denominations on the basis of theological formulations of the nature of the church and its relation to the general culture. It is within this context and in this spirit that the historical examination of the free churches in America is—or ought to be—proceeding.

Notes

Preface

1. The several quotations from and about Philip Schaff are taken from his *America: A Sketch of the Political, Social, and Religious Character of the United States of North America, in two Lectures, Delivered at Berlin with a Report Read Before the German Diet at Frankfort-am-Maine, September 1854* (New York: Charles Scribner, 1855), and from Perry G. E. Miller's "Editor's Introduction" to the Belknap Press of Harvard University Press 1961 reprint.
2. Sidney E. Mead, "Prof. Sweet's Religion and Culture in America; a Review Article," in *Church History*, XXII (March, 1953), 33-49.

Chapter I. The American People: Their Space, Time, and Religion

1. George Santayana, *Character and Opinion in the United States* (New York: Charles Scribner's Sons, 1920), p. 168.
2. J. Hector St. John Crèvecoeur, *Letters from an American Farmer*, reprinted from the original edition with a Prefatory Note by W. P. Trent and an Introduction by Ludwig Lewisohn (New York: Fox, Duffield & Co., 1904), p. 54.
3. Philip Schaff, *Church and State in the United States or the American Idea of Religious Liberty and Its Practical Effects* (New York: G. P. Putnam's Sons, 1888), p. 23.
4. Stephen Vincent Benét, *Western Star* (New York: Farrar & Rinehart, Inc., 1943), p. 145.
5. Francis Parkman, *The Oregon Trail*, Introduction by Mark Van Doren (New York: Farrar & Rinehart, Inc., 1931), p. 133.
6. Bernard DeVoto, *Across the Wide Missouri* (Boston: Houghton Mifflin Co., 1947), p. 371.
7. Benét, *op. cit.*, p. 144.
8. Implications of this view are developed by Walter Prescott Webb in *The Great Frontier* (Boston: Houghton Mifflin Co., 1952); see review by Ray Allen Billington in *Mississippi Valley Historical Review*, XL (June, 1953), 107-8.
9. Cf. Hamlin Garland, *A Son of the Middle Border* (New York: The

Macmillan Co., 1917), pp. 437-38: "All my schooling had been to migrate, to keep moving. 'If your crop fails, go west and try new soil. If disagreeable neighbors surround you, sell out and move—always toward the open country. To remain quietly in your native place is a sign of weakness, of irresolution. Happiness dwells afar. Wealth and fame are to be found by journeying toward the sunset star!' Such had been the spirit, the message of all the songs and stories of my youth."

10. DeVoto, *op. cit.*, p. 349.
11. Vernon L. Parrington, *Main Currents in American Thought* (New York: Harcourt, Brace & Co., 1927-30), III, 387.
12. Garland, *op. cit.*, pp. 463, 440, 452.
13. See William Henry Milburn, *The Pioneer Preacher; or, Rifle, Axe, and Saddle-bags, and Other Lectures* (New York: Derby & Jackson, 1857).
14. "A Reply to Mr. Williams His Examination: and Answer of the Letters Sent to Him by John Cotton," in *Publications of the Narragansett Club* (Providence, 1862), 1st ser., II, 19.
15. "The Simple Cobler of Aggawam . . . ," in Perry G. E. Miller and Thomas H. Johnson, eds., *The Puritans* (New York: American Book Co., 1938), p. 227.
16. Crèvecoeur, *op. cit.*, p. 66.

Chapter II. From Coercion to Persuasion: Another Look at the Rise of Religious Liberty and the Emergence of Denominationalism

1. Evarts B. Greene, *Religion and the State: The Making and Testing of an American Tradition* (New York: New York University Press, 1941), p. 37. See also Joseph P. Thompson, *Church and State in the United States* (Boston: James R. Osgood & Co., 1873), p. 55.
2. As quoted in Frederick J. Zwierlein, *Religion in New Netherlands* (Rochester, N. Y.: John P. Smith Printing Co., 1910), pp. 140-41, 117, 118-19.
3. Perry G. E. Miller, "The Contribution of the Protestant Churches to Religious Liberty in Colonial America," in *Church History*, IV (March, 1935), 57-66.
4. As quoted in W. W. Sweet, *Religion in Colonial America* (New York: Charles Scribner's Sons, 1942), pp. 151-52.
5. Zwierlein, *op. cit.*, p. 261.
6. *Ibid.*, pp. 257, 256.
7. Greene, *op. cit.*, pp. 52-53.
8. *For the Colony in Virginia Britannia. Lavves Diuine, Moral and Martiall, &c.* (Printed at London for Walter Burre, 1612); in Peter Force, *Tracts and Other Papers* (Washington: Wm. Q. Force, 1844), III, #ii, pp. 10-11.
9. *Virginia's Cure: Or an Advisive Narrative Concerning Virginia. Discovering the True Ground of That Unhappiness, and the Only True Remedy.* As it was presented to the Right Reverend Father in God *Gvilbert* Lord Bishop of London, September 2, 1661 (London: W.

Godbid, 1662), reprinted in Force, *Tracts . . . , op. cit.*, III, #xv.

10. Perry G. E. Miller and Thomas H. Johnson, eds., *The Puritans* (New York: American Book Co., 1938), p. 639.

11. For the general factors at Work, see Roland H. Bainton, "The Struggle for Religious Liberty," in *Church History*, X (June, 1941), 95-124. Professor Winthrop S. Hudson has argued that English Independents had developed a "denominational" conception of the church which, in spite of the rigors of the New England way, tended always to make its leaders inherently uncomfortable with persecution of dissenters; see his "Denominationalism as a Basis for Ecumenicity: A Seventeenth Century Conception," in *Church History*, XXIV (March, 1955), 32-50. This suggests a fruitful area for further exploration.

12. As quoted in Charles M. Andrews, *The Colonial Period of American History* (New Haven: Yale University Press, 1934), I, 386.

13. Arthur Lyon Cross, *The Anglican Episcopate and the American Colonies* (Cambridge: Harvard University Press, 1924), p. 22.

14. In the *Massachusetts Historical Society Collections*, Ser. 4, II (1854), 1-113.

15. Willem Sewel, *The History of the Rise, Increase, and Progress of the Christian People Called Quakers, Intermixed with Several Remarkable Occurrences*, written originally in low-Dutch by William Sewel, and by himself translated into English, now rev. and published with some amendments (London: J. Sowle, 1722), p. 280.

16. See Sanford H. Cobb, *The Rise of Religious Liberty in America* (New York: The Macmillan Co., 1902), p. 69.

17. Andrews, *op. cit.*, II, 42.

18. Henry Melchior Muhlenberg, *The Journals*, trans. by Theodore G. Tappert and John W. Doberstein (Philadelphia: Muhlenberg Press, 1942), I, 67.

19. See Jonathan Edwards, "A Faithful Narrative of the Surprising Work of God, in the Conversion of Many Hundred Souls, in Northampton . . . ," in his *The Works of President Edwards* (New York: Converse, 1830), IV, 70-71.

20. As, e.g., Jonathan Edwards' words: "The Beginning of the late work of God in this Place was so circumstanced, that I could not but look upon it as a remarkable Testimony of God's Approbation of the Doctrine of Justification by Faith alone, here asserted and vindicated: . . . And at that time, while I was greatly reproached for defending this Doctrine in the Pulpit, and just upon my suffering a very open Abuse for it, God's Work wonderfully brake forth amongst us, and souls began to flock to Christ, as the Saviour in whose Righteousness alone they hoped to be justified; So that this was the Doctrine on which this work in its Beginning was founded, as it evidently was in the whole progress of it." *Discourses on Various Important Subjects, Nearly Concerning the Great Affair of the Soul's Eternal Salvation* (Boston: S. Kneeland & T. Green, 1738), p. ii.

21. As quoted in Wesley M. Gewehr, *The Great Awakening in Virginia, 1740-1790* (Durham: Duke University Press, 1930), p. 16.

22. In *ibid.*, p. 65.
23. From Leonard J. Trinterud, *The Forming of an American Tradition, A Re-examination of Colonial Presbyterianism* (Philadelphia: The Westminster Press, 1944), pp. 89-91.
24. W. W. Sweet, *The American Churches, an Interpretation* (New York: Abingdon-Cokesbury Press, 1948), pp. 30-31.
25. See, e.g., Winthrop S. Husdon's review of Sweet's *The American Churches, an Interpretation* (*ibid.*), in *The Crozer Quarterly*, XXV (October, 1948), 358-60.
26. Isaac Backus, *A History of New England, with Particular Reference to the Denomination of Christians Called Baptists*. 2d ed., with notes by David Weston (Newton, Mass.: The Backus Historical Society, 1871), II, 41. See also C. C. Goen, *Revivalism and Separatism in New England, 1740-1800* (New Haven: Yale University Press, 1962).
27. Ralph Barton Perry, *Puritanism and Democracy* (New York: The Vanguard Press, 1944), p. 80.

Chapter III. American Protestantism During the Revolutionary Epoch

1. "On the administrative side, the two most profound revolutions which have occurred in the entire history of the church have been these: first, the change of the church, in the fourth century, from a voluntary society . . . to a society conceived as necessarily coextensive with the civil community and endowed with the power to enforce the adherence of all members of the civil community; second, the reversal of this change . . . in America." Winfred E. Garrison, "Characteristics of American Organized Religion," in *Annals of the American Academy of Political and Social Science*, CCLVI (March, 1948), 17.
2. Robert Baird, *Religion in America* (New York: Harper & Brothers, 1844), pp. 110-11. Baird argued that religious freedom in Virginia was "mainly owing to the exertions of the Presbyterians, Baptists, and Quakers" while Jefferson contributed his "famous act" not because he thought "the great principles embodied in the measure were right" but because "it seemed to degrade Christianity." This, he added, is what "made the arch-infidel chuckle with satisfaction."
3. See Roland H. Bainton, "The Struggle for Religious Liberty," in *Church History*, X (June, 1941), 97.
4. M. Kaufman, "Latitudinarianism and Pietism," in *Cambridge Modern History* (New York: The Macmillan Co., 1908), V, 742.
5. Benjamin Franklin, *Representative Selections* with introduction, bibliography, and notes by Frank L. Mott and Chester E. Jorgenson, eds. (New York: American Book Co., 1936), p. 70.
6. Thomas Jefferson, *The Complete Jefferson, Containing his Major Writings, Published and Unpublished, Except his Letters*. Assembled and arranged by Saul K. Padover, with illustrations and analytic index (New York: Duell, Sloan & Pearce, Inc., 1943), p. 676.
7. John Wesley, *Sermons on Several Occasions* (New York: Lane & Tippett, 1851), II, 392.

8. Quoted in W. W. Sweet, *The American Churches, an Interpretation* (New York: Abingdon-Cokesbury Press, 1948), pp. 46-47.
9. Herbert M. Morais, *Deism in Eighteenth Century America* (New York: Columbia University Press, 1934), p. 13.
10. Note, e.g., how easily the youthful Franklin, brought up "piously in the Dissenting Way . . . soon became a thorough Deist" simply by reading orthodox refutations of Deism. Franklin, *op. cit.,* p. 55.
11. *Ibid.,* p. 12.
12. Letter to Sarah Franklin, November 8, 1764, in Benjamin Franklin, *A Benjamin Franklin Reader,* ed. by Nathan G. Goodman (New York: Thomas Y. Crowell Co., 1945), p. 237.
13. Franklin, *Representative Selections, op. cit.,* p. 70.
14. Gilbert Chinard, *Thomas Jefferson, Apostle of Americanism* (Boston: Little, Brown, and Co., 1944), pp. 103-4.
15. The phrases "right wing" and "left wing" of the Reformation have come into quite general use since the publication of the article by Roland H. Bainton, "The Left Wing of the Reformation," in *The Journal of Religion,* XXI (April, 1941), 124-34. According to Bainton's definition, "The left wing is composed of those who separated church and state and rejected the civil arm in matters of religion." These, he adds, were "commonly on the left also with regard to church organization, sacraments, and creeds." A more radical social definition of the two "wings" was coming into use before publication of Bainton's article. See, e.g., Ernest S. Bates, *American Faith* (New York: W. W. Norton & Co., Inc., 1940), chaps. 2 and 3.
16. Note, e.g., the "New Lights," Separate Congregationalists, and Baptists in New England, the "New Side" Presbyterians in the middle colonies, and the Presbyterians and Baptists in the Anglican South.
17. See, e.g., Connecticut's "Act for Regulating Abuses and Correcting Disorders in Ecclesiastical Affairs" of 1742, and the struggle for recognition of dissenters' rights under the English Toleration Act in Virginia.
18. Cf. with W. W. Sweet's "comparison . . . between the basic ideas of the popular religious bodies and those held by the intellectual liberals," in his "Natural Religion and Religious Liberty in America," in *The Journal of Religion,* XXV (January, 1945), 54-55.
19. It is said that Madison and Jefferson were intrigued by the practice of democracy in the Baptist churches and no doubt their interest in religious freedom was stimulated by their observation of the persecution of the Baptists in Virginia.
20. W. W. Sweet, "The Protestant Churches," in *Annals of the American Academy of Political and Social Science,* CCLVI (March, 1948), 45. The argument is more fully developed in his "Natural Religion . . . ," *op. cit.*
21. Cf. the position of John M. Mecklin in his *The Story of American Dissent* (New York: Harcourt, Brace & Co., 1934), p. 36: "It was the pressure of circumstances that brought the leaders of the dissenting sects into sympathetic contacts with Paine and Jefferson at the end of the eighteenth century. When the battle for religious and national liberty was finally won and the great principle of separation of church

and state safely embodied in the Constitution, Paine and Jefferson speedily lost their attraction for the dissenting sects."

22. Morais, *op. cit.*, p. 20.
23. Thomas C. Hall, *The Religious Background of American Culture* (Boston: Little, Brown, & Co., 1930), p. 172.
24. Morais, *op. cit.*, p. 121.
25. See Jefferson's letter to John Adams, October 28, 1813, in Stuart G. Brown, ed., *We Hold These Truths: Documents of American Democracy* (New York: Harper & Brothers, 1941), p. 114.
26. Morais, *op. cit.*, p. 15.
27. Franklin, *Representative Selections, op. cit.*, pp. 508-9.
28. See John C. Miller, *Crisis in Freedom: the Alien and Sedition Acts* (Boston: Little, Brown, & Co., 1951), *passim.* E.g., on p. 11 Miller notes that Hamilton regarded the Republicans from Jefferson on down as "Frenchmen in all their feelings and wishes." See also Charles D. Hazen, *Contemporary American Opinion of the French Revolution* (Baltimore: John Hopkins Press, 1897), p. 140.
29. Letter to Mrs. M. Harrison Smith, August 6, 1816, quoted in Sweet, "Natural Religion . . . ," *op. cit.*, pp. 52-53.
30. Jefferson's "An Act for Establishing Religious Freedom," in his *op. cit.*, p. 947. He argued consistently that where "reason and experiment have been indulged . . . error has fled before them. It is error alone which needs the support of government. Truth can stand by itself." (*Ibid.*, p. 675.) In his Second Inaugural he pointed out the salutary effects of such freedom. (*Ibid.*, p. 413.)
31. Quoted in Adrienne Koch, *The Philosophy of Thomas Jefferson* (New York: Columbia University Press, 1943), p. 26.
32. Quoted from *The Age of Reason*, in Thomas Paine, *Selections from the Works of Thomas Paine*, edited with an introduction by Arthur Wallace Peach (New York: Harcourt, Brace & Co., 1928), p. 232.
33. Joseph Priestley, *An History of the Corruptions of Christianity*, 2d ed. (Birmingham: J. Thompson, 1793), I, v.
34. *Ibid.*, xv.
35. See Henry Wilder Foote, *Thomas Jefferson: Champion of Religious Freedom, Advocate of Christian Morals* (Boston: The Beacon Press, 1947), p. 52.
36. "Always latent" because, to the deistic way of thinking, the orthodox view of revelation was particularistic; that is, given to a particular group at a particular time and place and hence not readily available for all mankind. See Arthur O. Lovejoy, *The Great Chain of Being* (Cambridge: Harvard University Press, 1936), pp. 288-89, 292, for a discussion of this aspect of rationalism. Cf. Paine, *op. cit.*, pp. 250-51.
37. In Paine, *op. cit.*, p. 232. *The Age of Reason* was written in France and as much to stem the trend toward atheism as to undermine the church, "lest in the general wreck of superstition, of false systems of government and false theology, we lose sight of morality, of humanity, and of the theology that is true." Although widely read in America, it seems always to have been somewhat alien to the real situation there.

The incongruity was noted by Lyman Beecher, who was amazed that "boys that dressed flax in the barn, as I used to, read Tom Paine and believed him," and that the rural youths in Yale College "called each other Voltaire, Rousseau, D'Alembert, etc., etc." after the denizens of the sophisticated French world. Lyman Beecher, *Autobiography, Correspondence, etc., of Lyman Beecher,* edited by Charles Beecher (New York: Harper & Brothers, 1864), I, 43.

38. Cf. Morais, *op. cit.,* p. 129: "The deism of Paine, Volney and Palmer, presented in a popular form, was designed to reach the masses in order to destroy their faith in traditional Christianity with its priesthood, dogmas and supernatural revelation. Its ultimate end was to replace the Christian religion by the religion of nature with its three-fold creed —God, virtue and immortality, a creed believed in even by devout Christians."

39. In Paine, *op. cit.,* p. 263.

40. The theological issues raised by Paine's *Age of Reason* apparently received only a very few replies on a "rational and scholarly plane." Most of the "replies" were primarily personal attacks on Paine. See Morais, *op. cit.,* pp. 163-67.

41. See also Vernon Stauffer, *New England and the Bavarian Illuminati* (New York: The Columbia University Press, 1918), pp. 229 ff; Howard Mumford Jones, *America and French Culture* (Chapel Hill:. The University of North Carolina Press, 1927), pp. 398-99.

42. Stauffer, *op. cit.,* pp. 126-27, 272 ff.

43. Miller, *op. cit.,* p. 74.

44. Jones, *op. cit.,* pp. 402-3.

45. This ground has been made familiar by the studies of Vernon Stauffer, Charles D. Hazen, Herbert M. Morais, G. Adolf Kock, Eugene Perry Link, and Howard Mumford Jones which are referred to earlier in this essay.

46. Beecher, *op. cit.,* I, 453.

47. Martin E. Marty, *The Infidel* (New York: Meridian Books, Inc., 1961).

48. See Albert Post, *Popular Freethought in America, 1825-1850* (New York: Columbia University Press, 1943), and my review in *The Journal of Religion,* XXIV (October, 1944), 293-94, Also, Sidney Warren, *American Freethought, 1860-1914* (New York: Columbia University Press, 1943).

49. Kenneth Scott Latourette, *A History of the Expansion of Christianity* (New York: Harper & Brothers, 1937-1945, 7v.), IV, 415.

Chapter IV. Thomas Jefferson's "Fair Experiment"

1. W. W. Sweet, *Religion in the Development of American Culture, 1765-1840* (New York: Charles Scribner's Sons, 1952), chaps. 1-5.

2. Robert Ellis Thompson, *A History of the Presbyterian Churches in the United States* (New York: Charles Scribner's Sons, 1895), p. 34.

3. Henry Steele Commager, *The American Mind, an Interpretation of American Thought and Character Since the 1880's* (New Haven: Yale University Press, 1950), p. 165. See also Winthrop S. Hudson, *The*

Great Tradition of the American Churches (New York: Harper & Brothers, 1953), especially chaps. 8 and 9.

4. J. L. Diman, "Religion in America, 1776-1876," in *North American Review*, CXXII (January, 1876), 42. This view is confirmed by Wilhelm Pauck, "Theology in the Life of Contemporary American Protestantism," in *The Shane Quarterly*, XIII (April, 1952), 37-50.

5. "Notes on Religion, October, 1776 (?)," in Thomas Jefferson, *The Complete Jefferson, Containing his Major Writings, Published and Unpublished, Except his Letters.* Assembled and arranged by Saul K. Padover, with illustrations and analytic index (New York: Duell, Sloan & Pearce, Inc., 1943), p. 944.

6. *Ibid.*, pp. 538-39.

7. Winfred E. Garrison, "Characteristics of American Organized Religion," in *Annals of the American Academy of Political and Social Science*, CCLVI (March, 1948), 17.

8. See the discussion in chap. 2, *supra.*

9. John W. Nevin, "The Sect System," in *The Mercersburg Review*, I (1849), 496.

10. W. W. Sweet, "The Protestant Churches," in *Annals of the American Academy of Political and Social Science*, CCLVI (March, 1948), 45.

11. Benjamin Franklin, *Representative Selections* with introduction, bibliography, and notes by Frank L. Mott and Chester E. Jorgenson, eds. (New York: American Book Co., 1936), pp. 69-70.

12. Jefferson stated this very clearly in his "Notes on Religion": "Whatsoever is lawful in the Commonwealth, or permitted to the subject in ordinary way, cannot be forbidden to him for religious uses: and whatsoever is prejudicial to the Commonwealth in their ordinary uses and therefore prohibited by the laws, ought not to be permitted to churches in their sacred rites. . . . This is the true extent of toleration." Jefferson, *op. cit.*, p. 945. See also R. Freeman Butts, *The American Tradition in Religion and Education* (Boston: The Beacon Press, 1950), p. 66.

13. See Conrad Henry Moehlman, *School and Church: the American Way* (New York: Harper & Brothers, 1944).

14. Diman, *op. cit.*, p. 40.

15. John Paul Williams, *What Americans Believe and How They Worship* (New York: Harper & Brothers, 1952), p. 371. Rev. ed. (New York: Harper & Row, 1962).

16. See, e.g., Timothy Dwight, "Vindication of the Establishment of the Public Worship of God by Law," Letter V, in *Travels in New England and New York* (New Haven: T. Dwight, 1821-1822, 4v.; London: Printed for W. Baynes and Son, 1823, 4v.); reprinted in Louis M. Hacker, *The Shaping of the American Tradition: text . . . and documents* (New York: Columbia University Press, 1947), I, 258-63.

17. Williams, *op. cit.*, p. 13.

Chapter V. Abraham Lincoln's "Last, Best Hope of Earth": The American Dream of Destiny and Democracy

1. Bronson Alcott, quoted in Alice Felt Tyler, *Freedom's Ferment, Phases of American Social History to 1860* (Minneapolis: The University of Minnesota Press, 1944), p. 172.
2. Charles A. and Mary R. Beard, *The American Spirit, a Study of the Idea of Civilization in the United States;* "The Rise of American Civilization," IV (New York: The Macmillan Co., 1942), p. v.
3. "Reply to Mrs. Eliza P. Burney, September 28 (?), 1862," in Abraham Lincoln, *The Life and Writings of Abraham Lincoln.* Edited, and with a biographical essay by Philip Van Doren Stern, with an Introduction, "Lincoln and His Writings," by Allan Nevins (New York: Random House, 1940; New York: The Modern Library, 1942), p. 728.
4. "Annual Message to Congress, December 1, 1862," in Lincoln, *ibid.,* p. 745.
5. "Message to Congress in Special Session, July 4, 1861," in Lincoln, *ibid.,* p. 668.
6. George Santayana, *Character and Opinion in the United States* (New York: Charles Scribner's Sons, 1920), p. 168.
7. J. Hector St. John Crèvecoeur, *Letters from an American Farmer,* reprinted from the original edition with a Prefatory Note by W. P. Trent and an Introduction by Ludwig Lewisohn (New York: Fox, Duffield & Co., 1904), pp. 55, 51, 54.
8. *Ibid.,* p. 53.
9. *Ibid.,* p. 61.
10. "The Religious Impulse in the Founding of Virginia: Religion and Society in the Early Literature," in *William and Mary Quarterly,* 3d ser., V (October, 1948), 492-522; and VI (January, 1949), 24-41. The quotations are in order from V, pp. 509, 503, 493, 510.
11. See Karl H. Hertz, "Bible Commonwealth and Holy Experiment," unpublished Ph.D. Dissertation (Chicago: The University of Chicago, 1948), p. 69.
12. *Ibid.,* pp. 65, 91.
13. Perry G. E. Miller, *op. cit.,* p. 514.
14. See, e.g., John Winthrop, "A Modell of Christian Charitie Written on Boarde the Arabella, on the Atlantic Ocean . . . 1630," conveniently found in abbreviated form in Perry G. E. Miller and Thomas H. Johnson, eds., *The Puritans* (New York: American Book Co., 1938), pp. 195-99.
15. "Winthrop's conclusions for the Plantation in New England," in *Old South Leaflets* (Boston: Directors of the Old South Work, n.d.), II, no. 50. Cf. William Bradford's chap. 4, "Showing the Reasons and Causes of Their Removal," in *Bradford's History of Plymouth Plantation 1606-1646,* edited by William T. David (New York: Charles Scribner's Sons, 1908), pp. 44-49.
16. Miller, *op. cit.,* p. 515.

17. R. G. Collingwood, *An Essay on Metaphysics* (Oxford: The Clarendon Press, 1940), pp. 188, 225-26. And note Ralph Gabriel's conclusion that "the foundation of this democratic faith was a frank supernaturalism derived from Christianity." And ". . . in the United States in the middle years of the nineteenth century, the existence of a moral order which was not the creation of man, but which served as the final guide for his behavior, was almost universally assumed by thinking persons." *The Course of American Democratic Thought* (New York: The Ronald Press Co., 1940), pp. 14, 15.
18. "Meditation on the Divine Will, September 30 (?), 1862," in Lincoln, *op. cit.*, p. 728.
19. John Locke, *Two Treatises on Civil Government* with an introduction by Henry Morley (London: G. Routledge and Sons, 1884), 2d Treatise, chap. 19. See Also Sidney E. Mead, "The People," *The Chicago Theological Seminary Record*, XXXIX (January, 1949), 20-26.
20. Quoted in Tyler, *op. cit.*, p. 1.
21. "Notes on Religion, October, 1776 (?)," in Thomas Jefferson, *The Complete Jefferson, Containing his Major Writings, Published and Unpublished, Except his Letters*. Assembled and arranged by Saul K. Padover, with illustrations and analytic index (New York: Duell, Sloan & Pearce, Inc., 1943), pp. 947, 944.
22. Lincoln, *First Inaugural*, in his *op. cit.*, p. 655.
23. James Madison, "A Memorial and Remonstrance on the Religious Rights of Man," in Joseph L. Blau, ed., *Cornerstones of Religious Freedom in America* (Boston: Beacon Press, 1949), p. 82.
24. "Annual Message to Congress, December 1, 1862," in Lincoln, *op. cit.*, p. 745.
25. "Message to Congress in Special Session, July 4, 1861," in Lincoln, *ibid.*, p. 668.
26. John Paul Williams, *What Americans Believe and How They Worship* (New York: Harper & Brothers, 1952), p. 371. Rev. ed. (New York: Harper & Row, 1962). See the discussion of Dr. Williams' thesis, *supra*, pp. 68-71.
27. "Reply to a Committee of Religious Denominations, Asking the President to Issue a Proclamation of Emancipation, September 13, 1862," in Lincoln, *op. cit.*, p. 720.

Chapter VI. When "Wise Men Hoped": an Examination of the Mind and Spirit of the National Period

1. Alfred North Whitehead, *Essays in Science and Philosophy* (New York: Philosophical Library, 1948), p. 114.
2. Allan Nevins, *Ordeal of the Union* (New York: Charles Scribner's Sons, 1947), I, 42-43.
3. *The Federalist, a Commentary on the Constitution of the United States*, being a collection of essays written in support of the Constitution agreed upon September 17, 1787, by the Federal convention from the original text of Alexander Hamilton, John Jay and James Madison, with an

introduction by Edward Mead Earle (New York: The Modern Library, 1941), p. 3.

4. Godfrey Rathbone Benton, Lord Charnwood, *Abraham Lincoln* (New York: Pocket Books, Inc., 1939), p. 32.

5. Nevins, *op. cit.*, p. 35.

6. "Experience as a Minister," in Theodore Parker, *Autobiography, Poems and Prayers,* edited with notes by Rufus Leighton; his "Works," Centenary ed., XIII (Boston: American Unitarian Association, 1910), p. 335.

7. Charles G. Finney, *Lectures in Systematic Theology* (Oberlin: James M. Fitch, 1846), p. 205.

8. Merle Curti, *The Growth of American Thought* (New York: Harper & Brothers, 1943), p. 371.

9. *Ibid.*, p. 372.

10. Charles A. and Mary R. Beard, *The American Spirit, a Study of the Idea of Civilization in the United States;* "The Rise of American Civilization," IV (New York: The Macmillan Co., 1942), pp. 332 ff.

11. As quoted in Curti, *op. cit.*, p. 371.

12. Lyman Beecher, *Sermons* (Boston: T. R. Marvin, 1828), p. 85.

13. John A. Krout, *The Origins of Prohibition* (New York: A. A. Knopf, 1925).

14. Alice Felt Tyler, *Freedom's Ferment, Phases of American Social History to 1860* (Minneapolis: The University of Minnesota Press, 1944), p. 355.

15. P. J. Staudenraus, *The African Colonization Movement, 1816-1865* (New York: Columbia University Press, 1961).

16. Arthur Bestor, "Patent-Office Models of the Good Society," in *American Historical Review,* LVIII (April, 1953), 505-26.

17. Parker, *op. cit.*, pp. 341-43.

18. Paul Tillich, "The World Situation," in Henry P. Van Dusen, ed., *The Christian Answer* (New York: Charles Scribner's Sons, 1945), p. 3.

19. James Bryce, *The American Commonwealth* (New York: The Macmillan Co., 1908), II, 870.

20. *The Blithedale Romance,* in Nathaniel Hawthorne, *The Complete Novels and Selected Tales,* edited with an introduction by Norman Holmes Pearson (New York: The Modern Library, 1937), p. 584.

Chapter VII. Denominationalism: The Shape of Protestantism in America

1. Kenneth Scott Latourette, *A History of the Expansion of Christianity* (New York: Harper & Brothers, 1937-1945, 7v.), IV, 424.

2. Thomas Jefferson, *The Complete Jefferson, Containing his Major Writings, Published and Unpublished, Except his Letters.* Assembled and arranged by Saul K. Padover, with illustrations and analytic index (New York: Duell, Sloan & Pearce, Inc., 1943), p. 940.

3. I have used the listing in Willard L. Sperry, *Religion in America* (New York: The Macmillan Co., 1946), p. 282. Cf. Edwin S. Gaustad, *His-*

torical Atlas of Religion in America (New York: Harper & Row, 1962), pp. 4-5.

4. See W. W. Sweet, *The American Churches, an Interpretation* (New York: Abingdon-Cokesbury Press, 1948), p. 42. Cf. Gaustad, *op. cit.*, p. 52.

5. The story of the numerical growth and geographical expansion of the churches is most adequately presented in Gaustad, *op. cit.*

6. Alfred North Whitehead, *Essays in Science and Philosophy* (New York: Philosophical Library, 1947), p. 115.

7. Latourette, *op. cit.*, IV, 428. See chap. 1, *supra*, for my development of these ideas.

8. John W. Nevin, "The Sect System," in *The Mercersburg Review*, I (1849), 499.

9. J. Hector St. John Crèvecoeur, *Letters from an American Farmer*, reprinted from the original edition with a Prefatory Note by W. P. Trent and an Introduction by Ludwig Lewisohn (New York: Fox, Duffield & Co., 1904), p. 66.

10. Richard W. B. Lewis, *The American Adam* (Chicago: The University of Chicago Press, 1955).

11. Quoted in Perry G. E. Miller, *Orthodoxy in Massachusetts, 1630-1650* (Cambridge: Harvard University Press, 1933), p. 160.

12. There was in America, in this sense, a widespread reversion to "primitive Christianity," somewhat as defined by Ernst Troeltsch, which has suggested to me the possibility of adapting the "frontier thesis" of Frederick Jackson Turner to the interpretation of Christianity in America in a more profound way than that of Peter Mode and W. W. Sweet. Turner's thesis hinges on the reduction to primitive conditions on the frontier, followed by rebuilding, incorporating new elements derived from the local situation. Regarding all of America as the "frontier" of Western Christendom, the prevailing ideal there was patterned after primitive Christianity. Hence we have the tendency to overlook all Christian history since the first century. The emergence of the denominational form represents the rebuilding, incorporating new elements—the subject of this essay. The rebuilding is still going on as American Christianity becomes increasingly conscious of world Christianity and of history.

13. See, e.g., Jerald C. Brauer, *Protestantism in America* (Philadelphia: The Westminster Press, 1953), which presents an interpretation woven around these two themes.

14. Nevin, *loc. cit.*

15. See chap. 4, *supra*, for a development of this idea.

16. Gaius Glenn Atkins and Frederick L. Fagley, *History of American Congregationalism* (Boston: The Pilgrim Press, 1942), p. 342.

17. Alexis de Tocqueville, *Democracy in America*, trans. Henry Reeve, 4th ed. (New York: J. & H. G. Langley, 1841), I, 335.

18. Herbert W. Schneider, *Religion in 20th Century America* (Cambridge: Harvard University Press, 1952), p. 44.

19. Quoted in *ibid.*, p. 45.

20. Rufus Anderson, *The Theory of Missions to the Heathen,* a Sermon at the ordination of Mr. Edward Webb as missionary to the heathen, Ware, Massachusetts, October 23, 1845 (Boston: Press of Crocker and Brewster, 1845), pp. 9, 5.
21. Wade C. Barclay, *History of Methodist Missions* (New York: Board of Missions and Church Extension of the Methodist Church, 1949-   ), II, 8.
22. See Winthrop S. Hudson, *The Great Tradition of the American Churches* (New York: Harper & Brothers, 1953), chap. 8.
23. Laymen's Foreign Missions Inquiry, *Re-Thinking Missions: a Laymen's Inquiry after One Hundred Years* (New York: Harper & Brothers, 1932), p. 326.
24. Hudson, *op. cit.,* chap. 9, "The Church Embraces the World."
25. See, e.g., Archibald G. Baker, *Christian Missions and a New World Culture* (Chicago: Willett, Clark & Co., 1934), "Introduction."
26. Laymen's . . . , *op. cit.,* p. 327.
27. By the same token, those whose conception of the mission enterprise has not changed materially have, within their limits, suffered less confusion—as witness, e.g., the Seventh-day Adventists and the "faith missions."
28. C. Howard Hopkins, *History of the Y.M.C.A. in North America* (New York: Association Press, 1951), p. 4.
29. John A. Hutchison, *We Are Not Divided* (New York: Round Table Press, Inc., 1941), p. 25.
30. Walter Rauschenbusch, *Christianizing the Social Order* (New York: The Macmillan Co., 1912), pp. 14-15.
31. C. Howard Hopkins, *The Rise of the Social Gospel in American Protestantism 1865-1915* (New Haven: Yale University Press, 1940), p. 302.
32. *Ibid.,* p. 316.
33. Winfred E. Garrison, "Characteristics of American Organized Religion," in *Annals of the American Academy of Political and Social Science,* CCLVI (March, 1948), 19.
34. *Ibid.,* p. 20.
35. Herman E. Kittredge, *Ingersoll, a Biographical Appreciation* (New York: Dresden Publishing Co., 1911), p. 23.
36. William G. McLoughlin, Jr., *Billy Sunday Was His Real Name* (Chicago: University of Chicago Press, 1955), p. 125.
37. Lyman Beecher, *Autobiography, Correspondence, etc., of Lyman Beecher,* edited by Charles Beecher (New York: Harper & Brothers, 1864), I, 156-57. Lyman Beecher, *Works* (Boston: J. P. Jewett & Co., 1852-1853), II, 155-56.
38. Samuel J. Baird, *A History of the New School and of the Questions Involved in the Disruption of the Presbyterian Church in 1838* (Philadelphia: Claxton, Remsen & Haffelfinger, 1868), p. 225.
39. Daniel Day Williams, *The Andover Liberals, a Study of American Theology* (New York: King's Crown Press, 1941), p. 7.
40. McLoughlin, *op. cit.,* p. 158.

41. See Arthur M. Schlesinger, Jr., *The Age of Jackson* (Boston: Little, Brown & Co., 1945), p. 51.
42. See, e.g., the detailed study by Walter B. Posey, *The Presbyterian Church in the Old Southwest, 1778-1835* (Richmond: John Knox Press, 1952).
43. Robert Ellis Thompson, *A History of the Presbyterian Churches in the United States* (New York: Charles Scribner's Sons, 1895), pp. 34, 95. Leonard W. Bacon, *A History of American Christianity* (New York: Charles Scribner's Sons, 1900), p. 176.
44. See chap. 3, *supra.*
45. John Wesley, *Sermons on Several Occasions* (New York: Lane & Scott, 1851), I, 346-55.
46. John Herman Randall, *Religion and the Modern World* (New York: Frederick A. Stokes Co., 1929), pp. 26-27.
47. In Perry G. E. Miller, ed., *The Transcendentalists, an Anthology* (Cambridge: Harvard University Press, 1950), p. 108.
48. Bela Bates Edwards, "Influence of Eminent Piety on the Intellectual Powers," in his *Writings* (Boston: John P. Jewett and Co., 1853), II, 472, 497-98.
49. Bacon, *op. cit.*, p. 404.
50. *Ibid.*, p. 194. Note Francis Parkman's comment on the French Jesuit who "was as often a fanatic for his Order as for his faith" and "ardently as he burned for the saving of souls, he would have none saved on the Upper Lakes except by his brethren and himself." *LaSalle and the Discovery of the Great West*, 12th ed. (Boston: Little, Brown & Co., 1880), p. 30.
51. Robert Baird, *Religion in America, or an Account of the Origin, Relation to the State, and Present Condition of the Evangelical Churches in the United States with Notices of Unevangelical Denominations* (New York: Harper & Brothers, 1845), p. 220.
52. *Ibid.*, pp. 269-70.
53. See, e.g., Lyman Beecher, *A Plea for the West*, 2d ed. (Cincinnati: Truman & Smith, 1835); and Horace Bushnell, "Barbarism the First Danger," in his *Work and Play* (New York: Charles Scribner's Sons, 1903), pp. 227-67.
54. Miller, *op. cit.*, p. 11.
55. Bacon, *op. cit.*, p. 195.
56. Talcott Parsons, *Religious Perspectives in College Teaching in Sociology and Social Psychology* (New Haven, The Edward W. Hazen Foundation, 1951), pp. 40, 39. Also published as Talcott Parsons, "Sociology and Social Psychology," in *Religious Perspectives in College Teaching* by Hoxie N. Fairchild *et al.* (New York: Ronald Press Co., 1952), pp. 329, 328.
57. Oscar Handlin, *The American People in the Twentieth Century* (Cambridge: Harvard University Press, 1954), p. 222.

Chapter VIII. American Protestantism Since the Civil War.
I. From Denominationalism to Americanism

1. H. Paul Douglas, "The Protestant Faiths," in Harold E. Stearns, ed., *America Now; an Inquiry into Civilization in the United States,* by thirty-six Americans (New York: Literary Guild of America, Inc., 1938), p. 514. See also Mark Sullivan, *Our Times, the United States, 1900-1925* (New York: Charles Scribner's Sons, 1926-1935, 6v.), II, chap. 5, "The American Mind: Orthodoxy," pp. 84-93.
2. See, in this connection, Alexis de Tocqueville, *Democracy in America,* trans. Henry Reeve, with special introductions by John T. Morgan and John T. Ingalls, rev. ed. (New York: Colonial Press, 1899), II, 9, 22.
3. Henry F. May, *Protestant Churches and Industrial America* (New York: Harper & Brothers, 1949), p. 39.
4. *Ibid.,* p. 4.
5. Quoted from Justice Story by Ralph Henry Gabriel, *The Course of American Democratic Thought, an Intellectual History Since 1815* (New York: Ronald Press, 1940), p. 23.
6. This and following quotations are taken from Andrew Carnegie, "Wealth," in *North American Review,* CXLVIII (June, 1889), 653-64. I have used it as reprinted in Gail Kennedy, ed., "Democracy and the Gospel of Wealth," in *Problems in American Civilization,* readings selected by the Department of American Studies, Amherst College (Boston: D. C. Heath & Co., 1949, 8v.) VI, 8.
7. Mary Bushnell Cheney, ed., *Life and Letters of Horace Bushnell* (New York: Harper & Brothers, 1880), p. 56.
8. Horace Bushnell, "Preliminary Dissertation on the Nature of Language as Related to Thought and Spirit," in his *God in Christ,* Three Discourses Delivered at New Haven, Cambridge, and Andover, with a Preliminary Dissertation on Language (Hartford: Brown & Parsons, 1849), pp. 16, 40.
9. As quoted by Winthrop S. Hudson, *The Great Tradition of the American Churches* (New York: Harper & Brothers, 1953), p. 172.
10. C. Howard Hopkins, *The Rise of the Social Gospel in American Protestantism, 1865-1915* (New Haven: Yale University Press, 1940), pp. 14-15.
11. Daniel Dorchester, *The Problem of Religious Progress* (New York: Phillips & Hunt, 1881), pp. 31-32.
12. Francis Wayland, *A Discourse Delivered in the First Baptist Church, Providence, R. I., on the Day of Public Thanksgiving, July 21, 1842,* 2d ed. (Providence: Printed by H. H. Brown, 1842), pp. 22, 23. Wayland here noted the gulf between profession and practice in the churches which is still obvious to observers. See, e.g., the three articles on "The New Role of the Laity" in *Annals of the American Academy of Political and Social Science,* CCCXXXII (November, 1960), 37-69: Paul Harrison, "Church and the Laity Among Protestants," pp. 37-49; John

J. Kane, "Church and the Laity Among Catholics," pp. 50-59; Marshall Sklare, "Church and the Laity Among Jews," pp. 60-69.

13. John Herman Randall, *Religion and the Modern World* (New York: Frederick A. Stokes Co., 1929), pp. 26-27.
14. George H. Gordon, "The Theological Problem for To-Day," in Lyman Abbott, *New Puritanism*, papers by Lyman Abbott, Amory H. Bradford, Charles A. Berry, George H. Gordon, Washington Gladden, Wm. J. Tucker, during the Semi-centennial celebration of Plymouth Church, Brooklyn, 1847-1897, with introduction by Rossiter W. Raymond (New York: Fords, Howard & Hulbert, 1897), p. 151.
15. Bela Bates Edwards, *Writings* (Boston: John P. Jewett & Co., 1853), I, 490.
16. Tocqueville, *op. cit.*, I, pp. 331, 330.
17. *The Writings of the Late Elder John Leland*, Including Some Events in His Life Written by Himself, with Additional Sketches, &c. by Miss L. F. Greene (New York: Printed by G. W. Wood, 1845), p. 249.
18. John Herman Randall, Jr., "The Churches and the Liberal Tradition," in *Annals of the American Academy of Political and Social Science*, CCLVI (March, 1948), 149-50.
19. Hudson, *op. cit.*, p. 161.
20. May, *op. cit.*, p. 91. Cf. Paul Tillich's comment that the churches which "replaced the one Church" after the Reformation "were supported either by the state or by the dominant group in society—the former predominantly in Europe, the latter especially in America. In both situations, the Churches largely surrendered their critical freedom. They tended to become agencies of either the state or the ruling classes." His "The World Situation," in Henry P. Van Dusen, ed., *The Christian Answer* (New York: Charles Scribner's Sons, 1945), p. 38.
21. Horace Bushnell, *Popular Government by Divine Right* (Hartford: L. E. Hunt, 1864), pp. 15, 12, 15.
22. Herman E. Kittredge, *Ingersolls a Biographical Appreciation* (New York: Dresden Publishing Co., 1911), p. 288.
23. Quoted by Edmund Wilson in *New Yorker*, XXX (April 3, 1954), 115, in a review of Frederick Law Olmsted, *Cotton Kingdom; a Traveller's Observations on Cotton and Slavery in the American Slave States*. Based on three former volumes of journeys and investigations, Arthur M. Schlesinger, ed. (New York: Alfred A. Knopf, 1953).
24. Henry Ward Beecher, "Home Missions and Our Country's Future," in *Home Missionary*, XXXVI (September, 1863), 112.
25. Avery Craven and Walter Johnson, *The United States: Experiment in Democracy* (Boston: Ginn & Co., 1947), pp. 417-18.
26. As quoted in Ralph E. Morrow, "Northern Methodism in the South During Reconstruction," in *Mississippi Valley Historical Review*, XLI (September, 1954), 213.
27. As quoted in Craven, *op. cit.*, pp. 430, 422.
28. Cf. Arthur M. Schlesinger, Jr., *Political and Social Growth of the American Peoples, 1865-1940*, 3d ed. (New York: The Macmillan Co.,

1941), p. v: "Yet the record as a whole sums up a people who, despite the ills to which mankind is prey, managed to fashion a way of life and a system of government which at every period of American history served as a beacon light for struggling humanity everywhere."

Robert Baird in *The Christian Retrospect and Register: a Summary of the Scientific, Moral, and Religious Progress of the First Half of the XIXth Century*, 3d ed. (New York: M. W. Dodd, 1851) held that no one will deny that "in all that relates to their MATERIAL INTERESTS our race has . . . made great progress since the commencement of the XIXth century" and that "the latter half of the century will show still greater progress, we are far from being disposed, either to deny, or to doubt." Further, "that there has also been a great progress in all that has a bearing on the MORAL AND RELIGIOUS INTERESTS of Humanity, during the same era, is a position which none can question." But, he added, the authors "are pained to be compelled to admit" that "the progress in the moral and Religious Interests of our race, during the period . . . has not equalled that of their Material Interests."

29. Gerald Birney Smith, *Current Christian Thinking* (Chicago: The University of Chicago Press, 1928), p. 189.
30. As quoted in Hudson, *op. cit.*, p. 175.
31. John Bascom, "The Natural Theology of Social Scence. IV. Labor and Capital," in *Bibliotheca Sacra*, XXV (October, 1869), 660.
32. Kennedy, *op. cit.*, pp. 1-2.
33. *Ibid.*, pp. 68-76.
34. John P. Crozer, *Standard*, XV (May 7, 1868), 4, col. 4.
35. Caroline Augusta Lloyd, *Henry Demarest Lloyd, 1847-1903, a Biography* by Caro Lloyd with an introduction by Charles Edward Russell (New York: G. P. Putnam's, 1912), II, 190.
36. Arthur M. Schlesinger, *The Rise of the City, 1878-1898*, "A History of American Life Series," X (New York: The Macmillan Co., 1933), p. 331.
37. As quoted in May, *op. cit.*, p. 62.
38. *Ibid.*, p. 14.
39. Francis Wayland, *The Duties of an American Citizens Two Discourses, Delivered in the First Baptist Meeting House in Boston, on Thursday, April 7, 1825* (Boston: James Loring, 1825), p. 29.
40. John Winthrop, "A Modell of Christian Charity," in Perry G. E. Miller and Thomas H. Johnson, eds., *The Puritans* (New York: American Book Co., 1938), pp. 197, 197-99.
41. Wayland, *The Duties . . .*, *op. cit.*, pp. 35-36.
42. *Ibid.*, p. 27.
43. As quoted in John R. Bodo, *The Protestant Clergy and Public Issues, 1812-1848* (Princeton: Princeton University Press, 1954), p. 241; from "Christ, a Home Missionary," in *Missionary Enterprise* (Boston, 1845), p. 93.
44. Kennedy, *op. cit.*, p. 76.
45. The following quotations are from chap. 14, "The Anglo-Saxon and the World's Future," in Josiah Strong, *Our Country, Its Possible Future*

and Its Present Crisis, with an introduction by Austin Philips, rev. ed. based on the census of 1890 (New York: Baker & Taylor Co., for the American Home Missionary Society, 1891).

46. As quoted in Sullivan, *op. cit.,* I, 47-48.
47. Winfred E. Garrison, *The March of Faith: the Story of Religion in America since 1865* (New York: Harper & Brothers, 1933), p. 174.
48. Hudson, *op. cit.,* p. 161.
49. Alfred North Whitehead, *Science and the Modern World,* "Lowell Lectures, 1925" (Harmondsworth, Middlesex, Eng., Penguin Books, Ltd., 1938), p. 240.

Chapter IX. American Protestantism Since the Civil War. II. From Americanism to Christianity

1. Alexis de Tocqueville, *Democracy in America,* trans. Henry Reeve, 4th ed. (New York: J. & H. G. Langley, 1841), I, 341.
2. Daniel Dorchester, *The Problem of Religious Progress* (New York: Phillips & Hunt, 1881), see particularly chap. 3 and the Appendix containing "Ecclesiastical Statistics."
3. The thesis is developed in Arthur M. Schlesinger, "A Critical Period in American Protestantism, 1875-1900," in *Massachusetts Historical Society Proceedings,* LXIV (June, 1932), 523-48. Cf. William Adams Brown, *The Church in America, a Study of the Present Conditions and Future Prospects of American Protestantism* (New York: The Macmillan Co., 1922), p. 140. The questions, said Brown, are: "Can the old religion still maintain itself under the strain of the new conditions? Can it sustain the theoretical test of the intellectual movement which we call modern science? Can it meet the practical test of the social and economic movement which we call industrialism, with its political counterpart in the rivalry of races and of nations for prestige and for power?" These, he suggests, are aspects of the same scientific movement.
4. Henry F. May, *Protestant Churches and Industrial America* (New York: Harper & Brothers, 1949), p. ix.
5. Ezra Stiles Ely, *Visits of Mercy or the Journals of the Rev. Ezra Stiles Ely,* written while he was Stated Preacher to the Hospital and Alms House in the City of New York, 6th ed. rev. (Philadelphia: Samuel F. Bradford, 1829), I, iii.
6. Horace Bushnell, "How To Be a Christian in Trade," in *Sermons on Living Subjects* (New York: Charles Scribner's Sons, 1903), p. 251.
7. John Bascom, "The Natural Theology of Social Science. IV. Labor and Capital," in *Bibliotheca Sacra,* XXV (October, 1868), 680, 682.
8. Bushnell, *op. cit.,* pp. 263, 248.
9. Andrew Carnegie, "Wealth," in *North American Review,* CXLVIII (June, 1889), 653-64. For convenience I have used it as reprinted in Gail Kennedy, ed., "Democracy and the Gospel of Wealth," in *Problems in American Civilization,* readings selected by the Department of American Studies, Amherst College (Boston: D. C. Heath & Co., 1949, 8v.), VI, 8.

10. Bascom, *op. cit.,* p. 675.
11. Kennedy, *op. cit.,* p. 7.
12. Charles Wood, "The Pauperism of Our Cities: Its Character, Condition, Causes, and Relief," in *Presbyterian Quarterly and Princeton Review*, III, new ser. (April, 1874), 225.
13. Kennedy, *op. cit.,* pp. 7-8.
14. Henry Ward Beecher, "Economy in Small Things," in *Plymouth Pulpit*, Sermons Preached in Plymouth Church, Brooklyn, September 1873-September 1875 (New York: Fords, Howard & Hulbert, 1874-1875, 4v.), IV, 463-64.
15. Review of Charles Loring Brace, *The Dangerous Classes of New York and Twenty Years' Work Among Them* (New York: Wynkoop & Hallenbeck, 1872; 3d ed. with an addenda, 1880), in *Presbyterian Quarterly and Princeton Review*, II (January, 1873), 189.
16. Wood, *op. cit.,* p. 226.
17. Bascom, *op. cit.,* pp. 659, 662, 658.
18. See, e.g., Wood, *op. cit.,* pp. 218-19. For a contemporary account see May, *op. cit.,* chap. on "The Face of the City," pp. 112-24.
19. C. Howard Hopkins, *The Rise of the Social Gospel in American Protestantism, 1865-1915* (New Haven: Yale University Press, 1940), pp. 216, 217.
20. May, *op. cit.,* p. 220.
21. Wood, *op. cit.,* p. 224.
22. Beecher, "Liberty in the Churches," in *Plymouth Pulpit, op. cit.,* II, 209.
23. Aaron I. Abell, *The Urban Impact on American Protestantism, 1865-1900* (Cambridge: Harvard University Press, 1943).
24. *Ibid.,* p. vii.
25. May, *op. cit.,* p. 63.
26. Ray Allen Billington, Bert James Loewenberg, and Samuel Hugh Brockunier, *The United States: American Democracy in World Perspective* (New York: Rinehart & Co., Inc., 1947), p. 358.
27. May, *op. cit.,* p. 108. See also Robert V. Bruce, *1877: Year of Violence* (Indianapolis: Bobbs-Merrill Co., Inc., 1959), for a detailed account of the upheavals during that year.
28. *Ibid.,* p. 107.
29. Billington, *op. cit.,* p. 450.
30. Bascom, *op. cit.,* p. 678.
31. Andrew Preston Peabody, "Wealth," in *Andover Review*, XIX (May, 1893), 329. The September, 1877, issue of the *North American Review* carried an article by Thomas A. Scott, president of the Pennsylvania Railway Company, entitled "The Recent Strikes" (CXXV, 351-62). Speaking of the railroad strikes in terms such as "a mob," "riot, arson, and bloodshed," and "insurrection," and arguing that "the conduct of the rioters is entirely inconsistent with the idea that this movement could have been directed by serious, right-minded men bent on improving the condition of the laboring classes," Mr. Scott suggested, first, the use of the injunction, and, second, the systematic disposal of federal troops throughout the nation (pp. 359-61). The same issue (pp. 322-26) also

carried an anonymous article signed "A 'Striker,' " and entitled "Fair Wages." Unlike the handling of the Scott article, the editor appended the following (p. 326): "Note.—In this case, as in all others, the Editor disclaims responsibility for the opinions of contributors, whether their articles are signed or anonymous."

32. These quotations from the *Christian Union*, the *Independent*, and the *Christian Advocate* are taken from May, *op. cit.*, pp. 92-93, 105.
33. *Ibid.*, p. 100.
34. Bascom, *op. cit.*, p. 678.
35. *Congregationalist*, LXXVII (July 14, 1892), 224, col. 4. In fairness it should be noted that on the first page of the same issue (p. 221, col. 6), the editors condemned the views allegedly expressed by Senator Palmer of Illinois as "nationalistic," and thought that, if enforced upon capital by law, they would "cause . . . temporary, if not permanent, disaster." Palmer was reputed to have said that "hereafter manufacturing establishments will have to be regarded as semi-public property, their owners to be regarded as holding the property subject to the correlative rights of those without whose services the property would be valueless. Laboring men are conscious of the right to continuous employment during good behavior. They will insist upon it. If employers have the right to hold over the heads of their employees the rod of dismissal American freedom will be gone."
36. "The Impending Question in the Industrial World," in *Andover Review*, XVIII (September, 1892), 272-78.
37. Charles W. Clark, "Applied Christianity: Who Shall Apply it First?" in *Andover Review*, XIX (January, 1893), 24, 25. The editor, noting that the author "died in 1891, at the age of twenty-seven," held the article to be "typical of the aim of the better mind of his generation, as the more earnest of our younger men are seeking to interpret Christianity to themselves and to their time." In the May issue, the *Andover Review* carried an article by Peabody entitled "Wealth" (see note 31, *supra*) which has the appearance of being conceived by the author as a reply to Clark's article. Peabody is described in the recent history of the Harvard Divinity School as "a sage Unitarian . . . defender of a conservative version of the Liberal Faith."
38. Francis G. Peabody, *Jesus Christ and the Social Question*, an examination of the teaching of Jesus in its relation to some of the problems of modern social life (New York: The Macmillan Co., 1900), pp. 5-6.
39. Bert James Loewenberg, "Darwinism Comes to America, 1859-1900," in *Mississippi Valley Historical Review*, XXVIII (December, 1941), 342.
40. *Ibid.*, p. 349.
41. See W. H. Roberts, "The Reaction of the American Protestant Churches to the Darwinian Philosophy, 1860-1900," unpublished Ph.D. Dissertation (Chicago: University of Chicago, March, 1936). Stow Persons discusses the way in which the theory of natural selection tended to undermine belief in design in his *Evolutionary Thought in America*, edited for the special program in American Civilization at Princeton University (New Haven: Yale University Press, 1950), pp. 424 ff.

42. Loewenberg, *op. cit.*, p. 339.
43. See, e.g., George H. Williams, ed., *The Harvard Divinity School, its place in Harvard University and in American Culture.* (Boston: The Beacon Press, 1954), pp. 169-72.
44. Loewenberg, *op. cit.*, p. 341.
45. Gaius Glenn Atkins, *Religion in Our Times* (New York: Round Table Press, Inc., 1932), pp. 249-51.
46. Loewenberg, *op. cit.*, spells this out in some detail.
47. Peabody, "Wealth," *op. cit.*, pp. 327-28.
48. Cf. E. E. Aubrey, "Religious Bearings of the Modern Scientific Movement," in *Environmental Factors in Christian History*, edited by John Thomas McNeill, Matthew Spinka, and Harold R. Willoughby (Chicago: The University of Chicago Press, 1939), pp. 361-79.
49. Hopkins, *op. cit.*, p. 14.
50. Charles Hodge, "Inspiration," in *Princeton Review*, XXIX (October, 1857), 662.
51. See, e.g., John Wright Buckham, *Progressive Religious Thought in America: a Survey of the Enlarging Pilgrim Faith* (Boston: Houghton Mifflin Co., 1919).
52. See Stow Persons, *Free Religion: an American Faith* (New Haven: Yale University Press, 1947).
53. For a treatment of transcendentalism as a religious movement see Perry G. E. Miller, *The Transcendentalists, an Anthology* (Cambridge: Harvard University Press, 1950), Introduction. In my review of this work I stressed the relationship of transcendentalism to the present "cults," in *Journal of Religion*, XXXI (January, 1951), 52-54. For a sympathetic treatment of these "cults" see Charles S. Braden, *These Also Believe, a Study of Modern American Cults and Minority Religious Movements* (New York: The Macmillan Co., 1949). In my review of this book I pointed out how New Thought was. beginning to invade the Protestant churches, in *Journal of Religion*, XXX (April, 1950), 142-44.
54. Perry G. E. Miller, "Jonathan Edwards to Emerson," in *New England Quarterly*, XIII (December, 1940), 616.
55. Mary Bushnell Cheney, ed., *Life and Letters of Horace Bushnell* (New York: Harper & Brothers, 1880), pp. 56, 192. Horace Bushnell, *God in Christ*, Three Discourses Delivered at New Haven, Cambridge, and Andover, with a Preliminary Dissertation on Language (Hartford: Brown & Parsons, 1849).
56. Aubrey, *op. cit.*, p. 368. Cf. Lyman Abbott, *Reminiscences* (Boston: Houghton Mifflin Co., 1915), p. 451, where he says he could disregard "the scientific arguments for Christian truth" and appeal "directly to human experience and . . . find evidences for Christianity in the hearts and consciousnesses of my hearers," for "the foundation of spiritual faith is neither in the church nor in the Bible, but in the spiritual consciousness of man."
57. Abbott, *op. cit.*, p. 461.
58. *Ibid.*, pp. 461-62.
59. Aubrey, *op. cit.*, p. 368.

60. Shailer Mathews, *The Faith of Modernism* (New York: The Macmillan Co., 1924), p. 23.
61. *Ibid.*
62. Cf. Billington, *op. cit.*, p. 425: "The settlement houses were remedial agencies devoted to the salvage of wrecked lives, but they gave scarcely any attention to the economic whirlpools that produced social catastrophe." However, "conceived as laboratories for social workers . . . they came to be infinitely more."
63. Dorchester, *op. cit.*, p. 41.
64. Henry Steele Commager, *The American Mind, an Interpretation of American Thought and Character Since the 1880's* (New Haven: Yale University Press, 1950), p. 165. The "bankruptcy" of theology among the Congregationalists is made explicit, e.g., by Washington Gladden in his *Recollections* (Boston: Houghton Mifflin Co., 1909). "My Theology," he noted (p. 163), "had to be hammered out on the anvil for daily use in the pulpit. The pragmatic test was the only one that could be applied to it: 'Will it work?'" He recalled with relish that Dr. John Todd, moderator of the council which installed him in the church in North Adams, in 1866 "skillfully conducted the examination over ground on which there was no chance of discussion, and after about twenty minutes, brought it to an abrupt conclusion. It was a palpable evasion, but I was not responsible for it. 'I thought,' said Dr. Todd to me after the examination, 'that you were a great heretic.' 'Perhaps I am,' I answered, 'but you didn't bore in the right place'" (p. 168).
Finally, he notes with obvious approval that, in the "creed drawn up by the committee of twenty-five" in 1883, "all the distinctively Calvinistic dogmas . . . were eliminated; there was no formal doctrine of the Trinity . . . election, in the Calvinistic sense, was not in it, nor was original sin, nor Biblical infallibility; and the sufferings of Christ on the cross were described as his 'sacrifice of himself'" (p. 288).
65. See Paul Tillich, "The World Situation," in Henry P. Van Dusen, ed., *The Christian Answer* (New York: Charles Scribner's Sons, 1945). This change of attitude is exemplified in Gladden, *op. cit.*, pp. 295-97.
66. *Congregationalist*, LXXVII (September 8, 1892), 289, col. 5.
67. Clark, *op. cit.*, p. 20.
68. Washington Gladden, "A Question That Ought To Be Settled," in *Congregationalist*, LXXVII (July 28, 1892), 237, col. 3.
69. Cf. Brown, *op. cit.*, p. 141: "There are two ways in which modern science has affected the task of the church. It has affected it as pure science by its challenge to the assumptions on which the older theology is based. It has affected it even more profoundly as applied science by the changes which it has brought about in the external environment in which the church must work."
70. Cf. Charles A. and Mary B. Beard, *The American Spirit, a Study of the Idea of Civilization in the United States*, "The Rise of American Civilization," IV (New York: The Macmillan Co., 1942), p. 18.
71. Gladden, *Recollections*, pp. 90-91. It is interesting to note that Gladden, who frankly advocated overhead control of the social and

economic realms (p. 314), just as frankly endorsed the regnant an-
archistic Congregational individualism in theological and ecclesiastical
affairs. "It had come to be recognized as Congregational doctrine," he
said with reference to the "creed" of 1883, "that no ecclesiastical body
existed, or could be created, with power to frame such a creed and impose it upon the churches—each church, by the primary Congregational
principle, having the right to make its own creed" (p. 287).

72. "The Monopoly Problem," in *Congregationalist*, LXXVII (September
    8, 1892), 289, col. 5.
73. Walter F. Adeney, *A Century's Progress in Religious Life and Thought*
    (London: James Clarke & Co., 1901), p. 183.
74. Abell, *op. cit.*, pp. 16-17.
75. Atkins, *op. cit.*, p. 230.
76. See chap. 7, pp. 118-120, *supra*.
77. Charles A. Berry, "Retrospect and Outlook," in Lyman Abbott, *New
    Puritanism*, papers by Lyman Abbott, Amory H. Bradford, Charles A.
    Berry, George H. Gordon, Washington Gladden, Wm. J. Tucker, dur-
    ing the Semi-centennial celebration of Plymouth Church, Brooklyn,
    1847-1897, with introduction by Rossiter W. Raymond (New York:
    Fords, Howard & Hulbert, 1897), pp. 245-46.
78. George H. Gordon, "The Theological Problems for To-Day," in
    Abbott, *ibid.*, p. 143.
79. Hopkins, *op. cit.*, pp. 284 ff.
80. *Ibid.*, p. 296.
81. Walter Rauschenbusch, *Christianizing the Social Order* (New York:
    The Macmillan Co., 1912), p. 20.
82. Adeney, *op. cit.*, pp. 171, 186.
83. Although the statement of "fundamentals" varied somewhat, the follow-
    ing six would usually be included: the inerrancy of Scripture in every
    detail; the deity of Jesus; the virgin birth; the substitutionary theory of
    the atonement; the physical resurrection; the imminent, bodily return
    of Jesus to earth. See Stewart G. Cole, *The History of Fundamentalism*
    (New York: Richard R. Smith, Inc., 1931), and Norman F. Furniss,
    The Fundamentalist Controversy, 1918-1931 (New Haven: Yale Univer-
    sity Press, 1954).
84. Aubrey, *op. cit.*, p. 375.
85. *The Fundamentals; a testimony to the truth*, Compliments of Two
    Christian Laymen (Chicago: Testimony Publishing Co., 1910-1915, 12v.)
86. Winfred E. Garrison, *The March of Faith: the Story of Religion in
    America since 1865* (New York: Harper & Brothers, 1933), p. 273.
87. Universal Christian Conference on Life and Work, *The Stockholm
    Conference, 1925, the official report* . . ., ed. by G. K. A. Bell (London:
    Oxford University Press, H. Milford, 1926), p. 140.

Index

Index

215

Index 217

Free churches, defined, 103
Free Individual, 92
Freedom, 12
   Charter of, 17
   Religious, 3, 13, 18, 35, 61 ff., 194
Freylinghuysen, Frederick Theodore, 29
Fundamentalism, 183 f., 211
Furniss, Norman F., 211

Gabriel, Ralph Henry, 198, 203
Garland, Hamlin, 9, 10, 163, 189, 190
Garrison, Winfred E., 18, 59, 122, 192, 196, 201, 206, 211
Gaustad, Edwin S., 199, 200
George, Henry, 162
Gewehr, Wesley M., 191
Gladden, Washington, 173, 176, 210
Goen, C. C., 192
Gordon, George H., 138, 180, 204, 211
Gorton, Samuel, 24
Gospel songs, 5, 10, 146
Great Awakening, 29, 37
Greene, Evarts B., 22, 23, 190

Hacker, Louis M., 196
Hall, Thomas C., 194
Hamilton, Alexander, 194, 198
Handlin, Oscar, 202
Harrison, Paul, 203
Harvard Divinity School, 209
Hawthorne, Nathaniel, 155, 199
Hazen, Charles D., 194, 195
Heman, Felicia, 19
Hertz, Karl H., 197
Historylessness, 108 f.
Hoar, George F., 154
Hodge, Charles, 171, 209

Hopkins, C. Howard, 121, 171, 181-82, 201, 203, 207, 209, 211
Hopkins, Samuel, 98
Hudson, Winthrop S., 120, 142, 154, 191, 192, 195, 200, 203, 204, 205, 206
Hutchinson, Anne, 14
Hutchison, John A., 201

Indians, 4, 5, 8
Infidelity, 52-54, 55 f.
Ingersoll, John, 123, 201, 204
Interdenominational groups, 116-117

Jackson, Andrew, 125, 202
James, Henry, 10
Jay, John, 198
Jefferson, Thomas, 35, 40-41, 43, 45-48, 51, 57-59, 61 f., 71, 72 f., 82, 87, 91, 96, 106, 192, 193, 194, 195, 196, 198, 199
Jones, Howard Mumford, 195

Kane, John J., 204
Kaufman, M., 192
Kennedy, Gail, 203, 205, 206, 207
Kittredge, Herman E., 201, 204
Koch, Adrienne, 194
Kock, G. Adolf, 195
Krout, John A., 199

Labor, 103 f.
Laissez faire, 13, 83, 139, 145, 150, 175, 177
Latourette, Kenneth Scott, 54, 103, 108, 195, 199, 200
Laud, William, 25
Lavves Diuine, Morall and Martiall &c., 23, 190
Lawrence, William, 147, 152, 155
Laws of trade, 158 f.

Tennent, Gilbert, 32, 33, 122
Thompson, John, 32
Thompson, Joseph P., 190
Thompson, Robert Ellis, 195, 202
Thoreau, Henry, 9
Tillich, Paul, 100, 199, 204, 210
Time, 4 f., 11, 13 f.
Tocqueville, Alexis de, 91, 93, 114,
    140, 141, 156, 200, 203, 204,
    206
Todd, John, 210
Toleration, 18, 20
Trinterud, Leonard J., 192
Troeltsch, Ernst, 200
Trollop, Frances, 91
Trowbridge, John, 143
Turner, Frederick Jackson, 200
Tyler, Alice Felt, 108, 197, 198,
    199

Uniformity, 17, 20, 27 f.
Universal Christian Conference
    on Life and Work, 211

Van Dusen, Henry P., 199, 204,
    210
Virginia, 23, 57, 77 f., 191, 193, 197
Virginia Charter, 17, 20
Virginia's Cure. . . , 23, 190
Voluntaryism, 96, 113 f.

Walker, Mary, 8
Ward, Nathaniel, 13, 18

Warren, Sidney, 195
Wayland, Francis, 137, 151, 203,
    205
Webb, Walter Prescott, 189
Wesley, John, 29, 40, 127, 192,
    202
Westphalia, Peace of, 2, 105
Wharton, Edith, 154
White, William, 124
Whitefield, George, 29, 30, 32, 122
Whitehead, Alfred North, xi, xii,
    34, 90, 96, 108, 155, 198, 200,
    206
Whitman, Walt, 155
Williams, Daniel Day, 124, 201
Williams, George H., 209
Williams, John Paul, 68-71, 196,
    198
Williams, Roger, 3, 13, 14, 19,
    58, 190
Williams, William R., 151
Wilson, Edmund, 204
Wilson, Henry, 144
Wilson, Woodrow, 176
Winthrop, John, 78-79, 151, 197,
    205
Witherspoon, John, 124
Wood, Charles, 159-60, 162, 207
Woolman, John, 98

Y. M. C. A., 120-21, 201

Zinzendorf, Nicolaus, 29
Zwierlein, Frederick J., 190